I'M SURROUNDED AND BEING ATTACKED BY 109S. COME AND HELP ME!

I was climbing at full throttle as fast as I could. As I came out of the cloud directly in front of me were two 109s. I pulled in behind number two easily. The leader had seen me and they began to turn. I easily stayed behind him and closed to about 100 yards and opened fire. It took only one good burst and he turned on his back and was soon falling apart. I found Johnny and flew him back safely to the field.

—Allan Christopher Deere, R.A.F.
Shot the first 109 in a Spitfire.

In all my combat I never lost a wingman under my leading. I almost lost a transferred bomber pilot who left my wing during an air battle with four Yaks. I interrupted my attack on one of the enemy planes to help him. I saw hits from the Yak striking the 109 and I immediately called to him to bail out. He did, and I sent the Yak burning to hell.

—Eric Hartmann
The Greatest Living Air Ace with a record of 325 Allied aircraft shot down.

THE ACES TALK

(formerly titled FIGHTER TACTICS AND STRATEGY 1914—1970)

Edward H. Sims

BALLANTINE BOOKS • NEW YORK

All rights reserved. Published in the United States by Ballantine Books, a division of Random House, Inc., New York, and
simultaneously in Canada by Random House of Canada, Limited, Toronto, Canada. Originally published under the title
FIGHTER TACTICS AND STRATEGY 1914-1970.

Herewith acknowledgment for permission to reprint excerpts
from the following sources:
From *Winged Warfare: An Air Combat Classic* by Lt. Colonel
William A. Bishop and Stanley M. Ulanoff, editor. Copyright
© 1967 by Stanley M. Ulanoff. Reprinted by permission of
Doubleday & Co., Inc.

From *No Parachute* by Arthur Gould Lee. Copyright © 1968
by Arthur Gould Lee. Reprinted by permission of Harper &
Row, Publishers, Inc.

Library of Congress Catalog Card Number: 76-95984

ISBN 0-345-28794-0

This edition published by arrangement with Harper & Row
Publishers, Inc.

Manufactured in the United States of America

First Ballantine Books Edition: February 1974
Third Printing: March 1980

**For
Bente**

---

and Edward and Robert—and the
fighter pilots of many skies
1914-70

Contents

PART FOUR The Second World War: Second Phase

PART FIVE Korea: First Jet War

PART SIX Vietnam: New Missiles and Methods

List of Illustrations

ACKNOWLEDGMENTS

The major undertaking of this book, the seeking out and interviewing of fighter pilots and air commanders in two World Wars and, to a more limited degree, in the Korean and Vietnam wars, was helped by two highly capable young historians, Hans Ring in Germany and Chris Shores in England. The various chapters relating the views of great fliers were in almost every instance edited by the pilots themselves.

Cass Canfield Sr. of Harper & Row, who originated the idea for a study of fighter tactics and strategy; Kenneth Parker, who also offered guidance, and the staff of Cassell and Co.; Wolfgang Schilling of Motorbuch Verlag and John W. R. Taylor of London are also due acknowledgment.

The fighter pilots of all four wars, the members of their families and the others who supplied me with combat reports or various other documents, records and diaries are too numerous to list in this brief appreciative note.

Mrs. John Smiley typed the manuscript carefully and capably. Mrs. Melvin Hughes, Mrs. Dorothy Ziegler and Mrs. Frank O'Cain also gave their assistance.

My thanks are due to General John C. Meyer, Vice Chief of Staff of the U.S. Air Force, who provided several tactical papers on jet fighters; General Robin Olds, Director of Aerospace Safety, U.S.A.F., who was particularly helpful; Air Vice-Marshal J. E. "Johnnie" Johnson, the leading R.A.F. scorer in the Second World War; Group Captain Douglas Bader, the legendary R.A.F. hero of that war; General Adolf Galland, chief of the German fighter arm in the Second World War; and Erich Hartmann, the top scorer of all time, who provided valuable information.

My wife, to whom this book is dedicated, was the inspiration for the work and helped in preparing the manuscript for the printer, at scramble-time.

All of the sciences and most of the arts have rich literatures which describe their theories and practices. Nearly all of these disciplines support the Ralph Waldo Emerson observation that "There is always a best way of doing everything."

But in the art of flying fighters—and particularly in air-to-air combat—the fighter pilot is faced with an extremely difficult task. The problem which confronts the fighter pilot is in determining that "best way" in a fast-changing situation that is without precedent to a certain degree. What makes the task particularly difficult is the large number of variables to be considered in a very short period of time. Compounding this difficulty is the dearth of authoritative source material that would be helpful in training the pilot.

I have recognized this shortcoming in fighter literature ever since I got into the art of flying. And that being the case, I was most pleased when Edward Sims—my friend of many years' standing—told me he was gathering the views and impressions of the world's foremost fighter pilots. I thought it to be a most worthwhile undertaking. My only regret was that such a work was not available before I faced the German Messerschmitts and Focke-Wulfes of World War II.

Now that I have carefully studied *Fighter Tactics and Strategy 1914–1970,* I appreciate even more how useful it would have been just to have had the first two parts of this book before going into combat. What Ed Sims has been able to do is compile the tactics, techniques and technology that gave one fighter pilot an edge over another. In recording the views of many successful pilots he has been able to highlight the important independent variables. One after another of these aces talks about aircraft position, speed, and maneuver capability, as well as pilot skill, vision and marksmanship.

If there is one common characteristic that comes out of this eclectic volume, it is the pragmatic nature of successful pilots. Granted, the fighter pilot strives to attack from above, out of the sun, with surprise, and fire at point-blank range. Nearly all of us would agree that this is the "best way." But a pilot can't always do the best thing, especially when his adversary is trying to do it too. So he has to take a flexible stance as he adjusts, modifies and adapts to get the desired results.

This is pragmatism at its best. And although the focus of this work is in flying air-to-air combat—where I am sure it will be very valuable—the lesson it teaches is universal. It says that those who have succeeded were able to adapt their own particular capabilities and limitations to gain the advantage they sought. It is a lesson that I believe everyone should learn and one that Ed Sims has documented with great care.

Gen. John C. Meyer
Vice Chief of Staff
U.S. Air Force

Washington, D.C.
November 1, 1971

Foreword by
Air Vice-Marshal J. E. Johnson, C.B., C.B.E., D.S.O., D.F.C.

In this excellent and thoughtful book, my old friend Edward Sims describes, through the words and views of great fighter pilots and fighter leaders, the development of fighter tactics and strategy from the string, canvas and wood airplanes of the First World War to the dramatic supersonic air fighting over northern Vietnam, vividly described by another distinguished comrade, General Robin Olds.

The author gives a unique account of the decisive role played by fighter airplanes during the later stages of the First World War. Later, in 1940, the Spitfires and Hurricanes of Fighter Command won the great defensive Battle of Britain and here, as the author points out, is history's most crystal-clear demonstration of the strategic influence of fighters. Later, in 1943–4, when the Royal Air Force lacked a long-range day fighter, the Americans with their splendid P.51 (Mustang) fighters won great offensive battles over northwest Europe which, in turn, exposed Germany to strategic bombing both by day and night, and thus hastened her downfall.

Later still, in Korea in 1950, the versatile American fighter-bombers stemmed the Communist advance to Pusan, and the U.S. Army Commander told me that, without the fighter-bombers, his men would have been driven into the sea.

Edward Sims concludes that even in this missile age there is still a strong requirement for manned fighters, and in my view he has more than proved his case.

Part One

ORIGINS AND DEVELOPMENT

AIR POWER AND THE FIGHTER PILOT

The rise of air power probably constitutes the most dramatic technological advance of the twentieth century. In this process, the competition for air leadership between men and nations, both civilian and military, has been keen, and the fastest forward strides have come in wartime.

The most colorful, perhaps the most fascinating, part of this evolutionary process has been the struggle between individual pilots, from many countries, to win superiority in the air in two World Wars and in lesser wars. How influential have these pilots been in the growth of military air power? What were their tactics and strategy in winning superiority, or supremacy, in the air?

These are formidable questions, too complex to be answered completely in one study. But in this book we examine them. Many of the views will be those of the world's greatest fighter pilots, spanning the period from 1914 to 1970, interviewed in various countries during the last four years. Most of them describe combat experiences which shaped their ideas on tactics and strategy, the major principles of which are still pertinent today.

No effort has been made in this study to define precisely in textbook terms where tactics end and strategy begins, for it is often a hard line to establish, as more than one expert noted during the interviews recorded in this book. Nor is this volume a complete history of either—I purposely avoid the much-overworked word "definitive." Instead, this book is written for those interested in the fascinating story of the air and the great pilots, and how they considerably affected the outcome of wars, establishing the principles of air power. In interviewing many of the greatest fliers of the century—from 1914 to 1970—one naturally uncovers exciting flying stories. And if an account of the development of air tactics and air power can be made enjoyable reading by including adventure in the telling, so much the better.

The intriguing question that arises from a study of fighter pilots and their tactics is whether they played a military role in recent wars commensurate with the publicity and fame which surrounded their names. In this century's two World Wars (to a lesser extent in Korea and Vietnam) fighter pilots who shot down the greatest number of their country's opponents became idols of their countrymen. The most successful were known to millions, even in enemy countries. They were respected by opposing pilots. Baron Manfred von Richthofen (the Red Knight, or Red Baron to a younger generation) is still world famous though he died in 1918 at the age of twenty-five. The legend of the R.A.F. in the Second World War, Group Captain Douglas Bader, "the legless wonder", was known to German pilots long before they captured him and honored him as their guest. There are numerous other examples of the fame achieved by the greatest aces.

Air fighting is, of course, colorful. It was also a novelty in the First World War. Fighter aces are always relatively young, and thus no one associates militarism or war guilt with them. Is this, then, the reason for their popularity and fame—and the fact that each country's news media paint them as national heroes? Or do the great fighter pilots contribute in a very important way to their country's war effort? In the following pages we will attempt to find out what they have really accomplished.

At the outbreak of the First World War in 1914, of course, few had any idea that pilots or air units would exert much influence on land battles. But perceptive pilots, and other keen observers of events, soon began to realize the tremendous potential of air power. By the third year of the war, 1917, the great von Richthofen was, in fact, called back to the front while on leave because the British Army had wrested air superiority from the Germans

over the Messines front, practically driving German Air
Service scouts from the skies. (British infantry was advancing unhindered by accurate artillery barrages, only possible
with up-to-date information obtained by aerial observation.) At Third Ypres and at Cambrai in 1917 strafing
had become a significant factor in the fighting. In the last
great German drive in the West (the first battle of the
Somme), which broke on 21 March 1918, heroic bombing
and strafing efforts by the greater number of Allied aircraft helped prevent the British retreat from turning into a
rout.[1] Air power was by that time, therefore, already a
major factor in the war on the ground.

By the latter half of that year General William
Mitchell, commanding the U.S. air forces, assembled
1,476 aircraft for the attack at St. Mihiel, and firmly believed the success of that drive was in large part due to
all-out night and day work by these air units.[2] General
Erich von Ludendorff reportedly remarked toward the
end of the war that Richthofen's presence at the front was
worth three divisions.

The role for fighters continued to grow in importance in
the Second World War. The Germans remembered the
tactical cooperation lessons of the last years of the First
World War and opened the Second with an air force tactically co-ordinated with the army to such a degree that
lightning victories resulted. Though the Germans enjoyed
inferior numbers in many instances in those years, the
swiftness of their advance, the disruption forced upon opponents, was a tribute to the Luftwaffe. Always, in those
opening campaigns, the pattern was the same. The
victim's air forces were paralyzed on the ground, perhaps
by surprise. Those units not destroyed were taken on in
an all-out, concentrated assault by fighters. Opposing air
forces were soon no longer able to interfere seriously with
the advancing panzers; German Stukas and other strafers
and fighter bombers then offered them pinpoint support.

---

[1] Floyd Gibbons, *The Red Knight of Germany*, Chapter 10;
Winston Churchill, *The World Crisis*, p. 782.
[2] Frank Platt, *Great Battles of World War I: In The Air*, p. 99.

For a time this combination was invincible. Note, however, that this concept hinged on the ability of German fighters to maintain air superiority. In the final analysis, therefore, on the Western front the fighter force was the key to successful ground operations. The great leaders of these fighter forces, then, were in a unique position to contribute to their country's cause and did so. Consider, for example, the value of Bader, in the Battle of Britain. With two artificial legs, chafing at the bit throughout the first phase of the desperately fought battle, he eagerly entered into the struggle when unleashed and on 30 August his squadron (242) brought down twelve enemy aircraft without loss. A week later, 7 September, he claimed eleven; two days later, with three squadrons, twenty; and on the climactic day, 15 September (Battle of Britain Day), with five squadrons, forty-two! Few can doubt the worth of this R.A.F. firebrand at this critical moment in history. Likewise, little doubt exists of the value to the Afrika Korps of Kapitän Hans-Joachim Marseille. His death in September 1942 had a disquieting effect on all German pilots in Africa and was even felt by Rommel's army. Why? In his last four weeks in action he had shot down fifty-seven Allied aircraft!

What were the tactical methods of such fighter pilots? How similar were their tactics in two wars separated by twenty years? How similiar were the tactics of the air aces in Korea and Vietnam? How did tactics vary in the different air forces? What were the basic strategies of the air forces in the two wars? Is the basic concept of tactical air power the same after Korea and Vietnam?

Recently I was asked, on the Mike Douglas show, an American television program, whether writing about air war and the achievements of fighter pilots is a glorification of war. My answer was that all wars are tragedies, but that young men have always fought for their country (as conscripted men in many cases) when war came, and probably always will—as long as there are wars. We must assume all agree on the madness of war, especially in today's nuclear world.

In knowing many of the surviving fighter pilots one

learns to appreciate better the futility of war, and the similarity of circumstances which engulf young men in each country when war comes. None were or are born killers. Even Erich Hartmann, who shot down 352 aircraft, the all-time record, is basically a gentle soul. In this volume we are primarily interested in their tactics in the air and the development by them of air fighting. The reader should not think of these fighter pilots as a special, ruthless or cold-blooded breed. They were great fliers and gunners, no doubt, and they fought very hard for self-preservation and victory, but aside from that they were very much like their fellow citizens and came from all walks of life. Their exploits in their century's wars are fascinating, because they pioneered tactics in the air. And thus in analyzing their accomplishments we are studying history—the beginning of the air age—in dramatic form.

The first use of manned aircraft in warfare was probably
in 1911, when the Mexican Government reconnoitered
rebel positions by air. That same year Italy used both aircraft and airships in a war against Turkey, some fitted
with bomb releases. In the Balkan war in 1912 aircraft
were again used, but it was not until the First World War
(1914-18) that aerial combat began.

The first air fighting in manned and powered aircraft
occurred in the very early days of the First World War,
by chance and design. Before 1914, military strategists
saw the role of aircraft as one of observation and reconnaissance. For that reason, practically all aircraft in existence at the beginning of the First World War were two-
seaters, designed more as stable observation machines
than as combat aircraft.

Contrary to some accounts, however, aerial combat of a
sort occurred almost from the beginning, though in crude
form.[1] Usually in the opening encounters the observer, or
pilot and observer, employed a pistol or rifle because none
of the air forces initially possessed aircraft armed with
machine-guns. The British were installing Lewis guns on
their two-seaters but the armament of the first four Royal
Flying Corps squadrons hurried to France consisted of
pistols and rifles.[2] Machine-guns had been considered too
heavy; they substantially restricted rate of climb.

---

[1] On 22 August 1914 Sergeant-Major Tillings of No. 2 Squadron (R.F.C.) claimed to have downed a German two-seater with
his rifle.

[2] J. E. Johnson, *Full Circle*, p. 5.

The great French ace, René Fonck, recalls in his memoirs his frustration as late as mid-1915 at passing very close to a German aircraft and being helpless to attack or defend himself:[1]

My plane (a Caudron G III) was not at all like a fighter plane. It was a slow, cumbersome biplane in which it was hardly possible to do anything other than reconnaissance or artillery range adjusting. Nevertheless, it took me more than once to Munster, and I often flew to observe troop movements in the area above Colmar.

On the way back from one of these flights I encountered my first Boche. We crossed each other's path with a loud roar of motors over the Sainte-Marie Pass.

I was unarmed, and if he had felt like duelling to the finish, I wouldn't have hesitated to try to charge into him to drag him down with me in the crash. Circumstances decided otherwise. Perhaps he was unarmed like me; perhaps he didn't feel in a fighting mood. At any rate, he made no attempt to attack me. However, he passed sufficiently close for me to be able to distinguish his features. If he let me escape in the hope of a better encounter, a similar opportunity never presented itself. But the adventure taught me a lesson. I no longer took off without carrying a good carbine, which I used many times later on, and with which I had some fortunate successes.

Don't think that you encounter a Boche hidden in the clouds every day. I finished the month of June without spotting a single one.

I went out, nevertheless, morning and evening to effect reconnaissance missions in the vicinity, sometimes on the Alsatian slope of the mountain chain, sometimes on the French slope. I gave range information for our artillery fire on the enemy gun batteries and trenches, but deep within me remained the hope of soon seeing an enemy aircraft appear on the horizon. The memory of my encounter at the Sainte-Marie Pass pursued me like an obsession, and I trembled with impatience at the idea of achieving a brilliant victory. Besides, like all rookies, I thought it easy to defeat an opponent, but difficult to encounter one. Many have

---

[1] Quoted in Stanley M. Ulanoff (ed.), *Ace of Aces.*

paid with their lives for this illusion brought on by their inexperience.

On 2 July my wish was realized. In the area of Munster, I spotted a Boche plane and attacked it with carbine fire. He escaped.

But machine-guns were being used. On 5 October 1914 Joseph Frantz of the French Air Force, in a Voisin pusher, shot down an Aviatik with a machine-gun. This was probably the first attack from behind in the blind spot, with a machine-gun, though R.F.C. Lieutenant L.A. Strange had fitted a Henri Farman with a machine-gun and attempted to bring down German aircraft with it as early as August 1914.

Roland Garros, using a gun designed by Raymond Saulnier which fired through the propeller, further broadened the new era of aerial dogfighting in February 1915. The French pilot's sensational innovation was crude and dangerous, consisting simply of metal plates attached to the propeller blades. The plates deflected bullets until the propeller itself was shattered. Garros, flying a Morane with courage and perhaps some luck, shot down five German aircraft in three weeks to become the first "ace" of the war and terrorized the German Air Service. To the dismay of the French Air Force, however, he landed behind German lines with engine trouble and was captured. The secret, crude though it was, was out.

Within forty-eight hours the German High Command in Berlin turned to a Dutchman, Anthony Herman Fokker, with a request that he design with all speed an answer to the Morane, which had been repaired and flown to Berlin.[1] Fokker and his associates quickly designed and built a most successful scout (a designation which evolved into pursuit, fighter and interceptor), the Fokker E-I. Its machine-gun fired through whirling propeller blades by means of a synchronized device which stopped the firing when a blade obstructed the path of fire.[2]

---

[1] Quentin Reynolds, *They Fought For The Sky*, p. 9.
[2] Bruce Robertson, *Air Aces of the 1914–1918 War*, p. 15.

It was now the Germans' turn to terrorize Allied pilots, though Berlin moved cautiously with its new aircraft and weapon, not seizing the initiative with vigor for months. But by the second half of 1915 Fokker E-Is, E-IIs and E-IIIs had almost cleared the skies of Allied observation aircraft and scouts.

The Allies had, however, captured one of Fokker's machines during the summer of 1915 and British and French engineers, with the help of Georges Constantinesco of Rumania, designed and built a gun which also fired efficiently through the propeller. With this gun the Allies managed to bring an end to what was then known as the Fokker scourge and by 1916 had gained the upper hand in the air. Two Royal Flying Corps pusher types, the D.H.2 and the F.E.2b, and the Nieuport II and Morane Type N of the French Air Force finally took the measure of the early Fokkers.

The margin shifted back to the Germans later that year (1916) when they introduced the Albatros D-I and D-II and Halberstadt tractor scouts—both biplanes. Throughout the remainder of the war the advantage passed from one side to the other as new aircraft and improved models of proved designs, and better engines, were introduced. At the end of the war, the British Sopwith Camel, with a 135-horsepower Clerget engine, a speed of 113 m.p.h. and two Vickers guns, had shot down more German aircraft than any other. It had been in wide use for some time and could remain airborne two and a half hours and climb to 19,000 feet or more. But the French Spad XIII (twin Vickers) was perhaps the best Allied scout of the war. General Billy Mitchell, commanding the American air forces, preferred it. It was powered by a 235-horsepower Hispano-Suiza engine and could attain 138 m.p.h., climb to 21,800 feet and remain airborne two hours.

Sixteen American squadrons were equipped with the Spad in 1918, including the First Pursuit Group, of which Eddie Rickenbacker, the most successful American fighter pilot of the war, was a member. American pilots had been less than completely happy flying the French Nieuport 28, with which they scored their first aerial victories. The 28

mounted but one gun, was structurally weak and was powered by an unreliable engine, the Gnome Monosoupape.
The Nieuport 29, however, which was becoming available
as the war ended, was highly regarded.

On the German side, probably the best fighter operating
in the last year of the war was the Fokker D.VII, with
twin Spandau guns and a speed of 118 m.p.h. The D.VII
could attain 20,000 feet and remain airborne an hour and
a half and was powered either by a 160-horsepower Mer-
cedes engine or (in the D.VIIF) a 185-horsepower
B.M.W. The Camel, Spad and Fokker surpassed by far
anything built in the United States in the First World
War. U.S. industry, starting late, did not produce a scout
of competitive performance.

Engineers and industry on both sides in the major
countries sought to outdo each other in the technological
race until the end of the war, and basic fundamentals of
aerial combat became well established before the end.
Tractor aircraft proved they could outperform pushers.
The trend became one of more and more powerful engines,
a natural evolution to support more guns and heavier
aircraft and to produce greater speed. Flying time became
acknowledged as of great importance to the attacker. By
the end of the war the British S.E. (Scouting Experimental) 5a, one of the better scouts, was capable of three-hour
sorties. (Interestingly, German designers didn't stress the
importance of endurance for scout operations. This same
thinking was to limit the performance of the Me.109 in
the Battle of Britain.)

Using these, the best machines their countries could
build, pilots fought it out in the air for about three years.
And although some in Allied countries—especially if they
have thoroughly digested wartime propaganda or post-war
assessments based on wartime loss figures—are not eager
to face the cold ink of an accurate scorecard, there is little
doubt that the German Air Service destroyed far more aircraft than it lost. The scores of the best Jastas (squadrons)
are eye-opening reading. The top three (2, 5 and 11) were
each awarded over 300 confirmed kills against the loss of
36, 17 and 15 pilots respectively. Taking into consider-

ation the fact that these Jastas lost more aircraft than men, the score is nevertheless disproportionate.

The Germans were usually outnumbered, usually fought over their own lines, and on the defensive. They pioneered close-flying formations and larger units acting under close control. These and other factors accounted for their impressive records. There were, of course, high-scoring Allied units at the front also.

German strategy was to fight over German lines. Since the prevailing wind is west to east, this strategy gave the Germans two major advantages. Allied aircraft more often than not had to return to their airfields to the west against a prevailing wind, which meant slow flying and the need for ample fuel; German pilots were closer to their bases and, in any event, could fly eastward with the prevailing wind on return flights. G.A.S. scouts, because of this strategy, required less fuel. Also, German pilots could usually crash-land in their own territory or parachute into their own lines after being disabled.[1] (A quarter of a century later, when the Luftwaffe mounted its offensive against the R.A.F. in 1940, Me.109 pilots could remain airborne for only ninety minutes. They had a tactical penetration in the Battle of Britain of only 125 miles. German fighter pilots thus had only ten or fifteen minutes' flying time in the target area, not enough in campaign to knock out an opposing fighter force.)

As the war progressed, the importance of speed became accepted and the two-seater observation craft became fair game for the scouts; it became obvious that the air force with the best scouts could clear the sky of enemy observation aircraft and protect its own. But not all First World War pilots would agree that speed was of paramount importance, as we shall see. Many believe maneuverability was of equal importance, and indeed the very effective three-wing scouts such as the British Sopwith Triplane and the German Fokker Dr. I were specifically designed to achieve great maneuverability and a high rate of climb.

---

[1] This German strategy, as analyzed by a First World War British pilot, is discussed in more detail in Chapter 7.

What became Holy Writ was that if one side possessed a faster scout that was also the equal of opposing scouts in maneuverability, its pilot held a definite advantage—being able to initiate and terminate combat at will—other conditions, such as altitude, being equal.

The argument whether maneuverability or speed was of greater importance continued up until the Second World War, with a majority leaning toward speed, because it enabled a pilot to overtake his adversary or to escape when at a disadvantage. Successful scout pilots on both sides learned to translate altitude into a speed advantage—thus the importance of ceiling. It is probably accurate to say that speed became a more and more important factor as firepower increased to such an extent that one quick burst could cripple one's foe; this was more likely in the Second World War because fighters by that time were carrying six or eight machine-guns or cannon. But First World War fighters were less heavily armed and dogfights lasted much longer.

By the end of the First World War pilots were flying at heights of up to 20,000 feet and higher, without oxygen. Though numbed by intense cold and suffering from a lack of sufficient oxygen, many sought these heights for safety and the advantage in bouncing the enemy by surprise with superior speed attained in a dive. Rate of climb, to attain altitude quickly and also to overtake and intercept, was therefore important, and has remained a measure of the performance of fighters since.

As noted, the 1941–18 war showed keen observers the potential of tactical air support in ground operations. Probably the first large-scale use of scouts for this purpose was at the Somme in 1915, when the R.F.C. put a hundred planes into the air in close bombing attacks to support that costly push.[1] The first really large concentration of German scouts was at Verdun in March 1916. Strafing was used effectively by both sides in 1917; at Cambrai, the British also employed tanks to achieve a breakthrough their army was unable to exploit. Allied strafing was effec-

---

[1] John Cuneo, *The Air Weapon 1914–1916*, p. 268.

tive in helping avoid a Dunkirk for the British Army in the spring of 1918,[1] as we have seen, and played a major role in disrupting German troop and supply movements in the general German retreat later in that year. General Billy Mitchell organized the first such use of U.S. tactical air power in the American attack at St. Mihiel in the summer of 1918.[2]

The Germans built the first long-range, strategic heavy bomber fleet, which bombed England late in the war.[3] It forced the British to recall scouts from France to counter the threat to civilians from these giant G-type bombers—which had a greater wingspan than the heavy British and U.S. bombers which raided Germany in the Second World War! Here was the beginning of planned fighter interception of a strategic bomber fleet, to be carried on on such a massive scale in both the Battle of Britain and the Battle of Germany some two decades later. In the First World War the British scouts were unable to turn back the German bombers, which were launched at night as well as by day. (The night attacks prompted creation of the first night fighters.) The big, four-engine aircraft carried 4,000 pounds of bombs, could fly eight or nine hours and were defended by six machine-guns. It was ironic that Hitler, or more rightly Göring, on whose advice Hitler depended, attempted two decades later to crush England by air with an air force which didn't possess a strategic bomber. And Britain, anticipating an aerial bombing onslaught—which it had experienced in the last part of the First World War—had made just enough preparation in the building of radar defenses and a good fighter arm to turn back the ill-prepared German thrust in the Second World War.

In retrospect, then, we can see that the beginning of practically every form of air combat stems from the First World War, that fighter tactics which proved sound in that war generally proved sound in the next. The Chinese had

---

[1] It was also effective in harassing German forces in their other 1918 offensives.

[2] General William Mitchell, *Memoirs of World War I*, p. 156.

[3] Raymond Fredette, *The First Battle of Britain 1917/18*, p. 132.

used rockets as weapons thousands of years before 1914, and balloons and gliders had been used for military purposes in earlier wars both in Europe and America. But in the First World War, for the first time, men went aloft in armed machines to bomb, strafe or shoot other airmen out of the sky. It soon became self-evident that the key to aerial superiority or supremacy was fast, armed scouts, flown by good pilots. The superior First World War scout could chase everything (except the heavy bombers) out of the sky, defend all its own aircraft, check on enemy movements and strafe enemy troops, communications and supply. What was evolving in 1918 in air tactics and strategy pointed to the dramatic, evolutionary air progress which so critically affected the Second World War's outcome. Some saw the air age coming. A few listened to them. And many refused to change traditional patterns of thinking. But we are getting ahead of our story. Let us see how combat tactics developed in the 1914–18 war.

3

PILOT TACTICS

In the first days of air fighting in 1914 tactics were naturally primitive and experimental. Pilots and observers (most of the airplanes were two-seater observation aircraft) had a go at their adversaries with pistols, shotguns, or rifles—or in some cases waved sportingly as they passed, in the belief that serious air fighting was impossible or not sporting among airmen, who had practically no chance to save themselves if their machines were set afire or destroyed in the air.

But it was not long before two-seater aircraft were regularly engaging in serious combat. The two-seaters fought in a variety of aerial patterns as their crews actually taught themselves how to fight. The rear cockpit machine-gun soon became a fixture and was turned on the enemy and fired by the observer. In pushers the observer occupied the forward cockpit. Two-seater and scout machine-guns initially fired over the propeller, but later fired through it. The forward-firing machine-gun, it was learned early, was suited to the offensive, including surprise attacks, while the rear machine-gun was a must for defense.

The weakness of the defense was quickly found to be that an attacker could approach from the rear, below, and not come within the range of fire of his intended victim—because the rear machine-gun's field of fire was blocked by the fuselage. This firing approach became the early favorite of the Germans when they enjoyed Fokker superiority in 1915, and both the early German fighter leaders Oswald Boelcke and Max Immelmann employed this tactic. Allied pilots also employed it, for there was an inevitable blind spot behind and below all two-seaters. What made this so often fatal was that two-seaters were usually slower than scouts. They couldn't run away and, if forced to stand and fight, their slow speed frequently frustrated even the best pilot's efforts to avoid attack from behind (and perhaps below), against which there was no adequate defense.

There were, in addition to the rear, other blind spots for two-seaters. Scouts with forward-firing guns could approach from slightly above, and off to one side, hidden from view and from counter-fire by the top wing. They could fire before they were detected, or dive below and fire as they pulled up slightly ahead and below, or attack from one side, hidden by the lower wing. The first great British ace, Albert Ball, employed and helped make famous the tactic of flying below an adversary and using his gun (then mounted on the upper wing) to shoot up and ahead (but not very far ahead) into his victim.

Deflection shooting, to become so effective in the Second World War, was attempted by scouts and observers from the early days of the First World War but was not as effective as attack from a blind spot. And, of course, there were firing passes of all kinds, from all angles, diving down on or zooming up under an opponent, as the business of dogfighting was learnt for the first time.

Later in the war some American pilots were very successful attacking in pairs—one firing from the blind spot to the rear, below, and the other firing from above. This, of course, complicated the defense. Elliot White Springs, fifth-ranking American scorer in the war, often employed such tactics. By this time pilots on both sides had long recognized the advantage in several scouts concentrating on a separated or single enemy machine. At this stage, as in the animal world, the stray caught by a prowling pack or squadron was in serious trouble.

As the general appreciation of the vulnerability of observation aircraft became accepted, the need for scouts also became accepted. As early as 1915 the Royal Flying Corps was requiring that observation aircraft sent over enemy lines be escorted by at least three other aircraft. These escorts were meant to be scouts. But in many cases there were not enough scouts, and observation aircraft escorted one another.

Nor did the Germans have enough scouts. But they began to acquire them in sufficient numbers first, in 1915, employing the Fokkers mentioned in the preceding chapter. The German pilot who proved what could be done with the new interrupter gear that Anthony Fokker attached to a German Parabellum gun was Oswald Boelcke. Boelcke was probably the single most important figure in the development of air fighting during the first part of the First World War. In July 1915 he was victorious in an air engagement that he had carefully planned beforehand—and his account provides us with the first detailed description of combat tactics.[1] The engagement was between two two-seaters (Boelcke's Albatros and a French Parasol), and Boelcke used superior height, concealment in the sun, clouds and sharp turns to allow his gunner finally to bring down the Frenchmen. This was his only victory in a two-seater.

Fokker, demonstrating his new monoplane, had refused to shoot down an Allied observer plane which he had had in his sights. Boelcke soon tested the Fokker plane and was delighted with its performance. He developed tactics methodically. He would climb to about 5,000 feet (most Allied craft flew below this) and conceal his aircraft in the sun on the German side of the lines. There he would wait until an unsuspecting foe approached and maneuver to descend unseen in a long, slanting dive, hoping to approach quite near before being spotted. He waited to fire until very close and used a series of short bursts, closing steadily until only a few yards distant. Then he would regain altitude and wait for another victim to appear. Using these tactics, Boelcke pioneered in air combat. He was using concealment, speed gained in a dive, forward-firing, attack from the rear and close-in shooting (the secret of a surprising number of aces in both wars). He was, in reality, developing tactics for a flying gun, which was what the forward-firing Fokker monoplane really was.

---

[1] J. E. Johnson, *Full Circle*, p. 13.

Boelcke noted that on several occasions while diving to attack he encountered, to his surprise, another aircraft very close, which he had not previously seen. He reasoned that a single pilot in a scout was highly vulnerable to surprise attack—no longer having the eyes of an observer for protection. He decided scouts should fly in pairs. As a result, he enlisted the partnership of another German pilot, Max Immelmann (they were both members of 62 Section at the time). They worked out a system of signaling one another in the air and began flying regularly together. Each pilot could cover the blind spots the other could not cover visually and detect an enemy aircraft approaching the other from the rear. Immelmann perfected what is still known today as the Immelmann turn. Using the superior performance of the Fokker, Immelmann dived on an opponent, fired as he completed a pass, then pulling up into what appeared to be the beginning of a loop. As he reached a vertical position, he kicked rudder hard left or right, dropped off on one side and swung back down into another dive at his foe, from the opposite direction. The advantage in this was that the aircraft didn't lose its speed and height advantage while attacking. Immelmann's tactic became widely copied.

Boelcke and Immelmann, so far as is known, were the first flying pair. So successful were they that other air forces adopted the flying-pair system. And from this first grouping was to come enlargements to flights of four, then squadrons and finally wings. These groupings were used in both World Wars; in the Korean and Vietnam wars it has been found that modern aircraft are very effectively employed in smaller units, even in pairs. And so in this sense, as Air Vice-Marshal J. E. Johnson has noted, in the last fifty years air fighting unit tactics have come full circle. Only in the last year or two, over North Vietnam, where ground defense has become highly sophisticated, has the trend turned back to formations, for defensive purposes.

The introduction in 1915 of guns firing forward through the propeller (such as Boelcke used) firmly established the tactic of gaining a position on an opponent's tail—still the best-known principle of air combat. This made the radius of turn almost all-important if one aircraft was slower than its opponent. This principle, of course, applied to both observers and scouts. The pilot who could turn inside his foe would inevitably end up on his tail, and with forward-firing guns this position was decisive unless the pilot ahead could dive away at greater speed or somehow evade his opponent's fire. The best pilots, however, were seldom thrown off their opponents' tail once they assumed that position, even though desperate, hectic flying and acrobatics often resulted. Richthofen, of course, knew the cardinal rule well. In one of his accounts of combat with a leading British ace, Major Lanoe Hawker, he describes how he triumphed applying this tactic:[1]

I must confess that it was a matter of great pride to me to learn that the Englishman I shot down on November 23 [1916] was the English equivalent of our great Immelmann. Of course, I did not know who he was during the fight, but I did know from the masterly manner in which he handled his plane and the pluck with which he flew that he was a wonderful fellow.

It was fine weather when I flew away from our airdrome that day. I was in the best of spirits and keen for the hunt. Flying at an altitude of about ten thousand feet, I observed three English planes. I saw that they saw me, and from their maneuvers I gathered that our hopes for the day's fun were mutual. They were hunting bent, the same as I. I was spoiling for a fight, and they impressed me much the same. They were above me, but I accepted the challenge. Being underneath and in no position to attack, I had to wait till the fellow dived on me. It was not long to wait. Soon he started down in a steep gliding dive, trying to catch me from behind.

He opens fire with his machine-gun. Five shots rip out, and I change my course quickly by a sharp turn to the left. He follows, and the mad circle starts. He is trying to get behind me, and I am trying to get behind him. Round and

---

[1] Quoted in Floyd Gibbons, *The Red Knight of Germany,* Chapter I.

round we go in circles, like two madmen, playing ring-around-a-rosie almost two miles above the earth. Both of our motors are speeded to the utmost; still neither of us seems to gain on the other. We are exactly opposite each other on the circumference of the circle, and in this position neither one of us can train our single forward-shooting machine-guns on the other.

First, we would go twenty times around to the right, and then swing into another circle going around twenty times to the left. We continued the mad race, neither gaining an advantage. I knew at once that I was dealing with no beginner, because he didn't appear to dream of trying to break off the fight and get out of the circling. His plane was excellent for maneuvering and speed, but my machine gave me an advantage by being able to climb better and faster. This enabled me at last to break the circle and maneuver into a position behind and above him.

But in the circling fight, both of us had lost height. We must have come down at least six thousand feet because now we were little more than three thousand feet above the ground. The wind was in my favor. Throughout the fight, at the same time we kept getting lower, the wind was gradually drifting us back across the German lines. I saw that now we were even behind the German lines in front of Bapaume, and my opponent should have noticed that it was time for him to back out of the fight, because he was getting farther into my territory.

But he was a plucky devil. With me behind and above him, he even turned around and waved his arm at me, as though to say, *"Wie geht's?"* [How are you?] We went into circles again—fast and furious and as small as we could drive them. Sometimes I estimated the diameters of the circles at between eighty and a hundred yards. But always I kept above him and at times I could look down almost vertically into his cockpit and watch each movement of his head. If it had not been for his helmet and goggles, I could have seen what sort of face he had.

He was a fine sportsman, but I knew that in time my close presence behind and above him would be too much for him, particularly as all the time we were getting lower and lower and farther behind my lines. We were getting so close to the ground that he would soon have to decide whether he would have to land behind our lines or whether he would break the circle and try to get back to his own side.

Apparently, the idea of landing and surrender never occurred to this sportsman, because suddenly he revealed his plans to escape by going into several loops and other maneuvers of equal folly. As he came out of them, headed back for his lines, my first bullets began whistling around his ears, because up to now, with the exception of his opening shots, neither one of us had been able to range on the other.

The battle is now close to the ground. He is not a hundred yards above the earth. Our speed is terrific. He starts back for his front. He knows I am right behind him and close on his tail. He knows my gun barrel is trained on him. He starts to zigzag, making sudden darts right and left—right and left—confusing my aim and making it difficult to train my gun on him. But the moment is coming. I am fifty yards behind him. My machine-gun is firing incessantly. We are hardly fifty yards above the ground—just skimming it.

Now I am within thirty yards of him. He must fall. The gun pours out its stream of lead. Then it jams. Then it reopens fire. That jam almost saved his life. One bullet goes home. He is struck through the back of the head. His plane jumps and crashes down. It strikes the ground just as I swoop over. His machine-gun rammed itself into the earth, and now it decorates the entrance over my door. He was a brave man, a sportsman, and a fighter.

Generally speaking, the development of tactics in the First World War can be divided into two phases, though no exact date can be applied to them. In the early phase individualists with great courage and skill and an aggressive nature ran up the highest scores. They were men like Britain's Albert Ball (44 victories), the Canadian Willy Bishop (72) and France's Georges Guynemer (53).[1] Such individualists sought out the enemy, often a lone scout, against great odds. The attrition rate among such individ-

---

[1] Guynemer, in 1917, shortly before his death, pioneered the nose-firing cannon, but it was not until the Second World War that this armament was widely used.

ualists became awesome as the war progressed. Following
Boelcke's tactics of formation flying, senior commanders
soon adopted larger, controlled formations. In the later
years the top-scoring aces, like Richthofen (80), "Mick"
Mannock (73) and James McCudden (58) employed
formation tactics, organized units working together to support each other.

Richthofen describes how he led his pilots in a report to
Sixth Army air forces in February 1917:[1]

The best method of flying against the enemy is as follows: The officer commanding the group, no matter how
large, should fly lowest, and should keep all machines under
observation by turning and curving.

No machine should be allowed either to advance or to
keep back. More or less, the whole squadron should advance curving. Flying straight on above the front in dangerous, as even machines of the same type of plane develop
different speeds. Surprises can be avoided only when flying
in close order. The commanding officer is responsible that
neither he nor any of his pilots are surprised by the enemy.
If he cannot see to that, he is no good as a leader.

Many of the most successful pilots, such as Richthofen,
were essentially cautious in choosing foes and the conditions for combat. Yet Richthofen, like Ball, was shot
down while abandoning caution, flying low over enemy
lines in pursuit of an opponent: both were probably
downed by machine-gun fire from the ground.

In summary, more than a dozen considerations applied
to aerial tactics by the end of the First World War. A partial list of these factors that every scout pilot considered in
evaluating his aircraft's and his own capability include,
not necessarily in order of importance: Speed; Armament;
Sturdiness of the aircraft—how much stress it could withstand in violent maneuvers; Ceiling; Engine and gun relia-
bility; Vision and field of fire of guns; Acceleration—of
crucial importance in escaping a losing fight or in overtak-

[1] Quoted in Floyd Gibbons, *The Red Knight of Germany*,
Chapter 6.

ing a fleeing opponent; Diving velocity—likewise of crucial importance in escape and overtaking; Rate of climb; Endurance (flying time); Maneuverability; Location—the scout in combat over his own lines enjoyed a major advantage because he could descend in a dogfight without as much fear of ground fire and, if forced to land, escaped capture; Position—the aircraft with greater height, or positioned between the sun and his adversary, held an advantage; Wind (more of a factor in 1914–18 than in 1939–45); Formation—as air fighting developed formations proved effective in combat, and scouts in formation, especially when attacking in large formations, enjoyed a tactical advantage over scattered or single aircraft.

4

FIGHTER STRATEGY

Air strategy was relatively simple in the opening phases of the First World War. The primary purpose of flights was to gain information about the enemy army, its movements, strength and disposition. Steadily that role expanded. Aircraft were soon employed to strafe and bomb enemy troops, to disrupt transportation routes and vehicles, to bomb enemy airdromes, to turn back enemy bombers or to escort their own. In the final years of that war they were massed for concentrated support of major ground offensives and had become a significant influence in such campaigns.

In tracing fighter strategy as it has developed, we must momentarily look beyond the First World War. It was in the Second World War that fighters really came into their own and proved decisive in many major campaigns—both on ground and at sea. The key to German success in the onslaught against France, Britain and the Low Countries in 1940 was that the Luftwaffe literally shot the French and British air forces out of the sky in the first five days of the offensive.[1] The German Army was, of course, superior to its adversaries and would likely have achieved the triumph denied it for four years in the First World War without this advantage, but aerial superiority was at the very least victory insurance. At the most, in protecting advancing troops and armored forces (panzers) from Allied

---

[1] J. E. Johnson, *Full Circle*, p. 116. It should be remembered, in analyzing the 1940 campaign, that the R.A.F. opposed the Me.109 on the continent at this time only with Hurricanes. The higher-performance Spitfire was kept in England.

strafing and bombing (which so handicapped German forces in France in 1918) and in its coordinated bombing and strafing of enemy forces it was decisive in producing victory in the "lightning war" (*Blitzkrieg*).

If the vigorous, effective German use of panzers in 1940 deserves most of the credit for that lightning victory, then the decisive role of fighters in the next strategic effort, the attack on England (the Battle of Britain), is beyond doubt. The air forces fought and decided this battle, the outcome of which determined the question of an invasion of England. In winning it R.A.F. fighters checked the German Army. Here was history's most crystal-clear demonstration of the decisive strategic influence of fighters. They were to prove decisive on other occasions as the war progressed, and in later years enabled British and American heavy bombers to carry on their strategic bombing offensive.

Of interest in this study of the strategic air war in 1939–45 is the realization that the Allies overestimated the effect of strategic bombing. The Germans, for their part, underestimated the need for a strategic air arm. The R.A.F., and the French Air Force also, began the war with little in the way of an effective, trained air arm for close cooperation with ground forces. In the 1940 crisis in France this cost them dearly.[1] Great hopes, however, were harbored in England for the strategic bombing bomber force. The Germans, who never had any serious intention of attacking England until 1940, had no strategic bomber arm with which to carry out the attack when it was ordered.[2] Emphasis in the build-up of the Luftwaffe had been placed on tactical co-operation with the ground forces. That meant stress on dive bombers and medium bombers. As it turned out, the medium bombers were good, but not fast enough to outdistance fighters. Elite, two-engine destroyer squadrons (Me.110s) were less effective than had been hoped, not capable of taking on fighters nor fast enough to escape them. The Stukas

[1] A. J. P. Taylor, *English History*, pp. 392, 485.
[2] Taylor, *English History*, p. 410.

(Ju.87s) proved highly vulnerable when not shielded by German fighters. All these types, then, were dependent for success on German fighters. As long as Luftwaffe fighters held aerial superiority, the entire strength of the Luftwaffe and the German Army could be brought to bear, but when German fighters were not masters of the sky the Luftwaffe's potential, and that of the Army, was appreciably reduced. This is a cardinal air power lesson of the Second World War.[1]

Britain failed to develop effective tactical air co-operation with its armies until the middle of the war. It was probably not until the battle of Alam Halfa, before El Alamein in 1942, that Allied armies after many costly defeats finally received the type of close air support that helped so much to bring about victory. Germany had won quickly in Poland in 1939, in Denmark, Norway, France and the Low Countries in 1940 and in Crete and Russia in 1941, employing the strategy of tactical support of her armies. She had only lost in Britain, where German fighters could not gain mastery of the skies. (The victory in Crete accomplished by the Luftwaffe had, however, been bought at an awful cost to the paratroopers.)

After success in North Africa, the Allies won in Sicily, Italy, France and Germany, utilizing superior air power in close tactical air cooperation with their armies. When the occasion demanded, even the strategic bomber forces were assigned tactical support tasks, such as in the invasion of France. The statements of most German Army generals, including Field-Marshal Karl Gerd von Rundstedt, commanding in the West, convey the conclusion that overwhelming Allied air superiority was the prime cause of the German Army's defeat. In the June 1944 invasion, German formations in reserve in France often required weeks to reach the front because the transportation system in France had been shattered from the air. In the Battle of the Bulge six months later the turn of the tide came when the weather cleared at Christmas and Allied fighter bomb-

---

[1] F. W. von Mellenthin, *Panzer Battles*, chap. 9, relates that protected Stukas silenced artillery at Sedan.

ers were able to concentrate attacks on German armor in the narrow salient. By this time, it is true, the Germans also faced a shortage of fuel. But enough had been allotted from reserves to the panzers for this offensive. The key factor was that it could not be brought up to the forward units because the Allied forces had now achieved air supremacy. Allied fighters kept the skies and roads open to their supply forces and denied them to the Germans.

(In Korea and Vietnam it has been found that tactical support can be carried a step further by the extensive use of helicopters, and these aircraft are now a major element in any tactical air grouping, serving as fast troop transports as well as gunships.)

Strategic air power was seldom applied in the Russian campaign in the Second World War. The Luftwaffe was primarily designed for tactical support, the Russian concept was the same. Russian fighters were not even equipped with oxygen. Their role was intended to be close to the ground, strafing the enemy or protecting other Russian aircraft strafing the enemy. The Luftwaffe could have advantageously employed a strategic air arm to bomb Russian industrial centers and transportation routes after the German Army stalled at the gates of Moscow in December 1941, but little was available.

If the Luftwaffe had possessed a strategic long-range bombing fleet in 1941 it could have more effectively employed it in Russia than against Great Britain. For one lesson of the Second World War, concerning fighters and heavy bombers, was that a determined fighter force can inflict intolerable loss on heavy bombers. (This was true in the early years only in the case of daylight attacks, but as night fighters developed it also applied to night attacks.) The British had a strong fighter force by 1940 and by that time were building twice as many fighters per month as the Germans, contrary to the widely held and popular belief among those in Allied countries that the Luftwaffe held an overwhelming numerical advantage.[1] Moreover,

---

[1] Burton Klein, *Germany's Economic Preparations for War,* p. 410; Chester Wilmot, *The Struggle for Europe,* p. 54.

the R.A.F.'s fighters were equipped with oxygen and superchargers for high-altitude flying. The Russian Air Force was not so equipped and thus a strategic long-range bomber offensive against Russian industry and transportation in 1941 would very likely have been highly effective. Luftwaffe fighters, of course, would not have been able to escort the bombers—they were without sufficient endurance to do so effectively even in the Battle of Britain— but this would not have been a prerequisite in Russia.

It is not necessary to dwell at length on strategic bombing in a study of fighter tactics and strategy, but it should be kept in mind that massacres of R.A.F. bombers without fighter escort by day in 1940 (by German fighters using ground radar in some cases) turned the R.A.F. to night bombing.[1] Heavy losses of its bombers by day in the Battle of Britain turned the Luftwaffe to night bombing the same year. In both cases defending fighters checked the attempted daylight strategic bombing offensive. Three years later, when the U.S. Army began the build-up of its Eighth Air Force in England, a long-range, strategic, heavy bombing force, both the British and Germans initially felt that defending fighters would make daylight attacks by the B-17s and B-24s too costly. That is exactly what threatened to occur in the autumn of 1943, and only through the use of long-range fighter escorts, primarily the seven-hour P.51 Mustang, was the Eighth Air Force able to continue its daylight bomber attacks, which produced more accurate bombing of military targets than did night attacks. It was fighters, again, which determined the fate of a strategic air effort.

A final note concerning the strategic bombing of Germany in the Second World War is in order. During that war the people in Allied countries were impressed daily with newspaper headlines telling of the number of tons of bombs dropped on Germany (and Japan and Italy) and the tremendous military damage accomplished. After the war it was learned that many of these bombings had little

---

[1] J. E. Johnson, *Full Circle*, p. 115.

military effect—especially the night bombings. German industry, for example, produced far more war material, tanks and aircraft in the last year of the war, despite all-out strategic bombing, than in any other year of the war. But what is even more interesting are indications that the heavy bomber offensives of the R.A.F. and U.S.A.A.F. over Germany cost the attackers more dearly than the defenders.

A. J. P. Taylor believes that British strategists were obsessed with independent bombing and that this obsession led to many of England's disasters in the war. He feels it was a mistake to adopt terror bombing tactics.[1] Whether one agrees or disagrees, it is now obvious to all that the cost of many of these bombing missions was exorbitant. On some nights the R.A.F. lost more than ninety heavy bombers—more than the Eighth Air Force lost in any single daylight attack. The loss of so many heavy bombers represented the loss of almost a thousand highly trained personnel, plus the heavy bombers themselves, in a few hours. If, as sometimes happened, most of the bombs dropped fell miles from the target, or if the raid was on a city and failed to weaken the enemy's morale—which was often true—the sacrifice is highly questionable. On some of the U.S. daylight bomber attacks in late 1943 and early 1944 German fighters shot down sixty or seventy heavies and damaged others. Here again the loss was six or seven hundred trained airmen, plus others wounded on cripples which limped home, plus the loss of many expensive machines, in a few hours. Considering that the "round-the-clock" bombing offensive against Germany continued on a day-and-night basis for years, it is rather easy to understand why total loss figures were not quickly released either in England or America after the war. Many of these attacks were heavy defeats and the effect of the whole strategic bombing offensive against Germany was overrated for most of the war.

German fighters brought about this result in Europe. Japanese fighters failed to accomplish the same result in

---

[1] A. J. P. Taylor, *English History*, pp. 541, 551.

opposing the U.S. bombing of Japan. The larger U.S. bombers employed in the Pacific were in the end, as in Europe, escorted by fighters. The Japanese fighters, however, were not as effective and radar defense was not as well organized. Moreover, this offensive began in the last stages of the war in the Pacific, when the Japanese were up against overwhelming numerical odds in every weapons category. Earlier in the Pacific war, specifically in the campaign against Rabaul, where the Japanese had concentrated strong fighter forces, it was found that fighter escort of attacking U.S. bombers was necessary to hold down losses.

As fighters became recognized as necessary for bomber protection in both World Wars, so too did they become recognized as necessary for protection of naval forces, particularly in the Second World War. The first advocacy of this new military principle came between the World Wars, but it was not until 1940 and 1941 that the lesson was permanently implanted. Royal Navy losses from Luftwaffe attack off Norway in April 1940 because of inadequate fighter protection, the reluctance of either the German Army or Navy to move across the English Channel without adequate air protection, losses of Royal Navy warships around Crete to German air attack, and the loss of two Royal Navy capital ships off Malaya to Japanese air attack and the loss of Dutch, American and Australian warships in the Pacific, in the opening days of the war, due to the absence of defending fighter aircraft, well illustrated the lesson. The Pearl Harbor disaster falls in this category in a sense but it was also a sneak attack, which owed some of its success to its infamous nature.

In the First World War there had been much controversy over the proper strategy for scouts. R.F.C. dogma was aggressiveness, flights over the enemy's lines daily, and so on. The German Air Service adopted defensive tactics, generally, using offensive tactics only in major offensives (such as at Verdun in 1916). The British believed the Germans failed to understand the capability of their air arm. The Germans, conserving their forces and losing fewer aircraft, were satisfied their strategy was best. The

French, until they were badly mauled employing over-aggressive tactics, and the Americans later in the war, generally followed the British example in that war and losses were heavy.

By the time of the Second World War, it had become self-evident, or did in its opening phases, that fighters were the key to offensive and defensive air operations, that a combination of both their offensive and defensive capacity was necessary in any strongly opposed strategic campaign, whether on land, sea or in the air. Fighter forces on the defensive were successful in the Battle of Britain and in the Luftwaffe defense of the continent in 1941–2. Such successes were gratifying but didn't win positively; rather, they thwarted the enemy's strategic plan.

An offensive success of fighters in the strategic campaign known as the Battle of Germany (against a strong fighter defense) enabled the Allies to carry out their bombing strategy and was therefore decisive.

Interesting questions have been raised by the nature of air operations in the Korean and Vietnam wars. As noted above, helicopters have come into their own as transport strafers. But it should be kept in mind that in both these wars U.S. Air Force fighters held virtual command of the skies over the battle areas, and thus the helicopters were not subjected to heavy attack from enemy fighters. The Communists in both conflicts were tied to the claim that these conflicts were revolutionary struggles and therefore neither North Korean nor North Vietnamese fighters were often seen over the battlefields. U.S. Air Force fighters shot North Korean fighters out of the sky by at least a ten to one margin on those occasions over a period of time when the Communists tested their forces against American fighters. But in Vietnam the margin was very close. What might happen to helicopters in a war when fighter forces are equally balanced and employed over the battlefield is an unanswered question. Certainly they would need protection from fighters and it seems reasonable to conclude that their effectiveness would diminish in such a war unless friendly fighters enjoyed superiority or perhaps supremacy.

Another recent evolution which bears directly on the strategic role of fighters is the development of small, highly potent nuclear bombs. A fighter carrying such nuclear weapons considerable distances assumes the role of a strategic bomber as well as that of a tactical aircraft. Because of this increased power of destruction, a modern fighter can carry out a bombing mission which formerly required many bombers. Other fighters are often needed for protection. It has been found that today's faster jets can, against all but highly sophisticated defenses, operate effectively in twos and fours—smaller formations than were used in the Second World War and in the last years of the First for bombing or other missions.

In one other operational phase, the Korean and Vietnam wars could have been misleading. Because the enemy was usually employing guerrilla tactics, rather than moving armies openly across the countryside, tactical air operations against enemy armor have been limited (as were tactical air operations of the enemy against U.S. armor). Transports were often found and attacked, but seldom did tactical air power have an opportunity to operate against massed armored units conducting a major, concentrated offensive. When strategic bombers were employed, as they were regularly in Vietnam, targets were areas where troop concentrations, supply routes, equipment and so on were thought to be located. Relatively little tactical air co-operation, on a concentrated mechanized enemy, was seen.

The lightning victory of the Israeli Army in 1967, however, demonstrated to some extent the potential of modern tactical air power efficiently employed. The Egyptian Air Force was decimated in the first hours of that campaign and thereafter Israeli fighter bombers concentrated on enemy armor with devastating effect. It was the German pattern of 1940 over again, and illustrates what can be done today in the field of tactical air co-operation with armored units. With guided missiles and rockets under their wings, the tactical punch of modern fighters is more devastating than ever. Some believe that the day is approaching when

fighters with even more modern equipment will be re-
mote-controlled, both in interception and tactical roles.

But we have carried fighter strategy ahead far enough;
what we are now concerned with is the development of
tactics and strategy as described by some of the great fliers
of the First World War. They, after all, established most
of the principles of air war in effect today.

Part Two

THE FIRST WORLD WAR

5

EARLY DAYS

One of the outstanding fighter aces of the early days of the First World War was Duncan Grinnell-Milne, now in his seventies and living comfortably in South Kensington, London. A full gray moustache and erect bearing give him a trace of that long-ago military look, and he still vividly recalls the air fighting of more than fifty years ago, fighting in which he was shot down or forced down on numerous occasions, once falling captive to the Germans for two and a half years, until he escaped to fly again in 1918.

In November 1915 his airdrome (and that of the Royal Flying Corps' Sixteen Squadron) was near Merville in France; the grass field was L-shaped, on a bend in the River Lys. Pilots lived on a barge on the river. They were flying B.E.2Cs twice daily at that time in a bombing campaign against the rail junction at Don. Each aircraft carried two 112-pound bombs and at this stage of air bombing pilots first flew over the target to set up aim and then made a second run to drop the bombs. An observer sat in the front cockpit manning a Lewis .303 machine-gun.

The morning of the 28th, which was to be different, was cold. Pilots, dressed in trench boots, fleece-lined caps and flying-coats, breakfasted on the barge. Poplars were visible on the banks, and a short distance beyond were the squadron's brownish canvas hangars. The news came that enemy aircraft had crossed the lines. An anti-aircraft battery at the front had telephoned squadron headquarters—a nearby farmhouse. Four pilots, including Grinnell-Milne, were ordered to chase the Germans back. He and his observer, Captain C. C. Strong, were quickly off to begin the chase.

Grinnell-Milne buckled into the open cockpit behind a ninety-horsepower air-cooled engine and gave it a few strokes. There was pressure and he shouted that the switch was off. A crewman pulled the propeller blade around and backed away. Grinnell-Milne, in brown leather gauntlets reaching almost to the elbow, switched on, called out "Contact!" and eased on a little throttle to start the engine.

One pilot, in a small, single-seat Bristol Scout, had already taken off. Grinnell-Milne's was the first two-seater off, headed north. Climbing at 65 m.p.h., without goggles, he began a turn and almost at once saw a big, white Albatros two-seater far above at 9,000 feet, flying parallel to the lines. The Albatros was faster but the German hadn't seen him. Grinnell-Milne began a climbing approach at full throttle, wondering whether he would have time to reach the enemy before he turned back to the east. To gain the best chance Grinnell-Milne headed into the east, to be ahead of the Albatros when he turned homeward. The climbing chase began over Neuve-Chapelle and continued on a straight course to Armentières, by which time Grinnell-Milne had about reached the Albatros's level, his adversary having now descended to about 6,500 feet. Then the Albatros turned eastward, headed home!

Grinnell-Milne, with full throttle and nose slightly down, managed to pull in front of him, in the direction of the sun, the enemy pilot obviously looking behind into the west, perhaps blinded by the sun ahead. The two aircraft were about five miles into German lines. The Albatros throttled down, beginning his glide toward Lille. Grinnell-Milne let him overtake and he passed on the right. Strong opened fire as he did so, firing perhaps twenty or thirty rounds only.

The Albatros turned left in front of the B.E. and Strong began to change the gun to the forward mounting. Grinnell-Milne was surprised there was no return fire. By the time Strong was ready to fire again, from the forward mount, the Albatros was turning quite steeply and after only a few rounds he was diving so steeply that Grinnell-Milne couldn't follow. He then realized that the enemy was hit; he was going down, out of control! They watched, fascinated. And then Grinnell-Milne heard the crack of bullets. An Albatros was above him. Two more enemy aircraft approached from the east. After a desperate, running fight he managed to make it back to the base, holed in many places but victorious.

It had been an aerial victory of slow, difficult early-war tactics. Later in the war British pilots in Camels and S.E.s, much faster, would dive on their victims, often from behind. In these early encounters, however, the chase and the general conditions of flying were often more difficult than the encounter itself. The arrival of faster scouts was to change all this, though many First World War pilots believed maneuverability the most important single consideration in air combat even in 1918.

After his escape from a German prisoner-of-war camp in 1918, Grinnell-Milne flew an S.E.5a scout. It was light on the controls, could dive at 275 m.p.h. and side-slip rapidly. One of the experiences he survived in it was described in the *Daily Telegraph Magazine* as a First World War dive-bombing attack.[1]

According to the account, he was carrying bombs on that day and dropped two on an artillery battery. The upward force of the blast touched off by the bombs tossed the S.E.5a's tail up and pushed the nose down. The control stick jammed and he headed straight down towards the ground, a few hundred feet below. As the nose began to lift, the aircraft struck—by great good fortune on the down side of a hill. The undercarriage was torn off and the tip of the propeller blade was carried away. One side of the fuselage was stripped bare of its tail-plane and elevator. But in this condition he managed to reach British lines, where he crashed and was knocked unconscious.

The S.E.5a that Grinnell-Milne was flying toward the end of the war was one of the best British fighters. Like the Camel, its performance was superior to earlier English

---

[1] *Daily Telegraph Magazine* No. 182: 29 March 1968.

fighters. It was supplied to squadrons in 1917 and 1918 (the first were delivered in March 1917) and was faster than the French Spads and Nieuports, though less maneuverable than the Nieuport. Though Grinnell-Milne admits that it was unable to turn with the D.VII (probably the best German scout in wide use at the end of the war), because of its firepower, speed and high ceiling, it, with the Camel, enabled the Allies to regain air superiority in 1918. (The S.E.5a was the model of the S.E.5 produced in greatest numbers and was powered originally by a 200-h.p. Hispano-Suiza engine or one of the British-built equivalents. It could attain a maximum speed of 120 m.p.h. and climb to 19,500 feet. The French went into production of S.E.5as in 1918.)

Contrasting the performance of Grinnell-Milne's 1915 B.E.2C, which flew at 75 m.p.h., climbed at 65, and which carried two airmen and one machine-gun, with the two machine-guns (Vickers and Lewis) and high performance of the one-seater S.E.5a, one can measure the technical progress achieved between 1915 and 1917.

Grinnell-Milne recommends, for those who wish to learn what the air war was like for scouts in those days, *Flying Fury,* the story of the most decorated of British pilots, James McCudden, who shot down 57 enemy aircraft and rose to the rank of major after starting the war as an air mechanic. One can read more about his own remarkable career in *Wind In The Wires.*[1] He was awarded the Military Cross and Distinguished Flying Cross and has lived through another war and another quarter of a century, to see man reach the moon.

The slow mission of 1915 described above is a far cry from the combat to be examined in succeeding chapters. Grinnell-Milne was flying with an observer-gunner in a two-seater and it required half an hour to get into firing position—which was off to one side and slightly above his foe. Then from the one gun fired by the observer perhaps forty rounds in all were fired. There was no return fire. In

---

[1] Duncan Grinnell-Milne, *Wind In The Wires*; James McCudden, *Flying Fury.*

piloting the B.E.2C, Grinnell-Milne was in the position of being able to hear and see the gun fired, but other than gaining a good firing position he played a limited role in shooting down his opponent. By the end of the war all this had radically changed.

Scouts were much faster one-seaters. Fighting usually took place between organized formations, which sometimes flew as high as 20,000 feet. And it was seldom that one got in a shot at an enemy plane flying alongside—the victim continuing to fly straight ahead. The scouts of later years fired through the propeller and pilots sought to get into a position on their adversary's tail, and much dogfighting ensued as a result, as we shall see.

THE RICHTHOFEN GESCHWADER

On Südlich Auffahrtsallee, in one of Munich's nicer residential sections, lives Carl August von Schoenebeck, the youngest scout squadron leader on the Western Front in 1918, a member of Jagdgeschwader I, popularly known as the "Flying Circus". The Richthofen Geschwader (as it is also called) was the most efficient aerial fighting organization of the First World War. Established in June 1917, by the end of the war in November 1918 it had destroyed 644 Allied aircraft against a loss of 56 pilots killed and 52 wounded!

The slightly graying man with dark bushy eyebrows who greeted me at the door of an impressive stone house was surprisingly young and nimble—though in his seventies. We walked through rooms of old Dutch furniture onto a terrace overlooking a small pool. A garden stretched out from the back of the green-shuttered house. Sitting in the shade, where a breeze eased the heat of the day, Frau von Schoenebeck and a daughter joined us and we began our discussion. Von Schoenebeck still flies his own aircraft, often to the Ruhr, though Frau von Schoenebeck thinks it's time he consider slower transportation. The brown eyes are still clear and alert and he talks rapidly, full of the same energy, according to Frau von Schoenebeck, he has exhibited all his life. His physical condition is impressive and both Frau von Schoenebeck and their daughter expressed to me their astonishment at his never-failing energy.

"Yes, I flew with Richthofen, and once while flying in close formation with him a British pilot almost shot me down. It was in August or September 1917 and we were flying against the English, who were very sporting. I was in a D.III Albatros and behind Richthofen on the right. The British pilot had a large B painted on his machine and was flying an S.E.5 (one of the best, if not the best, British scouts of the war). Richthofen had seen this machine a few days earlier and was on the lookout for it. It was thought to have been flown by a famous pilot. When I spotted the British scouts Richthofen had already seen them, as he usually did. They were above us—six or seven of them—and we began a turn to the right.

"Down came the S.E.5s, the scout with the B on it leading. After I turned right he was suddenly on top of me, firing. I hadn't known he was heading for me. They had come down from some three thousand feet higher and had great speed. My aircraft was hit. One bullet entered my back but only just under the skin. The D.III took forty-eight bullets in a short time. I managed to evade further damage well enough to escape, landing at a Belgian field, Courtraix, where I managed to get out myself. Richthofen later apologized to me, saying he was just a little too late in turning!"

Von Schoenebeck wondered if the pilot who had attacked him could have been Albert Ball, but since this was in late summer of 1917 it couldn't have been. The famed Ball, after achieving 44 aerial victories, disappeared on the afternoon of 7 May that year. Richthofen had previously met Ball in the air and the Germans claimed it was Lothar von Richthofen (brother of the more famous Manfred) who had shot Ball down, though some on the British side disputed the claim. Be that as it may, discussion of this encounter led the conversation to the subject of Richthofen and his training and leadership methods, which von Schoenebeck recalled. He had been posted to Jasta 11 in 1917, the Jasta Richthofen led personally until 24 June, when he was made commander of the newly formed Geschwader.[1]

---

[1] After 24 June, Richthofen's brother Lothar normally led Jasta 11, though Manfred von Richthofen sometimes led his old Jasta after he had become commander of the Geschwader.

Richthofen, he recalled, showed a keen interest in each new member of Jasta 11 while he led it, interviewed each new pilot, took each on a flying test, then criticized the novice's mistakes and complimented him on the good points. He saw that all new pilots were allotted ammunition with which to practice gunnery, sometimes flying with them (it is said he often put over ninety per cent of his bullets into the ground targets). When the new pilot was ready, he took him on the first patrol and watched him very closely in the air, to help him react correctly in critical situations. Many were surprised by what Richthofen had learned of their flying habits in a short time. His tactics were those he had learned from Boelcke and his own experience and ideas. In the air he stressed a constant search of the sky and particularly a close watch behind, von Schoenebeck recalled.

I asked him what the most important performance factor in combat was.

"The most important was rate of turn; it was highly important. Second was speed. Of course, one needed a combination of good performance features. Looking at the Second World War for a moment, the Spitfire could perform better than the Me.109 at some altitudes because it had greater maneuverability. The Me.109 was faster, in my opinion.[1]

"Our best scout in the First World War was the Fokker D.VII with the B.M.W. engine. I think the S.E.5 was the best R.F.C. scout of that war. The British scouts could often turn sharply. I wouldn't say, as many claim, that the English were over our lines more.[2] They were, of course, very sporting and we were more military. I remember

---

[1] This is a matter of dispute between Spit and Me.109 pilots; performance was similar and different models of one aircraft flying against different models of the other accounted for some of the controversy. Performance manuals show the Spit, generally speaking, a bit faster.

[2] The overwhelming weight of evidence is that they were. But toward the end of the war, when von Schoenebeck flew, this may not have been as pronounced as in earlier years. See Chapter 7.

once, however, in October of 1917, when three R.F.C. scouts flew over our field at a height of about 1,200 feet. Richthofen said this was puzzling, especially when they returned some thirty minutes later and flew over the field again at the same height. It was about midday, and when one of them was brought down he told us he had thought German pilots would be eating lunch. He and his comrades had made a bet they could fly over our lines and return safely during the lunch hour. You might be interested to know that when English pilots were downed and brought to our base they lived with us, without guard, ate and slept with us, until they were taken off to prison. They were very sporting. The one we shot down that day at the lunch hour gave us a check for the bet he had lost which we dropped to his comrades.

"Our bases, of course, were usually located near some fine château, which we could utilize for living-quarters. We joked that whenever someone came upon a splendid château he would very likely find that an airfield had been created nearby. The aircraft at my field were parked only about four hundred yards from our château, under green tents."

Von Schoenebeck served in the Second World War also—as head of the Luftwaffe mission to Bulgaria and later in the headquarters of the General of Fighters. "I think we need slower fighters today. I'm speaking of the need to cooperate tactically with ground forces. Many of today's fighters are so fast the pilot can't drop a bomb accurately. I know it's said that with automatic equipment it can be done better but I believe the pilot's eyes are best. How can anyone know where the targets are likely to be found? If we were faced with the job of defending against the Russian Army, we would need fighters and bombers which could operate against advancing armor. Pilots would have to use their eyes. I think the U.S. Air Force learned something about this in Korea and Vietnam. The slower support aircraft in some ways were better."

I inquired about the victories von Schoenebeck achieved and the greater number of Allied aircraft de-

stroyed in the First World War. He believes one reason
for the high German score is that the Allies had so many
more aircraft in action. We looked at many pictures, one
of Richthofen and himself taken at Courtraix in the autumn of 1917, one of a De Havilland he had shot down,
and several of Richthofen's funeral. He said all pilots in
the Geschwader believed Richthofen was brought down
by ground fire.[1]

In discussing tactics in the two World Wars he stressed
that maneuverability was the most important single factor
in scout combat in the First, though perhaps not as important in the Second. Scouts, he said, were unable to interfere decisively in bomber attacks in the First World
War because the bombers flew so high and scouts had
such a difficult task to climb and intercept. This was
to change in the Second World War, when fighters were
more heavily armed, and could fly at great heights. They
then had the speed to get off the ground and climb to interception altitude before the bombers escaped—and also
they had the help of radar plotting at ground installations.
Thus fighters in the Second World War had become more
decisive than in the 1914–18 war, he believes.

It scarcely seemed possible that the energetic conversa-
tionalist and flier sitting before me that day had been a
scout pilot in a war more than fifty years before. Visiting
him almost makes one a believer in the theory that pilots
who survive wars have excellent chances for long life.

Von Schoenebeck later sent copies of some of the pictures we had looked at. One was a picture of a very serious young man of seventeen or eighteen, hair neatly
combed, in his best uniform, with rumpled cap in hand (a
flying tradition in dress which persists to this day) posing
for his picture more than fifty years ago. Von Schoenebeck's expression is the faith of youth. That so many such

---

[1] This is now more or less accepted in Allied countries; books
have been written in recent years on the subject—one proving a
British gunner was responsible, another an Australian, and so on.
For many years it was widely believed that the Canadian fighter
pilot Roy Brown had shot Richthofen down.

young men on both sides died doing what circumstances and fate decreed is a heavy thought; their obvious youth and belief in their cause made them fair game for the carnage that was the lot of their generation.

7

THE SPRINGTIME OF LIFE

The British, at Cambrai in 1917, launched the first large-scale, successful tank attack of the war. Though tanks had been used that summer in the slaughter called Third Ypres, in which the British suffered over 300,000 casualties to the Germans' less than 200,000, they had been employed ineffectively in the mud. And infantry losses in the long Third Ypres campaign, from late July to November, so devastated the British Army's infantry no reserves were available to back up the Cambrai tank attack. There were also virtually no cavalry forces available to follow the tanks. Nevertheless, 381 tanks were assembled at Cambrai and launched in massed formation without preliminary bombardment. They quickly advanced five miles on a broad front and captured more territory than the British Army had gained in Flanders or on the Somme in massive, and costly prolonged attacks earlier in the war. Some 10,000 German prisoners were captured, and 200 guns. British losses were slight. But because there was little infantry to follow the tanks, this revolutionary success could not be exploited. When the Germans massed reserves and counter-attacked, they regained most of the lost territory.

One British pilot flying several times daily over that battle front in 1917 was Captain Arthur Gould Lee of 46 Fighter Squadron. For much of 1917 British pilots had openly admitted that the Germans had better machines; their life expectancy was tragically short because of this and their unchanging aggressive tactics. But at last, shortly before Cambrai, they were equipped with Camels. Lee was nevertheless shot down three times in the ten days of the battle—on the 22nd, 26th and 30th. It was still a hectic time in the air.

Long years after the war he assembled the daily letters he had sent his young bride during that year and published them in book form. (So indelibly impressed in his memory was the failure of Allied air forces to equip their pilots with parachutes—the Germans began using them in 1918—that he named his book *No Parachute*.) He had survived his wife by many years when the book was published in 1968 and the dedication to her read: "To my first wife Gwyneth Ann who died long ago and to whom these letters were sent in the springtime of life."

Arthur Gould Lee, now a retired Air Vice-Marshal of the Royal Air Force, lives in London in a comfortable Kensington flat, not very far from that of Duncan Grinnell-Milne, the subject of Chapter Five. He has become a successful writer since his retirement after the Second World War, having published eight non-fiction books, and has thus retained and refreshed his memory on military history. Since he attained high rank, attended special command schools and remained in the R.A.F. until after the Second World War, his concentration on flying did not end abruptly in 1918 and he is something of an authority in the field of scout tactics and strategy in the First World War.

He is critical of the basic British strategy championed by Major-General (later Air Marshal) Hugh Trenchard of the R.F.C. which meant, in essence, almost constant offensive patrolling over enemy lines, and believes this strategy cost many planes and lives unnecessarily and was largely ineffective. He feels it scandalous that Britain failed to provide R.F.C. fliers with efficient aircraft until mid-1917 and that already proven parachutes—which would have saved the lives of many pilots and observers who fell with their aircraft or burned to death—could have been supplied early in the war.

"For most of the war we were definitely outclassed, especially below 15,000 feet," he recalled. "Until the latter part we were fighting with one gun while German aircraft opposing us had two. They were more often than not faster. The enemy could turn away and leave us or outclimb us. Once in a fight, we couldn't easily get away. We just had to fight it out.

"The most exacting part of flying for me was strafing. By 1917 much ground strafing was taking place. Earlier that year, flying a Sopwith Pup, I often fought the D.III. I must say I disliked shooting up troops. The odds were too much against us. We dropped bombs, and shot up enemy troops, in the Cambrai attack and in the counter-attack. And then sometimes we went up and found a fight. One of my climactic days came over Cambrai.

"It was on 30 November that I was shot down for the third time in eight days. The 46th Squadron was stationed at Izel-le-Hameau, west of Arras. Bishop and Ball had served there. It was only about eighty yards uphill from squadron headquarters to the field's three hangars. Our Camels were in front of them. It was a big airdrome serving three squadrons. We could get off the ground quickly from the mess, in an emergency. Our Camels were chocolate brown and light green. I flew in a wool-lined leather coat, a red, knitted scarf—important to keep out the draught—mask, goggles and mittens, plus long sheepskin thigh boots. We would belt ourselves in, though there was, of course, a fitter and a rigger, check the altimeter, Very pistol on the right, for emergency signaling, and be sure we had a map on the board at the left of the cockpit. We checked the fine adjustment, a little aluminum lever on the left, and the petrol gauge on the dash, an ancient automobile-type gauge. Then we would push down the brown wooden pump handle on the right to get sufficient pressure for starting. We had it practiced to the point where we could dash out of the mess and be airborne in one minute.

"Takeoff went like this. When the pressure was sufficient I would shout, 'Ready.' The crewman would reply, 'Switch off, sir.' I would confirm it was off and call, 'Suck In.' He turned the prop three or four times and shouted, 'Contact, sir', and I replied, 'Contact', and turned on the ignition switch. He gave the prop a jerk downward and it caught and I revved up the engine. It wasn't too loud and usually started with a puff of white smoke. After I saw the revs were right I throttled back and pushed the first shell in the chamber of each Vickers by moving metal levers about nine inches apart in front of me. That pushed the first .303 bullet into the chamber of each. Our aluminum gun belts were unlike those used in ground guns. The links broke apart as each bullet was withdrawn and slid away down a chute. When you had fired all 600 bullets there was nothing left of the belt. Having two guns was a vast improvement over the one in the Pup. And by this time we had the new Constantinescu hydraulic interrupter mechanism which gave a quicker rate of fire. I seldom lost both guns at the same time in the Camel, which was a great advantage over the Pup.

"We had just been equipped with the Camels, which were powered by 110-horsepower Clerget engines; we lived in an orchard, in Nissen huts. The 30th was a misty morning. I was on the dawn patrol—I had sometimes flown as high as 22,000 feet in Pups on these patrols. The Germans were reacting to our tank breakthrough with a counter-offensive of their own. The first sortie took off at 8:40 and we landed at 9:30. At 10:10 I was up again leading a patrol with bombs—four twenty-pound Coopers, designed to burst sideways to destroy troops. We dropped our bombs on the advancing enemy and were down again at 12:15. There was hard fighting and we all accepted the fact that we had to get off as often as we could. Major Philip Babington walked into the mess where we were eating and said: 'Get off again as soon as you can.'

"I waved my hand and the chocks were removed, signaled the other pilots with thumbs up and turned into the wind and took off. We flew in two vics this day. In my vic Dusgate was on my left and Cooper, a Scotsman, on the right. 'George' Bulman was leading the second vic—he later became famous as the Hawker test pilot and developer of the Hurricane. The second vic usually flew on the port side, and slightly to the rear. On this day, the third mission of the day, we were loaded with four bombs each and were to strafe the Huns. I wrote to my wife, describing the sortie, the next day:[1]

Because the squadron now has many new pilots who can't be thrown into this ground-attack work, and because Odell, Wilcox, Hughes and Ferrie are on leave, eight of us have to do everything, and the strain of it is beginning to tell. We had a quick lunch, but we hadn't much to say. Personally, I hadn't much spirit for yet another low job, but not a hint could I give of that. I was leading it!

I set out at 2:15, this time with Bulman, Thompson, Cooper, Dusgate and Blakeley. The weather was fairly clear, with cloud at 3,000–4,000. At the salient the air was positively lousy with D-Vs at all levels, but especially over Bourlon. There were also the Hun ground-strafing two-seaters which were being chased off by Camels and S.E.s. It was impossible to stay in formation with bombs on, so again I gave the break-up signal, and off they went to find their own targets, except Dusgate, a newcomer, who by prior arrangement stayed with me.

My specified target was a house on the edge of Bourlon village, a H.Q. of some kind. I tried to sneak across the lines to get there no fewer than seven times, but each time V-strutters and Triplanes came rushing towards us, and we had to turn away. Some had red colorings, which meant Richthofen's Circus, and it was no good trying to fight them with bombs on.

By now I was doing the job almost automatically. All this trouble and risk to bomb a house, which might be empty, anyway. I thought, they're bound to get me this time, I can't always be the one to get away with it. But one becomes fatalistic very quickly. I don't even bother to touch wood since we started this trench-strafing racket.

At last, fed up with not being able to penetrate the screen of Hun planes, I went westwards, still followed by the faithful Dusgate, climbed up to 4,000 and flew five miles northwards in the base of the cloud, then approached Bourlon from the northwest. I saw the target, and gave the signal to dive. I'd been told to make four separate attacks, one bomb at a time, to make sure of hitting the house, but

---

[1] Arthur Gould Lee, *No Parachute*, pp. 187–92.

I'd instructed Dusgate to release all his four when he saw my first one go, then make his way back across the Lines and wait for me over Havrincourt Wood.

We dived steeply, and I let go at 200 feet. It must certainly have been an important target, for a devil of a lot of machine-gun fire came up at us. As I pulled out of the dive in a climbing turn, I glimpsed Dusgate, also climbing, but then I lost him. I saw the smoke of our bombs bursting— mine was a miss, but his were quite near. But the house hadn't been hit. I had to try again.

I honestly felt quite sick at the prospect. I felt I just hadn't the guts to dive down three more times into that nest of machine-guns, now all alert and waiting for me. I had to do it, but I told myself, only once. And I did it, in a sort of numb indifference. If they got me, they got me. I dived down, to 100 feet, and released all three bombs. Bullets were cracking round me. I swerved violently to the right, and skidded away at twenty feet, where they couldn't follow me. Whether I hit the damned house, I don't know. I wasn't interested in it any more. Marvelously, they hadn't hit me, but one bullet had broken the handle of the throttle control, and another had smashed into the Very pistol cartridges, which ought to have exploded and set me alight, but they didn't.

I flew due north to get a breather from the Bourlon mix-up. It was quite peaceful here, so for ten minutes I shot up anything that showed up, mostly transport on the roads. There were no troops for me to go for. Then I climbed up to the cloud base, at 4,000 and made south. I approached the western end of the wood, towards Moeuvres. The ground below and to my left was splashed with shell-bursts, and there were scores of machines swirling around in the air beyond. I wanted to keep clear of them until I'd found Dusgate, and made a line for Havrincourt Wood.

Suddenly a D-V passed across my front from the west, about 200 feet below. As it slid by, I saw the pilot looking out of the further side of his cockpit at the smoke of battle below. He hadn't seen me. I swung steeply down onto his tail, and caught him up so quickly he seemed to be coming back towards me. At twenty yards' range I pressed the triggers. The tracers flashed into his back. The machine suddenly reared up vertically in front of me, and I banked to the right to avoid him. He fell over sideways, and went down in a vertical dive. I swung over and followed him down for a thousand feet, but he was going too fast. He didn't pull out, and crashed west of Bourlon village.

As I was flattening out at under 3,000 there was a sudden crump! of archie. Then crump, crump, crump. Black bursts all around me—a clang in the cowling—a thud somewhere in front. My engine stopped dead. Not even a sputter. A great blast of noise came up from below—exploding shells, guns firing, trench mortars, the rattle of machine-guns, the continuous sharp crackle of rifle fire.

I swung towards the south. It wasn't petrol, there was no smell, but I switched over to gravity to make sure. No result, so I closed the throttle and switched off. There was heavy fighting going on ahead of me, and I was gliding down over the middle of it. I knew the Boche had been attacking here all day, and by now they might have broken through as they had in the south. A dull heaviness flooded over me. Was I for it at last? Was this where my luck ran out? I'd be made a prisoner—if the Boche troops didn't shoot me down.

I was now at 1,000, gliding steadily down, already being fired at from below. There were Huns flying to my left flank, and any one could knock me down with a single shot. I could do nothing but go ahead, and hope I'd get across. I was zigzagging, looking over the side trying to discover signs of khaki, but the figures I saw scurrying beneath were field grey, no doubt about that.

I was now at 300. The hubbub below came louder and louder. The light was bad, the air smoke-laden. I had to find somewhere to come down, but the ground ahead was a shambles of trees, hedges, guns firing, dumps, trenches. I spotted a short stretch of clear ground off to the right, about the size of a couple of tennis courts. But I was too high, and had to lose height in a side-slip. I held her off to land very slowly. I daren't look sideways—I had to concentrate on the landing. Which side of the Line would I be?

I put her down gently, she trundled to the edge of a trench, and was pulled up by the parapet. Field guns were firing somewhere near me. I sat there tensed, waiting for it, too petrified to look around. For five long, long seconds I just didn't know whether I was a prisoner or not. Then a couple of tin helmets appeared alongside the cockpit. I sank thankfully into my seat. They were ours, flat and basinlike, not the Boche coalscuttle.

I got down to the ground, and was quickly surrounded by troops, from whom I learned that I'd come down south of the Bapaume–Cambrai road, west of Graincourt, well under a mile this side of the fighting. The Hun had gained ground here, after fierce fighting, but there'd been no breakthrough. At length, one of the numerous officers around, a gunner, introduced himself as Lieutenant Mills, of "Q" Anti-aircraft Battery, situated half a mile or so distant, and did I need any help?

We found that the cause of my descent was a chunk of archie, which had gone through the cowling immediately behind the engine, and sliced off the H.T. leads, which were wound tightly round the shaft. There was nothing to be done, the machine would have to be salvaged. I asked Mills to send a signal to the squadron while I decided what to do.

The air above was crowded with planes, and for some time I stood and watched them fighting each other. During half an hour I saw three come down, one a flamer, but none near me. Both British and Boche archie were busy, sometimes overlapping, black and white puffs. I saw something I'd never seen before. A machine was hit by a shell, and blown to fragments. Bits of it fell quickly, such as the engine and pilot's body, but most of the rest seemed to float lazily down like leaves from trees in autumn.

As darkness drew on, the machines gradually thinned out until only odd ones were left. Then about twenty Tripes and V-strutters appeared, in a final sweep of the salient at 3,000. Lieutenant Mills, who had come back again, said they were the Circus. Two of them dropped down, and one dived after a solitary D.H.5 that came from the Cambrai direction, and fired successive bursts at him as they flashed across our front twenty feet up, the D.H. zigzagging along the road to Bapaume.

The second Hun came down at my Camel, and put a long burst into it. Mills and I dived into the trench at the first bullet, though he did no damage that I could see. But this little episode persuaded me that I'd had enough for one day. I wanted no more nights in smelly dug-outs, nor cadging other people's rations. More important, the Hun might yet launch his breakthrough at dawn, and where would I be then? An additional reason was the shelling that now began.

Mills promised to put a "Q" Battery guard on the machine, and after abstracting the watch from its case, and a map and my automatic, I set out for Havrincourt in an ambulance belonging to the 4th London Territorials, 47th Division, who were in the thick of the local fighting. Once there, it was dark, and I was soon groping around trying to find the road out of the salient across the nearby Canal du Nord. Nobody I spoke to had any idea.

After a quarter of an hour of wandering up and down the narrow streets I saw a light in a cottage and entered. I had a shock. The scene was one of blood and suffering, in a deadly, sickly smell of ether. Groaning men lay on stretchers against the walls. A couple of absorbed doctors, white coats over their uniforms, attended by R.A.M.C. orderlies, moved swiftly from one man to another, unhurriedly injecting, probing, cutting, stitching. Nobody took any notice of me. I watched fascinated while they cut away at the elbow the mangled remains of a forearm. An orderly placed it on a small heap of other amputated limbs on a ground sheet in a corner, festooned with bloodied lint and bandages.

Outside I drew a deep breath of relief. I thought of that Tommy waking up with no arm. There but for the grace of God . . . ! How the doctors and orderlies can work and live in such primitive conditions was beyond me. I realized that fighting in the air or on the ground isn't the only thing that needs nerve.

I continued on, stumbling into unseen obstructions in the darkness, until I suddenly slipped heavily into a deep trench. I couldn't climb out, so walked along until I came on a large dug-out filled with a cheery bunch of Royal Engineers, who passed me on to Captain Deddes, R.E., attached to 47th Division. He gave me a much-needed drink and something to eat, told me I was actually in part of the Hindenburg Line, and said I'd never get away by the Canal du Nord road, which was jammed with traffic, and I'd best go south of the wood.

The roads were pretty full even on this route. I got a lift to Trescault with a motorized machine-gun section on its way to Gouzeaucourt. To Metz on a gun-limber. To Royailcourt on a kind of baker's cart belonging to the R.E.s. And from there to Bapaume in luxury itself, on the driver's seat of an A.S.C. lorry.

Bapaume was crowded with troops on their way to the salient. At the busy Y.M.C.A., at one o'clock in the morning, I had coffee and biscuits, and telephoned the advanced landing ground for transport. Eventually, a Crossley came, and I reached Izel at three, having been nine hours on the road.

Four hours of sleep, and I was up again to go on patrol at eight. But I'll leave this to my next letter. Thompson did pretty well while I was amusing myself ground-strafing. He had more sense than to use up good bullets that way. He climbed up into the dog-fight levels and shot down two Albatri, both on our side. There's no news of poor old Dusgate, and I'm afraid he's gone down on the other side.

Second Lieutenant R. E. Dusgate was a prisoner of war. "In a letter sent to me, and still in my possession, his sister stated that he wrote from his prison camp that his engine was hit, like mine, by anti-aircraft fire, and that he landed without injuring himself. But in the German Air Force records he is shown as having been shot down by Oberstleutnant Lowenhardt, of Jasta 10, one of the units of Richthofen's Circus. I do not attempt to solve this discrepancy. Dusgate unfortunately died soon afterwards in captivity."

Earlier that day Lee had already bombed German troops quite effectively, also strafing many before they could disperse—with telling effect. Considering that he was only one of many engaged in such work, the effect of tactical air operations at this stage of the war (November 1917) is readily apparent. The dangers involved in such strafing were great, and Lee believes flying up and down fixed, well-fortified trenches was both ineffective and excessively dangerous, that better results at less cost were achieved by strafing roads and supply lines behind the front lines.

Asked to designate the most important performance criteria for a scout, he replied: "Height and speed. The rate of climb was also vital. Height gives you, of course, the tactical advantage. But you can't keep this indefinitely without speed. A good climb rate, obviously, gives you superior height first. So these are very important—and maneuverability. Maneuverability saved my life several times. The Hun just couldn't get on your tail and you could get on his.

"The Sopwith triplane was good because it could climb so fast. When pilots in triplanes found the fight going badly, they didn't dive out of it; they climbed out of it. It's significant that Richthofen never shot down a triplane. If our triplane had had two guns and had been a bit stronger it would have been a wonder. The Camel, most dangerous plane to fly, which killed more pilots learning to fly than any other because it would spin easily, shot down the greatest number of German aircraft but I don't think it could get away from the D-V.[1] No one realized the Germans had triplanes until, flying one, Richthofen attacked the 46th, in September 1917."

About Trenchard's strategy for the Royal Flying Corps, later the Royal Air Force, Lee is incisive.[2]

After the Battle of Messines in June 1917 air activity had to slacken because of the R.F.C.'s heavy losses in April and May, which forced General Trenchard, on 10 June, to instruct his Brigade Commanders "to avoid wastage of both pilots and machines, for some little time. My reserves at present are dangerously low, in fact, in some cases, it barely exists at all. . . . It is of the utmost importance, however, that the offensive spirit is maintained."

General Trenchard was right to sustain an offensive spirit. Where he erred was in identifying this with an offensive strategy which was, in effect, a territorial offensive. To him, as to his staff, and most of his senior commanders, for a British airplane to be one mile across the trenches was offensive: for it to be ten miles over was more offensive.

Influenced perhaps by naval doctrines—"seek out and destroy the enemy" and "our frontiers are the enemy

---

[1] Performance charts indicate the Albatros D-V's top speed at 116 m.p.h compared to the Camel's 113 m.p.h. (models flying in early 1918).

[2] Arthur Gould Lee, *No Parachute*, pp. 217–18.

coasts"—he applied them to the air, not appreciating that
they were largely irrelevant in a three-dimensional sphere.
In the air fighting of the First World War, despite the
siege-like situation on the ground, it was not a fighter
airplane's position in relation to a line of defenses that
measured the offensive spirit but the aggressive will of its
occupants to attack the enemy wherever he was encountered, at whatever odds.

The pursuit of a territorial offensive strategy of distant
patrols, together with the handicap of a prevailing westerly
wind, resulted in a large proportion of aircrew disabled by
wounds, or put out of action by faulty engines or gun jams,
falling into enemy hands. That the High Command should
uphold such avoidable wastage in 1917, when the R.F.C.
was desperately short of airplanes, air-engines and trained
pilots, is hard to fathom.

These direct losses were augmented by the wear and tear
on pilots and planes in chasing the mirage of air ascendancy over the lines by continuous standing patrols of
fighters along the whole British front, regardless of the
needs of the tactical situation, ground or air. While we
thus dissipated our strength, more often than not merely
beating the empty air, the Germans, in their so-called defensive strategy, concentrated forces superior in numbers
or equipment and engaged our scattered Line Patrols in
turn, and our Distant Offensive Patrols as and when it
suited them. The result was that in 1917 British air losses
were at times nearly four times as great as the German.

Though the real criterion of an offensive policy was not
place but aggressiveness, even this was useless without
efficient airplanes. The most rashly aggressive pigeon
won't get far with a hawk. Important as was the offensive
spirit in the air war, technical superiority was more vital,
not least because it conferred the initiative.

For the High Command to persist, despite the toll in life
and material, in continuously patroling the lines and in
sending obsolescent machines deep into German-held territory, was incomprehensible even at the time. In retrospect,
such obduracy seems as irrational as Haig's unyielding ad-
herence to attrition, and the no less stubborn Admiralty
resistance to escorted convoys.

Lee believes some of the mistakes of the First World

War were corrected in the Second, in which R.A.F. fighters played such a prominent part at the beginning.

As he unveiled a little of the story of an almost incredible survival as a scout pilot, he brought home with considerable impact the sacrifice of so many brave airmen who flew their sorties daily and risked their lives regularly for long periods.

"It's hard to believe, now, that I went through all the exciting hazards described in those letters," he said. "But you can put up with a lot when you are young."

8

A RESERVE OFFICER

It was a sunny autumn day in Munich, in 1968, and we got up from the table in the lounge and walked through the lobby of the Hotel Bayerische Hof, outside. Smiling, my stocky, brown-eyed companion extended his right hand. With an *auf wiedersehen* and a bow, he turned, putting on his hat, and walked briskly away. About five feet nine, a quick walker in a well-tailored blue suit, he didn't look back, and I followed him with my eyes until he disappeared around a corner. He was seventy-four then, the most successful surviving scout pilot of the Kaiser's Germany. He shot down forty-eight Allied aircraft in the 1914–18 war and survived a long list of incredible experiences, having met many of the best Allied scout pilots in aerial combat. Joseph Jacobs, fifth-ranking ace of the German Flying Service in the First World War, probably remained at the front on flying duty longer than any other celebrated German pilot.

We talked all morning about air fighting in the First World War, and about the tactics and the great fliers of that conflict, and I thought, as the famous fighter pilot, now a representative of a small crane factory, disappeared: "There goes a man poorly remembered by his country for a tremendous contribution."

"I went to the front in 1914 and stayed there for the rest of the war," Jacobs had begun. "I first flew the Dorner, a very primitive monoplane, in 1912. I left flying school at Hangelar, near Bonn, to join the Army in 1914. I flew as an observer, bomber pilot and artillery spotter—the Aviatik, LVE, Rumpler and other planes. Once I flew all the way to Paris in 1915. We flew against the

French and the British. They fought differently. Usually the French stayed over their lines, or very high. With our weak engines we couldn't get up to them. When they saw a Fokker they fled. This was in 1915, when I joined a Fokkerstaffel in the West, near Laon. It was hard flying.

"In the beginning I sometimes carried bombs—we threw them over the side with our hands—ten-kilo bombs. We carried six in the cockpit. I threw bombs on trains on several occasions. We also flew against balloons, which was highly dangerous. When it was very cold the balloons wouldn't burn. We then aimed at the top so that the gas would escape and came around again and ignited them. In 1915 when I began I had only a pistol in the cockpit for armament. We would fly at 10,000 or 12,000 feet, twelve to fifteen miles behind enemy lines. Later in the war I remember flying over Big Bertha, the gun bombing Paris. I've flown with Boelcke, the Eagle of Lille, Max Immelmann, and against many of the great Allied aces.

"In the air we liked to have height, speed and the sun behind. Mornings we always had the sun behind us in the east. We watched for the French planes and sometimes found one alone. The French ace Guynemer was an individualist. He was faster and surprised many of our pilots diving from above. Most of his victims were taken by surprise.

"The English came to us. Often when we shot down their machines they were sent back to our experts to be tested. The Camel was the best English scout of the war. The English pilots were good, as were the Americans. The best Belgian scout pilot was Willy Coppens.

"With Jasta 22, near Laon, I scored five victories. In June 1971 I became leader of Jasta 7 in Flanders. There I scored most of my victories. But I was stationary, not like Richthofen, who was moved to where the fighting was. And when Richthofen lost a pilot he immediately got a replacement."

I asked Jacobs what he considered the single most important performance factor in dogfighting.

"The most important thing is maneuverability. Our three-wing scout was best for this, though slower than the fastest planes of the war. But it could out-turn and out-climb the other fellow. Of course, speed and height—ceiling—were very important."

I asked him what qualities distinguished great scout pilots from average. "Good eyes was the greatest individual asset. Not just seeing the enemy but seeing the situation, sizing it up correctly and quickly. That was very important. Another important talent for the scout pilot was still hands. With a still hand he could get the maximum from his machine—glider pilots know that—and roughness at great speed can damage the aircraft as well as interrupt smooth airflow. For dogfights, the pilot should be a good flier. Individually, then, good eyes, being able to size up the situation quickly, keeping calm and flying smoothly and being able to handle one's aircraft—those were all characteristics of the best pilots.

"Our best flier might have been Werner Voss, our fourth-ranked ace. He had wonderful eyes and was a wonderful flier and often flew alone. Richthofen, who learned from Boelcke, was our most successful. Richthofen came later and flew in formations, which were the rule by the end of the war. After I had scored about twenty victories I concentrated on helping younger pilots learn. Often it was the younger pilot, who hadn't learned to take care of himself, who was lost very quickly if someone didn't keep a close watch on him on his first flights. In combat, of course, if a pilot has the three assets I mentioned earlier when the first sighting is made—height, speed, and the sun behind—he can take on heavy odds. When we had these advantages we sometimes fought ten times our number. In the actual fighting one of the tricks that probably saved my life was the slip-turn, a turn solely with rudder. The wing doesn't go up and those behind don't realize you're turning. A normal, coordinated turn is accomplished by aileron and rudder, lifting the wing and turning the rudder simultaneously. But in the slip-turn you're skidding around a turn, level, and it's difficult to detect, and the bullets meant for you miss on the outside. Generally, acrobatics are not good in aerial combat. Loops offer no advantage nor does the roll, which reduces speed.

"I often flew against the Spad. It wasn't so good for maneuvering but it had speed and could climb rapidly and was stable. In the last of the war I often flew as high as 19,000 feet but never bothered with oxygen. We had parachutes in the last of the war, also, which I don't think the Allied pilots had, and parachutes saved my life on several occasions. I was shot up or crash-landed many times."

I intervened to ask Jacobs when he came closest to death or capture during the war.

"It was probably in December 1917. You know, something interesting happened last year (1967) concerning that flight. I won the *Pour le Mérite* because of it and last year was the fiftieth anniversary of the award. A television producer made a film of the fight and afterwards I got a telephone call from another German pilot who had seen me go down that day in 1917. In the fifty years since we had never met! There are only five of us alive who wear the *Pour le Mérite* with the fifty-year gold crown.

"I was a lieutenant then, flying the Albatros D-V and led eight in all that day. We were stationed in a small hunting house near the Wyuendaalevelo Schloss near the German–Belgian border, not far from Lille. The little house was in a park and the Unteroffizier came in that morning with a good report on the weather. The report came from Paris each day, six or seven o'clock. We had a ready room out on the field, near the D-Vs, about 800 yards away. We had a car to carry us to the aircraft. After 1917 reports of enemy planes crossing the lines came to us from the front by telephone, and then we would start out to the aircraft immediately. At this time we were flying with the Fourth Army. A report came in that enemy bombers were heading for Brussels. We were to intercept them before they got there. It was good weather and we were soon off. Soon they came into view and I successfully engaged their leader. Then I went after another English pilot, but someone—friend or foe—hit me in the scrap. My motor was gone and the wind was very strong—blowing me towards the west. I was barely able to maintain control and knew that I would have to crash-land. I did my best to make the D-V reach German lines but I was in a bad way and came down about seventy yards from them. Yet I had been lucky. The German line at that point stuck out into the enemy's in a salient. Had I landed to the left or right, even a hundred yards, I would have been taken prisoner. The Albatros flipped over on its back when I touched down, but I managed to get out, then scrambled back to our lines. That was close—almost a victim in the air, almost a victim in the crash and almost captured by the enemy. It was getting dark and very cold when I finally reached safety."

Turning to service in the Second World War, I suggested tactics had changed a bit with faster and more power-ful aircraft. Jacobs, who had also served in the Luftwaffe, agreed, but felt manueverability had still been important in the last war. He asked, "Did you know the Russian Rata could out-turn the Me.109?"

"I never did get along with Nazis, Göring and the oth-ers. I remember once Göring telling some of us that when the Americans got into the war our pilots would be able to shoot them down easily because they would lack experi-ence. I answered we were already fighting some of them flying for the R.A.F. and that our pilots reported they were excellent. One of my captains was with me and he joined in, supporting my view. Göring didn't want to be-lieve what was coming."

The highest-scoring living German ace of the First World War reminisced about the famous scout pilots on both sides. "We heard more about Coppens, Guynemer, Nungesser, Navarre, Ball and McCudden than the rest. Of ours, Voss was very good. Boelcke was probably the best. He taught us much and Richthofen learned from him. I thought Gottfried Banifeld was one of the war's outstand-ing scout pilots. He flew with the Austro-Hungarian Navy, though one of his legs had been badly shattered in a crash before the war. He contributed much to the morale of fel-low pilots. Hauptmann Godwin Brumowski, of the Aus-tro-Hungarian Luftfahrtgruppen, was of course credited with forty-one victories."

Jacobs sketched for me the formation German scout squadrons favored in the last of the war, explaining the reason for its V-shape. Ten scouts might comprise the V, with the leader forward, and inexperienced pilots just behind. The best pilot flew in the rear, between the two widened legs of the V. Each aircraft, counting back from the point of the V, was stacked higher. Groups (Gruppen) were also stepped up higher from the lead group.

Jacobs sketched formations and answered questions with the quickness of a man in his forties (as I had noticed about other scout pilots of the 1914–18 war). He demonstrated in the sketches how guns fired and exactly where they were located on German scouts, in detail.

Of his awards, he is proudest of the *Pour le Mérite*, which entitles him to wear a small gold crown above the medal so popularized in films, which is sometimes called the Blue Max. But though he had won his country's highest award in the First World War and served again in another, he lives a modest life today and doesn't receive a pension.

As he wrote down the names of the other four First World War pilots who now wear the gold crown on their *Pour le Mérite* medals—Laumann, Degelow, Osterkamp and Christiansen—he seemed amused at my astonishment that, at seventy-four, he didn't receive a pension for his outstanding service to Germany in the war.

"You see, I was only a reserve officer," he said.

9

THREE AMERICAN ACES

Of the American aces of the First World War (relatively few in comparison with the Second), Edward Vernon Rickenbacker was top scorer, with twenty-six victories over balloons and piloted craft. Rickenbacker readily acknowledges that he learned the essentials of air fighting from Raoul Lufbery, an American ace born in France of French parents. Lufbery, for whom the famous defensive circling maneuver is named (and which apparently cost many Allied pilots their lives when they attempted to apply this First World War tactic to Second World War conditions), served only briefly with the U.S. Air Service—from January until May 1918, when he was killed. But he had served two years in the U.S. Army some four years earlier.

He was brought to Connecticut when of school age in 1891 and became an American citizen. He remained until he ran away from home, and school, at seventeen. Lufbery roamed the world after army service, and the outbreak of the war found him in France. He was already an aviator but had to join the French Foreign Legion—as an American—to serve with French forces and went to the front as the mechanic of his best friend, Marc Pourpe. He got permission to fly when Pourpe was killed, in December 1914, and was posted in October 1915 to a bombardment group in which he served for six months. He transferred to a training school for *pilotes de chasse* and, after having much trouble learning to handle a Nieuport, reached the front as a scout pilot in May 1916, serving in the Escadrille Lafayette. In the next eighteen months he became a marvelous flier and expert marksman, the unit's most famous ace.

Rickenbacker was assigned to the 94th Air Pursuit Squadron in March 1918—just two months before Lufbery's death (according to one source he was not transferred to the 94th until 8 April 1918). In his autobiography Rickenbacker writes that he flew with Lufbery as much as he could, even though at the time he had to go up unarmed, as the Americans had not yet received arms and ammunition. Lufbery taught him a "corkscrew" maneuver to employ when flying over the lines. Lufbery, according to Rickenbacker, would constantly turn his head and search the sky and ground while flying this maneuver. Initially this made Rickenbacker ill. But he continued at it until it no longer bothered him.

Rickenbacker's well-learned mastery of his aircraft and guns, and good tactics, were demonstrated when he shot down his first victim, a Pfalz, with Jimmy Hall (remembered as the author of *Mutiny On The Bounty*) on 29 April 1918. The two spotted the Pfalz before they were seen, a point which so many successful pilots, including Joseph Jacobs in the preceding chapter, have stressed as vitally important, and soon had a 1,000 foot height advantage. Since they outnumbered him two-to-one and had altitude (and, as a result, speed) on their victim, the Pfalz's chances were poor. But even this might not have produced victory had not Rickenbacker known his aircraft and appreciated the situation immediately, which led him to predict what the Pfalz pilot would do.

Rickenbacker reasoned that, knowing he could outdive the Nieuports, the Pfalz pilot would wing over into a dive at the onset of the attack or if things began to go badly. Rickenbacker wanted position to take advantage of the dive when it came. The German pilot soon saw one or both of the Americans and immediately began to climb. Hall engaged him and the Pfalz dived. Rickenbacker had maneuvered into position to intercept. Knowing the Nieuport's weakness—fabric on the upper wing peeling off in a high-speed dive—Rickenbacker was lower than Hall, in position, and started down after the descending Pfalz, caught him and opened fire from close behind. Bullets from both guns reached the unlucky victim. When he pulled back slightly on the stick, the spray found the cockpit and the Pfalz fell out of control, crashing to the ground. It was a quick, classic example of seeing the enemy first, seeing the opportunity, enjoying an altitude advantage and gaining the so-often successful tail position. To accomplish this in his first combat was an indication of the future aerial success to come to America's top-scoring scout pilot of the First World War.

Rickenbacker later experienced a close call with his Nieuport involving the aircraft's famous structural weakness. In a dive to avoid two attackers, the entire linen cover of his top wing ripped off and he went into a spin. He believes it pure chance that he happened to add throttle, which lifted the nose and brought him out of the spin. Thus American pilots were glad to swap their Nieuports for Spads and other, more sturdy scouts, as the year 1918 progressed.

Of all American scout pilots in the First World War, the man Rickenbacker describes as the "most daring" was Frank Luke, of Phoenix and German-American parents. (His father had been born in Dahlhausen, Prussia.) While Lufbery had scored most of his victories over a long period of flying with the French before the U.S.A. was in the war, Luke became the second-highest scoring American pilot of the war in seventeen days of 1918 preceding his death. Luke was credited with twenty-one victories, Lufbery with seventeen.

Luke is remembered as the balloon buster because he specialized in destroying observation balloons, dangerous targets. After an outstanding school record as an athlete, and some boxing, he volunteered, was trained in Texas and San Diego, and was first in his class to solo. He arrived in France in March 1918 and took flight training at Issoudun, finishing first in flying and second in gunnery. Because he was assigned to ferry duty, which disappointed him, it was not until July that he reached the front near Château-Thierry as a member of the 27th Air Squadron, First Pursuit Group. On 2 August, in a Spad, which had replaced the squadron's Nieuports, he claimed a Fokker as his first victim. While his commanding officer believed his story, few of the others in his squadron did. His claim was not confirmed. Even worse, his fellow pilots now disliked him. Whether it was this reaction of his fellow pilots or something else, his loneliness grew. A new commanding officer was considerably less kindly disposed to him. Nevertheless, in the following month, September 1918, he achieved immortality.

The St. Mihiel offensive opened on 12 September. (Rickenbacker says this was the first great combined air and ground assault.) General Billy Mitchell ordered American squadrons to attack enemy balloons. In the 27th Squadron, Luke and Joe Wehner (another German–American) volunteered for the job. Wehner was one of the few friends he had. Both were successful in shooting down balloons that day and two days later they began to hunt both balloons and enemy aircraft together. They developed a twilight technique that was to be further developed (into night-fighter operations) in the next war. They would attack the enemy in the last, fading light of day and land after dark. Night landings, of course, were far more dangerous than daylight landings.

The pair shot down three balloons on the 16th. Luke's greatest day was over the Rainbow Division on the 18th, when he shot down three balloons and two enemy aircraft to become the leading American scorer of the war. His technique was to dive from superior height, firing into his victim until he almost collided with it (the close-shooting secret of many successful pilots). He often landed at a nearby French field—or near where a victim went down, to get American ground personnel to verify his claim—his Spad riddled with bullet holes. But although he achieved great success on the 18th, it was a bitter day for him because his friend Wehner was shot down and killed while protecting him and probably saving his life.

His commanding officer sent him to Paris on leave in an effort to raise his spirits, but he cut short a two-week leave authorization after six days and returned to the squadron. He shot down a Fokker on the 26th and then, flying from a French field where he had spent the night trying to forget another comrade's death he shot down another balloon on the 28th, after which he spent a second (unauthorized) night with the French at their field.

The next day was his last and he went down in a blaze of glory, to die an unnecessary, curious death. From Verdun, where he had flown to see his old commanding officer, he took off late in the afternoon and shot down three balloons in a short time (having dropped a note to an American balloon unit specifying his victims). Then he engaged several of the enemy in a dogfight over German territory, about which few details are known, and perhaps shot down two of them. But he too was brought down, though not, it is thought, mortally wounded. Getting out of his Spad, behind the German lines, he sought water at a stream about fifty yards away. When approached by a group of Germans, he drew his pistol to fight it out and was killed. He had told fellow pilots at a dinner in his honor less than two weeks earlier that he would never be taken alive. He had meant it, though one wonders why.

French witnesses said he had been pursued by German aircraft even before he attacked the first balloon that afternoon, that after he had downed three he was wounded by enemy aircraft but continued to strafe the enemy, killing six German soldiers and wounding many more. They described his tactics as a dive from great height, to gain speed, and a leveling-out before he attacked the balloon from very close range. The end of the war had been less than two months away at the time of Luke's death. As it is, he remains the second-ranking American ace.

In October, only a month after Luke's seventeen victories, Rickenbacker increased his score rapidly, shooting down fourteen enemy aircraft to bring his total to twenty-six by 30 October.

Most of the U.S. aces of the war ranking just below these top three, Rickenbacker, Luke and Lufbery, had the training and experience of flying with the Royal Flying Corps or the Royal Air Force before American squadrons reached France. Many were well educated and the sons of wealthy parents—a number from Ivy League schools. Interestingly, the top three scorers had limited educations, Luke being a high-school graduate, Rickenbacker having ended his formal education at the age of twelve and Lufbery having run away from school at seventeen. Luke and Rickenbacker won the Medal of Honor, two of four American airmen in the war to do so.

Rickenbacker, the surviver of the three, was a cool thinker in the air and, while not one to refuse a fight, carefully sought the advantage when he went into combat and planned his tactics in advance. In this respect his tactics were similar to those of many of the more successful aces of the war, including Richthofen. The Second World War, to arrive twenty-one years after the First, would demonstrate again that most of the best fighter pilots carefully planned tactics and strategy, and again used height, speed, and a close approach.

10

SUMMER DAY, 1918

As the First World War progressed, scout pilots flew and fought in larger and larger formations, until by 1918 really large-scale air battles were taking place over the front lines almost daily. It is probably true to say that the feats which were achieved by a few individuals in the early air fighting of 1914 and 1915, and which made them famous, were regularly achieved in 1918 by hundreds of pilots whose names would remain relatively unknown. Air fighting had grown in scope to such an extent that what had been sensationally new just two or three years earlier was now commonplace.

One of the most successful British aces of the war was Captain L. H. Rochford (D.S.C. and bar, D.F.C.) with twenty-eight aerial victories; he was one of those who compiled an outstanding record in 1918. Rochford was originally a Royal Naval Air Service scout pilot and served in the same squadron, No. 3 Naval (203 R.A.F.), with Lieutenant Colonel Raymond Collishaw, now Air Vice-Marshal R.A.F. (retired), third-ranking R.A.F. ace of the war. Both gained many of their victories as Royal Naval Air Service fliers before the Royal Air Force was created in 1918 (the Navy had the better aircraft in the first years of the war). Both survived the war, and the next one, and are active and healthy as this book is prepared. One of Rochford's missions, in the summer of 1918, illustrates clearly the effectiveness of the tactics and teamwork which were the order of the day by that stage of the war. Rochford now lives in Bruton, Somerset, and recently described that day over fifty years ago.

Squadron 203 was stationed at Izel-le-Hameau (from

which Arthur Gould Lee flew in November 1917) and at this time was equipped with Camels. Rochford was commander of B Flight, consisting of five planes (some were made up of six). B Flight flew in a V formation, all aircraft at the same height. The Camels' top speed was 113 m.p.h. and they could reach 20,000 feet.

Before dawn on 22 July Rochford and Collishaw, the Squadron Commander, took off on a special bombing flight they had planned for some time. The target was Dorignies, an airdrome being used by the Germans. Rochford had been visiting friends at the 64th Squadron late into the evening before (there were several squadrons stationed on the big field at Izel-le-Hameau) and had gone to bed quite late. He had had only a little sleep when, while it was still dark, Collishaw woke him to inform him this was the morning of their long-planned bombing sortie. "We're off this morning," he had said cheerfully. Though not the morning he would have chosen, Rochford arose, dressed and accompanied Collishaw out to the two silent Camels in pre-dawn darkness. They took off separately. They carried four twenty-pound Coopers, two under each wing. Flying at 5,000 feet, less worried about archie than in daylight, they reached Dorignies. Rochford attacked first, firing all his ammunition into buildings and hangars from 200 feet. He then dropped three bombs on the living quarters and a fourth on a hangar which went on fire. Collishaw then attacked three machines, which were being brought out of a hangar, with machine-gun fire and dropped four bombs from 150 feet which burst among the huts. Before returning home, Collishaw attacked a hostile machine and shot it down in flames, as it was about to land on the airdrome.

Thus Rochford had enjoyed little sleep for twenty-four hours when he was ordered off at nine o'clock that morning to lead an offensive patrol behind enemy lines. It was a clear summer morning as five brown biplanes took off and climbed into the blue toward the rising sun, Rochford taking off last and the others moving into a V formation on his wings as he set course. They climbed steadily upward; on patrols over enemy lines height was a prerequisite, especially so because they were flying into the sun. By this time Rochford knew well the meaning of the Hun in the sun falling from above on surprised victims. The only way to avoid such surprise was to gain great height and to keep one's eyes on the sky above and to the east, especially in the vicinity of the sun. With height, chances were good that the Camels, not the enemy, could surprise their foe from above.

The altimeter steadily registered gains. B Flight was approaching 8,000 feet, now crossing the lines below, at 80 m.p.h. in the climb. Ahead, below, several of them spotted action at about the same time. An R.A.F. Armstrong-Whitworth two-seater was being attacked by two Fokker D.VIIs. The D.VII was much respected, perhaps the best German scout of the war, and Rochford lost no time dropping his nose and diving to the rescue of the hard-pressed observer. The fight was being waged at 5,000 feet, so B Flight had 3,000 feet in which to dive. The two-seater pilot was violently throwing his machine around in a desperate effort to save himself. The rear gunner was firing away at his two tormentors. Rochford came screaming into the vicinity to the rescue at nearly 200 m.p.h. Fortunately for the two-seater, the Fokkers didn't see the Camels plummeting down from behind and in seconds Rochford was maneuvering to align his sight on the Fokker not under fire from the Armstrong-Whitworth's gunner. He pulled back on the stick, leveled out somewhat, still at speed, and rapidly closed his victim, waiting until he was very close before opening fire with the Vickers 303s. Surprise was complete, and, as bullets from Rochford's Camel began to find their mark on the trapped D.VII ahead, the rear gunner in the two-seater began to find the range of the other Fokker. Almost simultaneously the two black-crossed D.VIIs fell, spiraling down, out of control, below. The A-W was saved and Rochford had scored a quick victory over one of the enemy's best scouts. It was a good start, coming on top of the before-dawn bombing mission. But the patrol had just begun.

The fight with the two D.VIIs had taken B Flight down to 5,000 feet, and now began the climb for altitude; they were dangerously low for a patrol over enemy lines. Headed south-east, they regained 8,000 feet and continued climbing. When they were at 10,000 specks in the sky to the east became visible. The specks were higher than the Camels! Rochford maneuvered into the south to bring the sun behind him, meanwhile continuing his climb hoping the enemy had not seen his five Camels. Soon he could make out the unidentified enemy aircraft—more D.VIIs, green on top and blue underneath. By this time he had put the sun at his back and felt the Fokkers had not seen them. They too were climbing and Rochford questioned whether the Camels could gain an altitude advantage. The D.VII was reputedly able to outclimb any other aircraft on the Western Front. But he would give it a try. The Camels with their Bentleys strained at maximum throttle and steadily increased height, 11,000, 12,000, 13,000. When they reached 14,000 feet, in thinning oxygen, Rochford was looking down on the green D.VIIs. They still had not spotted the Camels, now above and in the tactically superior position. By this time Rochford had maneuvered the Camels slightly to the east of the Germans. Both formations were flying southward.

Rochford gave the signal and the flight nosed over in a dive to fall on the D.VIIs from the rear. He picked out one of the trailing green biplanes, fixed his eyes on it and dived until he was approaching its level from behind, then pulled back on the stick and came racing up behind. He waited until the last moment ("I was too bad a shot not to get really close") and pressed both Vickers triggers. Almost immediately the Fokker in his sights shattered. He continued to pour bullets into his adversary until the German aircraft fell off on a wing and plummeted toward the ground far below, out of control. Other members of the flight were also scoring, and the five Camels accounted for four D.VIIs in this classic diving pass. It was out of the sun—utilizing speed, surprise and attack from the rear with deadly effectiveness. Rochford had not opened fire until twenty to thirty yards behind his victim.

Success was achieved with these tactics, including patience in avoiding a fight until an altitude advantage had

been gained ("I knew there was no use going into them
until I had height") and success in hiding in the sun, enabling the flight to dive out of it and catch the Fokkers by
surprise ("I had been in combat for eighteen months and
knew most of the tricks by that time").

Since he had had two scraps and was low on ammunition, as were some of the other Camels, B Flight headed
homeward after almost two hours of flying and reached
Izel-le-Hameau at 11.00, where all, except one pilot, landed safely, Rochford first and the others following. "We
were all very happy," he recalls, "although we were anx-
ious about Rudge, who was missing."

Although he used height, speed and close-in shooting to
achieve success in one pass on 22 July, Rochford believes
maneuverability was the most important single advantage
in dogfighting in the First World War. "We had the edge
in maneuverability with the Camel and Pup, though the
Germans were faster. That was true against the Albatros
and Halberstadt in 1916, and the D.III and D.V at times.
The secret of success was to get above them unobserved
and slip down like a bat out of Hell, getting as close as
you could before opening fire. That was far better than
splitting up into individual dogfights if you could get into
proper position.

"When I went into a scrap, I didn't feel any hate. The
Hun-haters usually got shot down in the end.

"Boelcke was first to fight in pairs. He had Immelmann
in his squadron and he realized that when he was attacking he might himself be attacked. He got Immelmann to
fly with him and stand guard to protect him from attack;
that was the birth of formations. While we in B Flight
flew in a V of five, some of our flights at this time were
flying in two Vs of three planes each. Other flights used
even different formations. But by this time it was a case of
formation flying. The usual thing was flights of five in one
V, and three of these made up a squadron.

"I did some troop strafing, but did not like it, and I
don't know how much good it did. In the Second World
War it did a great deal of good because we were using
rockets. In the Second World War, also, maneuverability

was not as important in fighter combat as speed. Fighters were then flying so fast they couldn't turn as tightly. But in the First World War, maneuverability was of primary importance. It's also true, by the way, that the Germans seldom came to us in the First World War. We had to go to them."

The day was drawing to a close and our discussion was at an end but Rochford wouldn't leave without a word of praise for Collishaw. "He was a marvelous pilot and a fine chap. He and I first met in February 1917 in No. 3 Naval Squadron on the Somme front. He was one of the best." Collishaw is the highest-scoring living R.A.F. ace today. He has maintained his interest in the First World War throughout the years and has compiled an amazingly thorough record of day-to-day casualties in 1917 and 1918 for the R.F.C., R.A.F. and German Jastas. His Air Casualty Register contains 26,000 names. Moreover, he has spent much time putting together the recently published list of Richthofen's victims, identifying seventy-seven. Information is missing only on victims 54, 58 and 78! Collishaw also compliments the First World War German system of automatically commissioning non-commissioned pilots when they scored a certain number of victories, noting that the R.A.F. didn't do so. He believes this is one reason why German N.C.O. pilots did better than Allied N.C.O. pilots in the 1914–18 war.

Rochford, like many other British pilots, feels Collishaw has been comparatively overlooked in the years since the First World War. One cannot talk about flying and the First World War with him for long without learning something about his old squadron leader. Collishaw, with sixty confirmed victories, may well have been the top-scoring Allied ace had he not been withdrawn from the front on several occasions for long periods. He didn't fly combat between late January and June 1918 because he was assigned to administrative duties. He got back into the air fighting in June and quickly ran his score from forty to sixty by the end of September. Then, however, he was sent to England and missed the last six weeks of fighting, a time when many Allied fliers achieved their greatest success. Thus in 1918 he was in action only about four months.

"You must look up Collie," Rochford repeated in parting. And then the ace who reported to the Somme in February 1917, and served and survived the rest of the war, said goodbye.

11

SPRINGS AND BISHOP FROM THE NEW WORLD

A successful American fighter pilot who flew with Ricken-backer in the 94th Squadron was Robert C. Cates. Cates had almost finished at college (Wofford) when he volunteered in 1917. After training in America and France he was posted to the front early in 1918. His assessments of the aircraft involved and conditions prevailing in the 1914–18 air war, and incidentally of the reasons that made Rickenbacker so successful, are highly interesting. It was in 1970 that we discussed pilots, aircraft and combat tactics, fifty-two years after the war had ended. His memory was still clear.

"The most important quality for a scout pilot in combat was the ability to judge speed and distance. This is more important than anything else, because in an engagement one hopes to dive on the other fellow and knock him down with one pass. Often that's all there is to the so-called dogfight, one pass—since one side or the other usually moves out of a scrap pretty quickly. That's one reason Rickenbacker was so successful. He had been a racing driver and could judge speed and distance better than the others. He could dive on an enemy plane and judge the speed so well that he knew when to pull out, and the distance so well that he knew exactly when to open fire.

"In movies about dogfighting in the First World War it often looks almost like a merry-go-round with planes all milling around and staying somewhat together. I never saw much of that. When people ask me I tell them it wasn't that way. Once in the Verdun area I happened to see a Fokker on the tail of one of my friends, who was diving in an effort to escape. I happened to be in the right position and dived after the Fokker and shot him down. That wasn't dogfighting. I told them later it was more luck than anything else. That's what victory often was—a matter of luck."

Cates offered interesting observations about German scout aircraft of the First World War. "The German machines were a whole lot heavier. They'd stay together in a dive. Our Nieuports—we were flying the 28 in 1918, Spads were better—wouldn't stay together. The wings were made like orange crates and the fabric would often peel off in a steep dive. The water-cooled Spads had more weight in the nose and the wings would stay together. The air-cooled Nieuport was good for maneuvering. One could get out of a tough mess with the Nieuport maneuvering. But they wouldn't dive as fast and were dangerous to dive. The Germans, with heavier aircraft, often dived to escape a bad situation. In general, taking in the whole war, the accepted view on our side was that the Allies had more manueverable planes, the Germans faster machines. But after the war, when I was still in service, we received many German aircraft and tested them. I never could get the performance out of them they did."

Could it have been that the speed of the German machines was often overestimated because they so regularly followed the tactic of diving from height? Cates thought there might be something to this. Of course, in combat there's a tendency to exaggerate the performance of the other machine, as well as the number of the enemy.

Cates believes larger formations were not always best, especially when the performance of some machines was less than that of the others.

"My buddy, Willie Palmer, always flew with me. We could do better as a pair. We'd often stay low, just above the treetops. It was sort of hit and run. Formations high up couldn't spot us that low, that close to the ground, and we were usually safe from attack. Others did that too. Frank Luke, an unusual sort of guy, was one of them. He lost his flying buddy, Joe Wehner, and it affected him so deeply that he decided he'd clean up all the Germans he could." (Luke, as we have seen in Chapter Nine, had lost still another friend shortly before his last flight, on which he was flying alone.)

Cates, who flew from the same field as Rickenbacker and Luke, is an admirer of the late Elliot White Springs, fifth-ranking American ace of the war and the most famous of all American pilots who served first with the British. "He was fearless," Cates observed. "There was a job to be done and he was out to do it, but he was also quite a liver!" Cates smiled as he recalled the colorful Springs, who served under Billy Bishop in 85th (R.F.C.) Squadron. Millions of Americans became aware of his exploits, for he became a successful writer after the war, after compiling an outstanding combat record.

Springs was one of the Ivy Leaguers (Princeton) so conspicuous numerically among top-scoring American scout pilots of the First World War. In his early days in England he distinguished himself with good-natured English hosts as much by teaching them to appreciate the merits of South Carolina eggnog, and how to mix a proper Mint Julep, as with flying ability. But he was an excellent pilot and Lieutenant Colonel Bishop, second-highest scorer in the R.F.C. with seventy-two aerial victories, liked what he saw in Springs and two inseparable buddies, John Grider and Larry Callahan. (They called themselves the Three Musketeers and an indication of their spirit lies in the names they gave their Camels in France—Eggnog First, Julep and Gin Palace II.)

In writing this book I spoke to Springs's daughter, who put me in touch with Marshall Doswell, who in turn enlisted the help of Miss Barbara Fenix, who was at that time sifting through the papers and records of the late pilot and as a result obtained his combat reports. They reveal that Springs and many Americans also used the buddy system, that in general engagements under the leadership of Bishop they employed two-to-one tactics to achieve many air victories. For example, the history of the 148th Aero Squadron, Aviation Section U.S. Army Signal Corps, describes a dogfight which took place on 24 September 1918 as follows:[1]

With three flights on patrol, Lieutenant Clay leading the bottom flight, the Blue Tails (German Fokkers) were sighted to the east. They could always be identified because four of them flew very close together. These four could be easily marked in the sky by their peculiar formation. They were at about the same height as the bottom flight of the 148th. Lieutenant Clay, knowing he would have the support of the other two flights above, led the squadron straight for the Fokkers, who outnumbered him by several planes. The Blue Tails were willing to fight and met the bottom flight head-on, starting a dogfight. In the meantime some of the Blue Tails held off in reserve and gained altitude. The two upper flights of the 148th held their altitude as they came over the fight. As C Flight seemed outnumbered, Lieutenant Kindley dove with his flight into the battle, soon followed by B Flight and Lieutenant Springs. Then the remaining Blue Tails came in, reinforced soon by four or five more Fokkers. By this time there were fifteen Camels and twenty or more Fokkers in the scrap, and it had become a question of luck more than good judgment, as Camels and Fokkers alike twisted, half-rolled, turned and dove, tracer bullets flying in every direction. The Huns knew they were good fliers and, being brave men, tried to bring down their opponents singly. This more than any other one thing proved their undoing, as the pilots of the 148th watched their chances and whenever a pilot was in trouble, two or more would help him out by shooting the Fokker down. One after another the Fokkers went down, seven in all. Then as quickly as it had started, the two sides separated and the 148th, dazed, but knowing they were victorious, started for home. Each man must have surely thought some of his comrades had gone down in that fight. A sigh of relief was enjoyed by all when all the machines had returned. Some of the planes, however, had to be condemned because the enemy's bullets had destroyed their usefulness. . . . The pilots who were

---

[1] W. P. Taylor and F. L. Irvin, *History of the 148th Aero Squadron*, p. 39.

credited with the Huns brought down were Lieuts. Zistell (two), Knox, Kindley, Clay, Springs and Wyly.

Nine days earlier Springs and a fellow pilot used two-to-one tactics against a Halberstadt near Epinoy. His combat report read: "Leading lower flight, we cut off a Halberstadt and attacked from east and below. After a good burst E.A. (enemy aircraft) turned west. Lt. Cunnius attacked from the rear above as I attacked from below and I observed his tracer going into observer's cockpit. E.A. dove east with smoke issuing from fuselage. Observer ceased to fire at me and followed him down to 500 feet and was forced to pull up due to ground fire. Later Lt. Ralston and I attacked a Hannoveranner over Bourlon Wood at 300 feet. E.A. disappeared after long bursts. Ground fire fairly active . . ."

Thus by this stage of the war Allied pilots were attacking regularly in pairs and it had become obvious that team tactics were highly effective. The day of the lone hunter was past, except for rare exceptions. Springs had attempted it and had learned his lesson. It was two weeks after he reached the front with Bishop and the 85th, and he was impatient to see action. Bishop was carefully training the inexperienced pilots and felt they were not yet ready. Yet Bishop, also impatient, flew off to the front lines and shot down a two-seater. He repeated the performance, getting two of the enemy, three days later. (He often flew alone throughout his career, a brilliant exception to the rule.) Still having seen no action, this was more than Springs could bear. On 4 June he took off, unauthorized, and made his way east to the lines looking for the enemy, alone. They found him before he found them and he was surprised from above by six Pfalz scouts. They shot him up from end to end. He was lucky to escape with his life and straggled back to the airdrome at Baizeux, near Albert. In attempting to land he crashed into Bishop's own plane, destroying both machines. Bishop watched him climb out of the wreckage. Springs, shaken, nevertheless refused to be cowed. He walked up to the great Canadian ace and passed his finger across the row of ribbons on his chest. "See those decorations," he said. "You're welcome to them." And he walked off. Later that night he went to his squadron commander's room and apologized. Next day Bishop took him with him and each shot down a Pfalz—Springs's first, which left him jubilant, so jubilant that he crashed his S.E.5 in landing. Bishop, noting that he had destroyed three squadron machines in two days, against one of the enemy, asked him which side he was fighting on.

There are many surviving Allied fliers of the First World War who believe Bishop was the best all-around pilot of the war. Many feel that his record of seventy-two victories is less than the truth. He was one of the few great aces who persisted in solo flights into enemy territory throughout the war, perhaps succeeding so often because of his remarkable marksmanship. This singular airman, holder of the Victoria Cross, rated gunnery by far the most important of the talents required for success in air combat. In *Winged Warfare* he expressed his views. They are worthy of a careful look:[1]

I had learned that the most important thing in fighting was shooting, next the various tactics in coming into a fight and last of all flying ability itself. The shooting, as I have said before, I practiced constantly and became more and more expert at it, with the result that finally I had great confidence in myself, and knew for a certainty that if I only could get in a shot from one or two of my favorite positions, I would be successful in downing my opponent.

To those who have never seen a war machine I would explain that to control one, the pilot has to manipulate but a single lever which we call the "joy-stick". It is very much like the lever with which you shift gears on an automobile, but it moves in four directions. If you want your machine to go down, the instinctive move would be to lean the body forward. Therefore, the fighting airplane is so rigged that when the pilot pushes the "joy-stick" forward, the nose of the machine points down. In the same way, if he pulls the "joy-stick" back, the nose goes up and the

---

[1] William Bishop, *Winged Warfare*, Chapter 17.

machine climbs at any angle he wants it to. In turning, it is necessary to bank the machine, otherwise it will skid outwards. It is also just as necessary that the machine is not banked too much. This is one of the first things a pupil is taught when learning to fly.

The "joy-stick" also controls the banking. . . . The pilot thus has both feet on the rudder bar, holds the "joy-stick" with his right hand, and with his left controls the engine of the machine by holding the throttle in his hand. He is always able to do anything he wishes, either with the engine or the machine itself. When firing the gun, he simply moves his thumb slightly along the "joy-stick" and presses the lever which pulls the trigger.

To be able to fight well, a pilot must be able to have absolute control over his machine. He must know by the "feel" of it exactly how the machine is, what position it is in, and how it is flying, so that he may maneuver rapidly, and at the same time watch his opponent or opponents. He must be able to loop, turn his machine over on its back, and do various other flying "stunts"—not that these are actually necessary during a combat, but from the fact that he has done these things several times he gets absolute confidence, and when the fight comes along he is not worrying about how the machine will act. He can devote all his time to fighting the other fellow, the flying part of it coming instinctively. Thus the flying part, although perhaps the hardest to train a man for, is the least important factor in aerial fighting. A man's flying ability may be perfect. He may be able to control the machine and handle it like no one else on earth, but if he goes into a fight and risks his life many times to get into the right position for a good shot, and then upon arriving there cannot hit the mark, he is useless. Unable to shoot his opponent down, he must risk his life still more in order to get out and away from the enemy, and that is why I put aerial gunnery down as the most important factor in fighting in the air.

Tactics are next important because, by the proper use of the best tactics, it is so easy to help eliminate risks and also so easy to put the enemy at a great disadvantage. Surprise is always to be aimed for. Naturally if one can surprise the enemy and get into a proper position to shoot before he is aware of your presence, it simplifies matters tremendously, and there should be no second part to the fight. But it is a very hard thing to do, as every fighting man in the air is constantly on the look-out for enemy machines. To surprise him requires a tremendous amount of patience and many failures before one is ever successful. A point to know is the fact that it is easier to surprise a formation of four or six than it is to surprise one or two. This is probably because the greater number feel more confident in their ability to protect themselves, and also are probably counting upon each other to do a certain amount of the looking out.

When flying alone or with just one other, it is always a case of constantly turning around in your seat, turning your machine to right or left, looking above and around or below you all the time. It is a very tiring piece of work, so it is but natural that when you have three or four other men behind you, you spend more time looking in the direction where you hope the enemy machines are, if you want to attack them, and to looking at any interesting sights which are on the ground.

In ordinary fight or duel we had tactics, of course, to suit the occasion. The great thing is never to let the enemy's machine get behind you, or "on your tail". Once he reaches there it is very hard to get him off, as every turn and every move you make, he makes with you. By the same token it is exactly the position into which you wish to get, and once there you must constantly strive for a shot as well as look out for attacks from other machines that may be near. It is well if you are against odds never to stay long after one machine. If you concentrate on him for more than a fraction of a second, some other Hun has a chance to get a steady shot at you, without taking any risks himself. To hit a machine when it is flying at right angles to you across your nose is very hard. It requires a good deal of judgment in knowing just how far ahead of him to aim. It is necessary to hit the pilot himself and not the machine to be successful, and also necessary to hit the pilot in the upper part of the body where it will be more certain to put him completely out of action at once. When a machine goes into flames it is largely a matter of luck, as it means that several of your bullets have pierced the petrol tank and ignited the vapor escaping from it.

In our tactics we used this cross shot, as it is called, considerably; mainly when, after a combat has been broken off for some reason, guns having jammed or the engine running badly, it becomes necessary to escape. Upon turning to flee, your opponent is able to get a direct shot at you from behind. This is decidedly dangerous; so, watching carefully over your shoulder and judging the moment he will open fire, you turn your machine quickly so as to fly at right angles to him. His bullets will generally pass behind you during the maneuver. The next thing to do is to turn facing him and open with your cross fire.

In fighting in company with other machines of your own squadron you must be very careful to avoid collisions, and it is also necessary to watch all of them carefully as well as the enemy, because it is a code of honor to help out any comrade who is in distress, and no matter how serious the consequences may seem, there is only one thing to do —dash straight in, and at least lend moral support to him. In one case I had a Captain out of my own squadron, a New Zealander, come eight miles across the lines after both his guns had choked, and he was entirely useless as a fighting unit, just to try to bluff away seven of the enemy who were attacking me. It was unnecessary in this case, as I had the upper hand of the few machines that were really serious about the fight; but it was a tremendously brave act on his part, as he ran great risks of being killed, while absolutely helpless to defend himself in any way.

All fights vary slightly in the tactics required, and it is necessary to think quickly and act instantly. Where a large number of machines are engaged, one great thing is always to be the upper man—that is, to be slightly higher than your particular opponent. With this extra height it is quite easy to dive upon him, and it makes maneuvering much easier. If, as is often the case, you are the "under dog", it is a very difficult position and requires great care to carry on the fight with any chance of success. Every time your opponent attempts to dive at you or attack you in any way, the best thing to do is to turn on him, pull the nose of your machine up, and fire. Often while fighting it is necessary to attack a machine head-on until you seem to be just about to crash in mid-air. Neither machine wants to give way, and collisions have been known to occur while doing this. We prided ourselves that we hardly ever gave way, and the German was usually the first to swerve. At the last moment one of you must dodge up and the other down, and there is great risk of both of you doing the same thing, which of course is fatal. It is perhaps one of the most thrilling moments in fighting in the air when you are only 100 yards apart, and coming together at colossal speed, spouting bullets at each other as fast as you can.

Once you have passed you must turn instantly to keep your opponent from getting a favorable position behind you, and then carry on the fight in the usual series of turns and maneuvers. An extraordinary feature of these fights which occupied any length of time, and entailed such maneuvering, was the fact that they were generally undecisive, one machine or the other finally deciding that for some reason or other it must quit and make good its escape. In nearly all cases where machines have been downed, it was during a fight which had been very short, and the successful bursts of fire had occurred within the space of a minute after the beginning of actual hostilities.

It will be noted that Bishop agrees with Cates, who expressed the view at the beginning of this chapter that most fights were usually brief. Bishop's stress on shooting carries weight because of his exceptional victory record. He also emphasized flying ability, including acrobatics, not for shooting down enemy aircraft while engaged in fancy flying but for giving a pilot confidence in his machine in whatever position he finds himself in, or must assume, in combat. But mastery of his guns, marksmanship, is what Bishop stresses repeatedly as the most important factor in air fighting.

There is a house in Baden-Baden in which live three Generals. One of them is General Theo Osterkamp, victor over thirty-two Allied airmen in the First World War, as a German Navy scout pilot, the present Ordenskanzler of the *Pour le Mérite* Order and commander of German fighter Geschwader in the Battle of Britain. Osterkamp is thin, of medium height, agile and sharp-featured. His blue eyes are hawk-like and one immediately feels the intenseness and concentration of this old eagle, as he was called by pilots he commanded in the Second World War—including Adolf Galland and the late Werner Mölders.

We entered a comfortable living-room, a large picture window at one end, and I asked the retired General, in a bright blue coat which contrasted with white hair, about air fighting in the First World War.

"I was in the Navy in the First World War," he said, "flying land fighters. We flew the Albatros D.III and D.IV, which had a bigger cockpit. They were not very maneuverable. The Spad was faster. Later I flew the Fokker D.VII, also the tri-decker (Fokker Dr. I). Interestingly, we never got our best fighter to the front. In 1918 I was sent to Dessau to test the new metal Junkers J7, forerunner of the J9. It was 20 m.p.h. faster than anything else we had. It would have been our best scout. But Fokker came out to test it and cracked it up, and since there was not time for Junkers to build another model before the tests, Fokker's new model was selected. In general, our fighters were heavier and that's why the Allied machines could often out-turn us. The same thing was true for much of the Second World War. The Me.109 was heavier than the Spit and though below 18,000 feet it was as good, and although it had a higher ceiling, it couldn't turn with English fighters because it had a heavier engine and tended to fly with the nose up. The Spit flew at a more level attitude and turned inside it. Of course, the weight gave us an advantage in diving away—in both wars.

"The most important advantage in aerial combat in the First World War was altitude. [Osterkamp's judgment fits with Edward ("Mick") Mannock's so-called golden rule —always above, seldom on the same level, never underneath.] The second most important thing was maneuverability. In that war we sometimes had rather long duels. My longest lasted about twenty or twenty-five minutes, very long for air combat. The third most important thing for the First World War pilot was the speed of his aircraft. That became a little bit more important in the Second World War.

"Our tactics as Navy fliers were different from those on the Western Front. We flew very high because of the accuracy of the flak. We developed high-altitude fighter tactics before anyone else. These were the tactics which were much used in the Second World War. There were no scrambles for us. We flew at 18,000 or 19,000 feet. Richthofen came to fly with us once. I told him that high-altitude combat was different, to be cautious. In the time his unit was with us I think their losses were something like seventeen for four or five victories. So it was a different air war.

"We sought altitude and then a diving pass on the enemy because we were not so maneuverable."

Osterkamp, who knew Richthofen well, and who trained with Boelcke, believes the secret of Richthofen's success was his wonderful marksmanship. "Richthofen was not the best flier we had in the First World War. In fact, he learned flying and formation from Boelcke. But he was a genius with the guns. That's something that cannot be taught. Only one other man was as good as Richthofen at gunnery, and he came along in the Second World War—Marseille."

Osterkamp supports the theories of Bishop in the preceding chapter—that shooting was the most important factor in combat success. The pilot he referred to as Richthofen's equal in marksmanship, Hans-Joachim Marseille, flew with the Afrika Korps in 1941 and 1942, scoring 158 aerial victories—losing his life when his engine caught fire over British territory. He stayed in the aircraft long enough to reach German lines before jumping. When he finally jumped he was struck by the tail. Marseille's shooting artistry was such that he could bring down several aircraft with little ammunition. Of course, he had better guns and sights, and a better aircraft, than did Richthofen a quarter of a century earlier.

I asked Osterkamp why German pilots scored more victories than Allied pilots in the First World War.

"In the First World War we had older pilots. They were more experienced. That was true partly because we were fighting over our own territory most of the time. When we had pilots shot down they usually returned to us, unless of course they had been fatally hit. So as we recovered most of our pilots they gained more experience. We didn't need so many young replacement pilots. On the other hand, Allied pilots were often taken prisoner and were lost for the war because we captured them after they had been forced down or had crash-landed behind German lines. This meant a steady flow of new, young pilots to Allied squadrons. So French and English pilots were, for most of the war at least, younger and less experienced.

"That situation reversed itself in the Second World War. It was the Luftwaffe which was forced to use young pilots then."

Osterkamp survived many narrow escapes in the First World War. The most "fantastic" escape he recalls was in a battle with the French ace Guynemer.

"The fight began at about 17,000 feet and we went at it all the way down to a hundred and fifty feet. A shell from the ground flipped me over on my back and I was upside down. I managed to dodge his bullets and get down but nosed up in a desperate landing. I also once had the distinction of being shot down by Albert Ball."

I asked Osterkamp how many members of the *Pour le Mérite* order were still alive. "There are just eighteen of us," he answered. "Four of those are fighter pilots." He showed me the stationery of the order, with a large engraved "Blue Max" at the top of the page, under which was written: *"Die Ritterschaft Des Ordens Pour Le Mérite."* As we were looking at it the paper slid off the top of the desk. Osterkamp's hand intercepted it before it was halfway to the floor. I laughed and told him he still had cat-like reflexes.

Frau Osterkamp talked with us for a time. When she left us, Osterkamp put his hands to his lips, and said, "I was in Hamburg recently and they let me fly one of the modern jet fighters." I was astonished. "But I don't want my wife to worry about it," he added.

On the walls hung many pictures of pilots and aircraft from both wars, several of them now dead. There was a picture of Osterkamp's teacher and old comrade, Gotthard Sachsenberg, who had scored thirty-one victories, one less than his famous pupil. Both had come from Dessau on the Elbe and both, with Joseph Jacobs, whom we met in Chapter Eight, went off to fight the Communists in 1919 after Germany lost the war.

Osterkamp is slim and wiry—has been since his flying days in the First World War. In fact, he was thought to be too sickly for soldiering and after being turned down found that the Volunteer Navy Flying Corps would accept him. He had been a forester in East Prussia and had already had brushes with the Cossacks, and scouting appealed to him. When the Army turned him down, it sent the German Navy its leading ace. He reached the front at the beginning of April 1917 (only five weeks before Ball went down) and began to score regularly. On 12 August 1918, when his friend Sachsenberg went on leave after receiving the *Pour le Mérite*, he had one of his greatest days, leading Marina Jasta 2 in combat with a formation of D.H.9s. In the resulting dogfight the D.VIIs led by Osterkamp accounted for nineteen of the R.A.F. planes without loss! It was not long afterward that he, too, re-

ceived the *Pour le Mérite*—about the time he was shot
down again, by three Spads.

He fell ill near the end of the war and was only dis-
charged from the hospital on 9 November. The war was
to be over in two days and he scored no more victories.
But flying with the Iron Division fighting against the
Communists in Lithuania, Estonia and Finland he and his
friends achieved considerable success in the Junkers D.I.
and CL.I. Then he and his comrades were ordered back
from the front by the German Government and their early
air fighting days were over. The pace had taken its toll,
however, and Osterkamp shortly afterward suffered a
breakdown and spent many months in the hospital.

When the new Luftwaffe was organized he joined, began a second air career, not as a fighter pilot this time but
as the head of the fighter school Werneuchen, near Berlin,
and thereafter commanding fighter units in the Second
World War. His recollections about that conflict, the campaigns and tactics of the fighter forces, constitute an inside
view of one in command of the Luftwaffe's best fighter
units, and we examine them and those of other pilots in
Part Three of this study, analyzing the air war of 1939–43.

THE SECOND WORLD WAR: FIRST PHASE

13

THE BEGINNING

At the end of the First World War scouts were flying at 130 m.p.h. and faster, diving at 200 m.p.h. and attacking with twin guns. Speed, fire-power, ceiling and other performance measurements had increased throughout the four years of the war. Engines of more than 200 horsepower were being built to give even greater performance. The role of aircraft had progressed from the original concept of 1914, observation, to wide tactical application and strategic design, as seen in the German Air Service's long-range bomber offensive against England. Tactics had evolved from primitive, limited means of fighting to the use of large formations organized for high-altitude, controlled combat.

Certain combat advantages were accepted by all: maneuverability, speed, ceiling, rate-of-climb, endurance, sturdiness, fire-power and many other capabilities were the sought-after measurements of aircraft. Good eyes, quick judgment, marksmanship, flying ability, prudence and other talents were recognized as qualifications of the successful scout pilot. At this stage of air development, the carnage which ended a way of life in Europe (and perhaps the world) and introduced Communism on the globe ended in November 1918.

All understood that in a new war aircraft would be faster and more potent in many ways. Future tactics and strategy, however, were debated. A theory originated in England, America and Italy which rapidly gained wide acceptance—that bombers would prove almost all-powerful in a new war. In the interval between the wars and into the first months of the Second World War, this school of thought held that well-armed, fast bombers could "always get through" and do the job. Hitler was one of those who emphasized the bomber; it was an offensive weapon and he was almost totally offensively minded. There were those in each country who held like views. The greatest difference between the democracies and Germany in the strategic concept concerning bombers at this time was that in Germany the bomber was projected primarily an army cooperation weapon.

The Germans had an advantage in shaping and training their air arm when they used some of it in the war in Spain to test equipment and practice tactics. In Spain they learned quickly that the day of the biplane fighter, with which several countries were to begin the Second World War, was over, and they developed effective ground cooperation tactics. In the decisive battle of the Ebro in 1938 the Nationalist Air Force played the major role in the opening days in checking the Republican advance.[1]

The Germans in this case were further developing a proven concept of the First World War; in the last two years of that conflict aerial bombing and strafing had become an important part of ground operations. The new concept in the democracies, strategic bombing, was a concept not as clearly established in the First World War. It had been demonstrated in that conflict that heavy bombers could be built to fly long distances and do considerable damage. But in the First World War there had been no final determination of the question whether bombers could sustain such an offensive in the face of sustained and determined scout resistance, nor of the question whether they could paralyze an enemy's industry. The Germans had discontinued dirigible attacks on England because of heavy losses, but when they launched heavy bomber raids the British were not prepared for that faster form of air assault. At first, German bomber losses were slight. So seriously did the British take these bomber as-

---

[1] José Varios, *Combat Over Spain*, p. 224.

saults, however, that scout squadrons were withdrawn from the Western Front to defend against them. German losses increased, due to scout interception and other causes. Nevertheless, modernists in the interval between the wars believed the early German success with relatively slow bombers showed what might be accomplished in the future, what was indeed inevitable in the future with fast, well-armed bombers. Both Britain and the U.S.A., following this concept, embarked on a heavy bomber program years before the outbreak of the new war in 1939.

Thus in the years between the wars the democracies—impressed by German bomber attacks on England and France in the First World War—placed heavy emphasis on a large strategic bomber force and, to some extent, forgot the lessons of tactical aerial cooperation with ground forces of the last years of the war, which they had pioneered. The Luftwaffe emphasized bombers but its bombers were medium and fighter bombers designed to cooperate with the Army primarily. Though Germany had pioneered in the field of long-range heavy bombing (the strategic bombing concept), the Luftwaffe did not build a heavy bomber force. Its mediums were to conduct independent bombing in addition to cooperating with the Army.

Despite this emphasis on bombers, the key to air operations in the Second World War turned out to be the scout (its name changed to pursuit or fighter), as had been the case in the First World War. Even the fastest and most heavily armed bombers, it was discovered, couldn't penetrate hostile air space and carry out strategic bombing in the face of determined fighter interceptions without suffering unacceptable losses—unless fighters accompanied and protected them all the way. Therefore, the fighters being built in Germany and England during the late thirties held the key to success in the opening campaigns of the 1939–45 war. There were, basically, only three which counted in the first two years of the war—the Messerschmitt 109 and the Hurricane and Spitfire. Germany was a fraction ahead, but only a fraction. The Luftwaffe had chosen the Me.109 over the He.112VI and two other entries in 1935 and used the Me.109B in the war in Spain after the Hein-

kel 51 biplane had been clearly outclassed by the Russian-built Rata and the American-built Curtiss P.36. At
the outbreak of the war the Me.109 was probably the best
high-altitude fighter in the world. Only the Spitfire, of
which there were but a few, equalled it in overall performance—being slightly superior in speed at medium altitude and having a better turning radius. The Me.109
(which incidentally is properly labeled the Bf.109, for
Bayerische Flugzeugwerke) had a higher ceiling, could
outdive and possibly outclimb the Spitfire (though this is
still debated) and was equipped with a fuel injection engine which continued to operate under negative-gravity
conditions. In his introduction to William Green's book,
Famous Fighters, Johnnie Johnson says the Spitfire was
the best conventional defensive fighter of the war and that
the P.51 Mustang was the best offensive fighter (because
of its range). At the beginning of the war, however, the
R.A.F. was primarily equipped with the Hawker Hurricane, another excellent fighter, which bore the brunt of
the onslaught in the Battle of Britain. The Hurricane's performance handicap was that it was slower than the
Me.109; but it was very sturdy, had a fine rate of climb,
and a high ceiling—about equal to the 109's.

The Me.109E was the first mass-production Me.109. By
the end of 1939 it had replaced earlier models in first-line
units. Thirteen Gruppen of forty fighters each were operating with the 109E when the war began. Its performance
was, briefly: speed 354 m.p.h. at 12,300 feet, ceiling 37,-
500 feet, a combat range of 412 miles, initial climb rate
of 3,100 feet per minute. It was armed with two 20-mm.
cannon and two 7.9-mm. machine-guns.

The Spitfire I, the model which most often met the
Me.109 in the Battle of Britain, possessed a maximum
speed of 362 m.p.h. at approximately 19,000 feet,[1] a ceil-

---

[1] The apparent 8 m.p.h. advantage of the Spitfire is misleading.
At lower altitude the 109 was probably faster. In any event, the
speeds of individual aircraft vary. German pilots are convinced
the 109 was faster at most altitudes flown in 1940. See Adolf
Galland, *The First and The Last*, p. 37.

ing of approximately 35,000, a combat range of 395 miles and an initial climb rate of 2,500 feet per minute. The Hurricane was about 40 or 50 m.p.h. slower, with a greater combat range (approximately 500 miles) and a slightly better climb rate, but performed less well at higher altitude. Both R.A.F. fighters were armed with eight .303-inch machine-guns. The Battle of Britain was fought by these three fighters, primarily, and the medium bombers, fighter bombers (destroyers) and dive bombers (Stukas) of the Luftwaffe, the latter two types being largely withdrawn after suffering heavy losses in the opening phases. Thus the great interest shown in these fighters throughout the world, then and since.

The strategy employed by the air forces of Germany on one side and France and Britain on the other in 1940 followed between-the-wars planning. Having developed effective ground-air operations in Spain (Wolfram Freiherr von Richthofen, cousin of the great First World War ace, had headed Germany's Condor Legion operating there), Germany struck on land with a new type of mechanized war, the *Blitzkrieg*. It was a combination of fast-moving armor and infantry, working closely with bombers, fighter bombers and fighters. It was immediately successful (as it had been in Poland in 1939).

When the Luftwaffe attempted a strategic bombing offensive with an air force designed primarily for co-operation with the army, and encountered what Johnnie Johnson called the world's best defensive fighter, the Spitfire, supported by the Hurricane and operating with certain advantages (fighting over their home territory and directed by radar), it met defeat. Actually the Me.109s performed quite well, shooting down more R.A.F. fighters than they lost. This achievement was due in part to better combat formations, the superior level of combat training enjoyed by German fighter pilots and the average performance superiority of the German fighters (most of the R.A.F. defenders being Hurricanes). It was the slaughter of German bombers, dive bombers (Stukas) and fighter bombers (destroyers), plus the greater (and growing number of British fighters toward the end of the Battle of Britain, which brought about the Luftwaffe's defeat.

The Luftwaffe had not been designed to conduct such an offensive. R.A.F. fighters had been designed to fight just such a campaign, the British not having forgotten German bomber attacks in the First World War. In looking briefly at this 1940 aerial campaign, it should be noted that the time Britain gained from the period between the Munich agreement of September 1938 and the outbreak of the Second World War in the autumn of 1939 later enabled the R.A.F. to win the Battle of Britain. Had the British gone to war in 1938 and fought the battle either that autumn or in 1939 they would have done it without Spitfires (except for a few pilot models) and with only a few Hurricane squadrons. The R.A.F. biplanes would almost certainly have been swept from the skies, as were biplanes of the Polish, French and other air forces. (Hitler had perhaps been right in pushing his generals to attack in the west in 1939.) The Luftwaffe was well ahead of the R.A.F. in modern fighter strength in 1938, but was no longer so by 1940. In the time between Munich and the Battle of Britain—almost two years—the British had set about building modern fighters at a feverish pace and in the summer of 1940 they began the battle about even (possibly ahead) in first-line fighter strength and outbuilding Germany two-to-one or better. This fact is still magnificently resisted by many who cling to the popular and fictional notion about relative fighter strength in the Battle of Britain, so often reflected in films, fictionalized features and inaccurate books. The author of this book and other serious researchers of the air war have offered the less romantic facts regularly in publications in recent years; Bruce Robertson, writing in *Air Pictorial*, pointed out recently that the R.A.F. never faced a desperate situation in the supply of modern fighters, that in the opening week of the Battle of Britain Fighter Command could have put 1,000 fighters in the air. Air Vice-Marshal J. E. (Johnnie) Johnson, writing after the war, says, Fighter Command had 800 modern fighters operational in May 1940.[1] By contrast, though it included some 2,700 aircraft of all types, the Luftwaffe assault force began the Battle of Britain in August with about 800 single-engine fighters. And since fighters would determine the outcome of this exclusively aerial campaign of the war, the Luftwaffe faced quite an assignment. Its fighter arm enjoyed the three advantages mentioned earlier but faced the disadvantages of inadequate range, being tied too closely to the bombers in a defensive role and fighting over enemy territory (which meant loss of pilots and planes forced down). It also faced the best radar defense system in the world and for a time its leaders didn't realize it.

Luftwaffe fighter pilots, flying combat formations perfected in Spain and utilizing proved principles of the First World War, entered the Second using the basic unit of a pair (Rotte) of widely separated fighters. They were separated by about two hundred yards so that each pilot could cover the other's tail, or blind spot, though this was traditionally more the responsibility of the wingman. This basic unit was easily added to. Another pair constituted a Schwarme and the four fighters spread out four-abreast just as Boelcke's pilots had done in the First World War. When several fours (flying in what is called the finger-four formation) joined to make a squadron (Staffel), the units of four were staggered in height and weaved back and forth as a means of mutual search and protection.

Unfortunately for many French and British pilots, the combat formation lessons of the First World War had been largely forgotten by those who wrote their training manuals. The R.A.F. in particular entered the Battle of Britain flying in vics and other V formations, too closely spaced for effective operation. R.A.F. pilots were also saddled initially with fixed patterns of controlled firing passes. These formations and tactics were soon proved disastrous

---

[1] J. E. Johnson, *Full Circle,* p. 119. In June, July and August (the Battle of Britain began in August) 1,418 fighters were produced in British factories.

(but not soon enough for the unfortunate) and were abandoned by various units as the light dawned.

Luftwaffe fighter pilots, knowing they had a fine high-altitude aircraft, liked to employ the same tactic their fathers used successfully in the First World War, a high diving pass out of the sun. Since the Me.109 could outdive both the Spit and Hurricane, this was a logical tactical maneuver. Often it was not possible, however, because the Me.109s were tied closely to the bombers. On these occasions R.A.F. fighters often held the altitude advantage and dived on the bombers or both bombers and fighters. In their defensive role in 1940, the R.A.F. fighters' better maneuverability—so important in the First World War—was a major asset, though somewhat offset by the Me.109's greater diving speed, which enabled its escape in a disadvantageous situation. As the war progressed, the advantage of maneuverability proved to be less important than in 1914–18 primarily because the faster fighter, or that with greater ceiling, tended to limit the engagement to one pass, and, with the greater firepower of Second World War fighters, one pass was often sufficient. If it were not, it was often true that, approach speeds being so great, the two fighters were sufficiently separated after the initial pass that either could get away—but not always. There was still dogfighting. It was merely faster and of briefer duration.

Most of the combat principles of the First World War remained valid. A few years ago I asked Douglas Bader what combat conditions should be sought, and his reply was, "Height, sun and getting close."

Just as Mannock taught his pilots in the last years of the First World War to attack from astern, approach close and shoot straight, and to perfect team tactics including ambush and decoy, exactly the same rules were found to apply to fighter combat in the Second World War. Most fighter pilots scored when they managed to assume a stern position. They were successful when they got so close that it was hard to miss. Deflection shooting, however, was more widely and successfully used than in the First World War.

Mutual protection achieved in formation was lost when one pilot flew alone, which proved highly dangerous—as it had in the last part of the First World War. In other words, the ground rules of the First World War were soon accepted by fighter pilots of the Second, with a few modifications.

Aircraft were improved, and new ones introduced (but not at the First World War pace) throughout the war. That is why it is difficult to compare, for example, the Me.109 and the Spitfire. We have briefly compared the performance of the Me.109E of 1940 and the Spitfire I of that same year, but from then until the end of the war new, higher-performance models of each were introduced, so that at times one outperformed the other. In the later years of the war, and after the Japanese and Americans had entered, new models were produced in England, Germany, America and Japan (the Japanese began with an advantage over U.S. fighters with the famed Zero-Sen).

By the end of the war propeller fighters which could fly well over 400 m.p.h. were being built in all the advanced countries. In Germany the Me.262 was flying in combat at speeds in excess of 600 m.p.h. Among the best fighters not already mentioned were the U.S. Thunderbolt P.47, the German Focke-Wulf 190, the British Mosquito and Tempest, and the Japanese Tony (Type 5), Frank (Ki-84) and George (Shiden-Kai).

A close comparison shows that fighter speeds did not increase proportionately from beginning to end, as much in the Second World War as in the First, except in the case of the breakthrough by the jet—almost twice as fast as the fighters with which England and Germany began the war. The greatest difference in the air between the two wars was the decisive influence of fighters so often in both tactical and strategical roles in the Second World War, whereas they had scarcely ever been decisive in a strategical role in the First World War and only at times decisive tactically.

Fighters often determined the fate of land campaigns, sea campaigns, strategic bombing campaigns and logistical operations in the Second World War. The great fighter contribution of the United States was in introducing the long-range fighter, the P.51 Mustang, which Johnnie Johnson called the best offensive fighter of the war. The Mustang gave fighters, for the first time, the range to determine the outcome of strategic, long-range, offensive campaigns and made them a global weapon. By the end of the war they were flying from England to the easternmost parts of Germany and over Austria and western Czechoslovakia. They were flying from island bases equal distances—600 and 700 miles—to Japan. Such an offensive concept had not been foreseen for fighters in the interval between the wars nor in the first year or two of the war, and the performance of the Mustang from late 1943 until the end of the war showed what could be done with even faster jets in the post-war years, with range even farther extended. The Mustang over Germany in late 1943 and 1944 definitely wrested the initiative from the German fighters which, until the autumn of 1943 at least, appeared on their way to checking the U.S. daylight strategic bomber offensive.

In Part Three of this book we give the views of leading aces of the Second World War on fighter tactics and strategy, interesting accounts of missions exemplifying conditions up to the end of 1943, and their opinions on the growing role of air power. The pilots were interviewed, as was the case with First World War aces, in the United States, Germany and Great Britain. Their combat experience qualifies them as experts in the field of air warfare. They include both day and night fighter pilots.

Night-fighter combat was developed to a high degree in the Second World War, fighters in that eerie struggle carrying two crew, one a radar operator, and relying on directions from the ground to locate their opponents. The night war in the air grew into a battle as vast and costly as the day struggle, the Bristol Beaufighter and Mosquito and Me.110 and Ju.88 assuming important roles as fighters, in addition to the others already mentioned.

In our first visit to one of the great aces of the Second World War, we concern ourselves with the morning of 11 May 1940, the day after the beginning of the German offensive in the West which was to bring about the collapse of France. In this swift, mechanized assault the Luftwaffe demonstrated the degree to which it had perfected tactical aerial cooperation with panzers and its method of knocking out an enemy air force in a matter of days.

14

CHAOS IN FRANCE

A famous R.A.F. fighter ace of the Second World War (at twenty-three the youngest Wing Leader in the R.A.F.) was Roland P. Beamont, D.S.O., O.B.E., D.F.C. Beamont's record is especially fascinating because of the variety of his accomplishments, in various fighters, from the beginning to near the end of the war. He was finally shot down in October 1944 by flak over Germany, there to spend the last seven months as a prisoner.

He began his combat career as a Hurricane pilot in France, trying unsuccessfully to stem the German offensive in May 1940, which quickly overran Holland and Belgium as well as France. Two years later he was given command of a Typhoon squadron assigned the task of checking the almost daily bombing of London and the South Coast towns by the F.W.190. The Luftwaffe had introduced the 190A in November 1941; it had soon established superiority over the Spitfire V, then in use, an edge it probably maintained until 1943. The F.W.190's speed advantage induced the Luftwaffe to use it for hit-and-run raids, as they were called, on the British capital as well as other targets. For some time Spitfires had been unable to catch these annoying low-level invaders. Beamont, in late 1942, was posted to Manston, on the south-east coast of Kent, with a squadron of the new Typhoons and was soon able to exact a respectable toll of the 190s. In the last relatively ambitious daylight raid on London by the 190s, on 20 January 1943, Typhoons caught and shot down five of them.

Beamont flew the first Typhoon night intruder mission over enemy-occupied France. He then did considerable strafing and bombing in the Typhoon. He became the first wing leader of a Tempest wing (a variant of the Typhoon) in 1944. Flying a Tempest, he overtook many V.1s (the pilotless jet "flying bombs") and was credited with destroying thirty-two of them out of the Wing's total of 632. After scoring ten confirmed aerial victories, several unconfirmed, plus the thirty-two victories over V.1s, and having destroyed numerous trains and vehicles strafing in France, he was offered a job at Hawkers, which had designed the Typhoon and where he had worked earlier. With ninety-four missions completed, he decided to increase the total to one hundred and then accept. On his next mission—13 October—after strafing a troop train, he made one last pass to have a look. A small-calibre shell struck the coolant housing of his Tempest; without coolant liquid, which leaked out rapidly, his engine overheated and seized. Forced to crash-land, he destroyed his aircraft with an incendiary bomb carried for that purpose and evaded Hitler Youth and Wehrmacht for an hour but was finally captured and taken prisoner.

When I met Beamont he was a Director of the British Aircraft Corporation's Preston Division, often flying a private aircraft to work. His vivid description of flying the Hurricane I in the grim days of May 1940 illustrates the disadvantages (such as poor formations) and trying conditions Allied pilots confronted in France at that time. The short period of resistance of 87 Squadron, twelve days, before it was withdrawn to England reflects the Luftwaffe's superiority. The May 1940 air struggle also illustrates the great advantage of superior numbers, which the Luftwaffe attained by concentration in many cases and which so often in both wars produced disproportionate losses on the outnumbered side. As Beamont remembered those days:

"In November 1939 I was posted to France and joined 87 Squadron, near Lille. On 10 May 1940 I was sick but went up to the front to have a look. I was nineteen. I saw troops with First World War rifles and much horse-drawn equipment. We heard a mechanized attack was coming and the squadron actually moved on the 10th. Tom

Mitchell, like me a Pilot Officer, who had spent the night with me in Lille, and I found them on the 11th at Senen, near Mietz. I was still somewhat sick. We reported to the Squadron Adjutant and then to the C.O. He sent us to our flight commanders. I was asked by my Flight Commander, Bobby Vose Jeff, if I was fit and I said I was.

"The field was grass with a hump in the middle. Six Hurricanes, a flight, were on one side and six on the other—but you couldn't see the other side because of the hump. We had heard the guns firing all night in Lille and were told the 87th had shot down four enemy planes on the 10th. I was placed on stand-by to replace one of the pilots who had gone off for breakfast, though it was late in the morning, and was waiting out on the field with other pilots.

"The Flight Commander received a phone call—we had a field telephone near a ditch where our ammunition was stored. It was Squadron Headquarters, located at a farm half a mile away. Squadron had had a call from Wing Headquarters. After brief words Vose Jeff put down the phone and announced: 'Okay, chaps, we're off to Maastricht.' The Germans were crossing the river there, on the Belgium–Luxembourg front, and our Battles were attacking the bridges. We were to patrol and give them protection. We ran out to our Hurricanes—these had the fixed propeller. I was flying in the lead vic of two in B Flight, the second six of the squadron formation. I was to keep position just to the right and rear of B Flight Leader in the leading vic of our trailing section. The fitter jumped out of the cockpit as I scrambled in and fastened the parachute and seat belt straps. The C.O. rocked his ailerons and soon we were all rushing out to take off as fast as we could. We prided ourselves in being able to get off in less than two minutes. It's a wonder we didn't have an accident taking off, not being able to see the other chaps for that hump, but we all got off safely.

"We were supposed to patrol over Maastricht at 15,000 feet and had been told to expect heavy enemy activity. We set course, climbing at 180 m.p.h. There wasn't much radio talk. The TR-9 radios weren't very reliable. On about one of every two missions they failed. It was a clear day and our climb continued for some minutes. We were warned over the radio that there were bandits in the general area of Maastricht–Brussels. My gunsight, the GM-2, was on. Its horizontal lines could be moved in order to fit the wingspan ahead and get the proper range. But our guns weren't turned on. We continued to climb for about twenty-five minutes and were at good altitude. Then suddenly someone shouted, 'Bandits—eleven o'clock high.' I saw the twin-engine aircraft, but wasn't sure what they were. Immediately the voice of the C.O. came over the microphone: 'Echelon starboard for attack—go!'

"We all slid inside him as he began a sharp turn to the right, flat out. But things became confused. As we maneuvered to attack the grayish, twin-ruddered bombers—they had radial engines—other aircraft swooped down on us from above. I was suddenly alone with my flight leader. It happened so fast—I had had only a hundred and fifty flying hours at this time—I was thoroughly confused. Me.110s were diving into us and moving out front as they pulled out. I picked out a bomber and prepared to open fire. But an Me.110 went by me and moved out front. At first I hesitated, then opened fire on the Dornier—one of the bombers. The range was considerable. The bombers began to turn to the left, I followed, and suddenly Vose Jeff popped up in front of my guns from below and I stopped firing. At that moment I saw a Hurricane plunging earthward off to my left, a 110 on his tail. I winged over left and dived to get on the 110's tail, full throttle. But they had pulled too far away. Suddenly I noticed white tracers to the right. It took a second to register, then I turned left as tightly as I could, making two circles with full power. There was nothing behind me after that. The sky seemed empty. Up ahead I saw a Dornier turning right. I closed as fast as I could and though I wasn't in a position to fire from the rear I tried a full one-deflection shot. The eight Brownings scored hits on his raised port wing and engine as he turned. I could see more strikes; his port engine began to smoke and he nosed down. I moved in closer and fired another burst. His port engine stopped and he nosed more steeply down. I could see more hits and he headed toward a cloud below and we went into it at 3,000 feet—I was above and off to the right. I broke out of the cloud at 2,000. There was no sight of the Dornier. I was over a forest, wondered where I was, guessing it was probably the Ardennes. Then I saw flak bursts—blackish, 20-mm. stuff—in front. I immediately dived to 100 feet and set course west. Suddenly, again white streaks shot past in front of me. I looked behind and got a shock. A Dornier was after me!

"I was out of ammo but didn't know it and I executed a sharp port turn, as sharp as I could, to get behind him. I was getting into position after about one and a half turns. His rear gun began firing at me. I lined him up in my gunsight and pressed the trigger button. Only three or four rounds came out. Every time I got close the rear gunner opened fire. The Dornier was only fifteen or twenty miles an hour slower than I was. I knew I had to get away, being out of ammunition, that I'd have to make a break for it. On the Hurricane we had a boost override for emergency power of about three minutes and I knew I would have to use it to gain enough distance to get away. I pushed the little round, colored knob for overboost; it could blow the gaskets if used for more than three minutes. I then rolled into a hard starboard turn, which separated us by about 700 yards before he turned and came after me. He fired but the distance was too great, and I pulled away. I was lost and scared and guessed that a 350-degree compass heading would get me back in the vicinity of Brussels, or where I might see the coast and find a landmark. I flew for some minutes—it was getting late—and finally saw the coast. Off to my right I recognized Dunkirk and then I knew I had to turn south-east. I finally found the field and landed, greatly relieved to be down. The squadron had lost several planes and had written me off. I claimed a probable but everything was so confused there was no confirmation.

"For the next five days we were up every day and I think I shot down about five in all in that period but at that time the squadron didn't pay much attention to claims and we weren't encouraged to write intelligence combat reports unless we were absolutely certain of the result, which was very difficult under such conditions. I remember that the next day, the 12th, Me.109s shot down three of our Hurricanes by diving from above and coming up under a vic. We were stacked down in close formation. On the 13th I claimed a probable. I had a Ju.88 spinning down and then an Me.109 streaming smoke [Beamont got a confirmation on this day, his first in France] and I think I got two 110s. In those five days, then, I hit a number of planes. They were not the first, however; in January I had caught an He.111 over the Channel and hit him and he went into the sea.

"By the 22nd, just twelve days after the German attack had begun, 87 Squadron was down to four aircraft. We had lost half our pilots. We were recalled to Yorkshire for refitting and rest and remained there for a month. I went back on ops in June, at Exeter, just in time for the Battle of Britain, but the Battle of France was over then and all our squadrons had been withdrawn to England."

The Beamont account is a remarkably vivid illustration of combat at the beginning of the war. Only a few months later German bombers such as the Dornier which attacked him at 100 feet would probably have refrained from taking on a fighter. But at this opening stage of the war the German bomber crews thought their aircraft were as fast as British fighters, and they believed they enjoyed a reasonable chance in dogfighting with them. They were to learn better at Dunkirk and over England a few weeks later.

The Luftwaffe caught the Hurricanes by surprise on the 11th diving from above (one wonders if it was out of the sun) as the British fighters went for the Dorniers—the classic pattern of Richthofen and others in the First World War. It appears that none of the twelve Hurricane pilots saw the Me.110s before they were amongst 87 Squadron. It is interesting to note in this day's fighting that the Luftwaffe was using the Me.110 as top cover, as fighters would be used. This reflects the belief of the Luftwaffe command at the beginning of the war that the Me.110

was capable of meeting enemy single-engine fighters on somewhat even terms. This was a misplaced hope. Yet against the Hurricanes the Me.110 was not so greatly overmatched and with the element of surprise and superior formations in these opening days Me.110 units sometimes pulled it off without suffering heavy losses. On other occasions, however, the Me.110s were rudely treated.

This account of the second day of the shooting war also illustrates the aggressiveness of Luftwaffe pilots. Both the Me.110s and Dorniers attacked fighters persistently, individually as well as in formation.

Beamont was to fly better and better fighters throughout the war. When he took over 609 Typhoon Squadron at Manston, the new fighter contained bugs, which he helped to remove, but in spite of them the very fast Typhoons of 609 shot down a number of F.W.190s in the first four months of operation.

In 1944, when his wing of Tempests became operational (just before D-Day), he was piloting a fighter which could outperform anything in the war at that time below 20,000 feet. "The Tempest, with a Saber engine, could achieve 418 m.p.h. at 2,000 feet. This compares with the Mustang P.51's 395 m.p.h. and the Spitfire 14's 380 m.p.h. at this altitude.

"We met F.W.190s over Arnheim once and out-turned them at 20,000 feet. I flew nearly all the fighters during the war, the Me.109G6, the F.W.190, and so on. The P.51 was the best for going to Berlin, of course. The F.W.190 or Spit 9 was best at 30,000. The Spit 9 was more fun to fly than any of them. But below 20,000 feet, the Tempest was the best by far."

15

SHUTTLING FROM ENGLAND TO FRANCE

One of the great fighter pilots of the Second World War who believes fighters and dogfighting will be part of the picture in any future war is R.A.F. Air Vice-Marshal Harold Arthur Cooper Bird-Wilson, C.B.E., D.S.O., D.F.C. His opinion will be shared later in this book by U.S. Air Force General Robin Olds, at present (1971) Commandant of Cadets at the Air Force Academy at Colorado Springs. Olds was a highly successful fighter pilot in both the Second World War (the author served with him in the 479th Group) and in the Vietnam war.

Bird-Wilson doesn't feel the day of dogfighting is over because of the higher speed of modern jets or because of their sophisticated weapons systems. He points out that the faster jet fighters or interceptors fly the stronger they must be built—to withstand the stresses produced by great speed. "Today's jets can take a substantial amount of damage," he said. "And in Vietnam the MiG-21s and Phantoms, with sophisticated weapons, are still going round and round—dogfighting—as fighters have done for fifty years."

But we are getting ahead of our chronology of air tactics, and the stage of air fighting with which we are concerned in this chapter is that in which R.A.F. fighters proved that twin-engined Me.110s could not hold their own in combat with them. The Luftwaffe command had expected them to when Me.110 destroyer squadrons, often with picked crews, were formed. The fighting described by Bird-Wilson, however, one week after Roland Beamont had flown against Me.110s in Hurricanes, shows that early in the 1939–45 war the old First World War dogma that even the best two-seaters couldn't survive against one-seaters was re-established. Bird-Wilson's experience in these days also testifies to the successful tactics of the Luftwaffe in its onslaught against the West in 1940 and to his squadron's condition after resisting that concentrated assault for several weeks.

He was serving with 17 Squadron at the time (May 1940), having begun the war still not fully recovered from the effects of an air accident in 1938. Thus he was just becoming operational as the war erupted. The squadron was flying Hurricanes, shuttling from England to France on a daily basis, in order not to be caught on French airdromes by German ground or air forces. Its base in England was Hawkinge, a grass field two miles north-west of Folkstone. His description of the 18th, a day the squadron flew to France and saw action, and his comments on operational conditions in France at the time, are enlightening.

"At seven-thirty in the morning the batman awoke us and told us it was a sunny day. After breakfast we walked down to the field, an old one with four wood and brick hangars and on which our brownish-green Hurricanes—there were twelve in the Squadron—were scattered about. It was a most peculiar grass airdrome, something like a bowl. One landed downhill from any direction; in those days we landed in threes.

"We waited at the hangar hut; inside was an operations airman at the telephone and a station Intelligence officer. There was a big map on a sixteen-by-twelve table. After a time the phone rang and the Squadron Commander was called. On this morning he was A Flight Commander, W. A. Toyne; Squadron Leader Tomlinson, the C.O., had crashed while trying to out-turn a Ju.87 the day before. It was Sector Headquarters at Biggin Hill. We were to take off immediately and escort two V.I.P. transports to Merville airdrome in France, where we would come to readiness for operations during the day. We took off in threes and flew in three flights of four aircraft, each line astern. In the air we used Blue, Red and Yellow designations rather than A Flight or B Flight, etc. We relied mostly on hand signals, and after taking off closed our hoods and assembled. The last pilots in each flight of four took off together and joined the squadron after getting airborne—the number four in Red Flight, which was in the middle and led by the C.O., was the weaver. He weaved back and forth and searched the sky to guard against surprise bounces and was affectionately known as tail-end Charlie. I was flying as Blue Two this day, in the flight on the left. Yellow Flight was the four line-astern Hurricanes to the right.

"We were to rendezvous with the Bombay and Douglas transports near Manston and picked them up on schedule, but they were slow and it was forty-five minutes before we saw them down safely and landed ourselves at Lille Marcq, north of Lille. There we had tents and, as at Hawkinge waited. It was not long before Toyne was called to the phone. It was the British Expeditionary Force Operations Room, which reported enemy aircraft shooting up refugee civilians nearby. We scrambled immediately and headed south. We were flying toward Seclin, only about ten minutes away. With guns on and eyes scanning the sky ahead we soon made out a Dornier 215 twin-engine bomber escorted by two Me.110s ahead and below. Toyne ordered Red and Yellow Flights to go after the escorting 110s and we in Blue Flight were to go for the 215. We banked left and climbed for altitude from which to make a diving pass. But they saw us and dived for the tree-tops. The 110s left the 215 to its fate but we were now diving on all of them and had greater speed. I closed in on the 215 and managed to make the first pass, hitting his starboard engine with a good burst. I think that burst also killed the rear gunner.

"Other members of Blue Section followed my pass on the 215 and in a short time it crashed in a field near Douai. I then caught sight of a Hurricane—that of Pilot Officer Ken Manger—being hotly pursued at tree-top height by an Me.110, which in turn had three Hurricanes on its tail. The Me.110 crashed in flames shortly afterwards in an open field. To the members of the Squadron the myth of the maneuverability of the Me.110 was dispelled by this flight.

"All twelve of us now returned to Lille Marcq, most of us jubilant, Pilot Officer Manger a little shaken. As we looked down from the sky at the French countryside, it was a pathetic sight to see that all the roads leading west were crammed full of a moving mass of civilian refugees fleeing in advance of the approaching German Army. Exactly what was happening in the land battle was only known to a very few and all we knew at Squadron level was that our forces were being pushed back rather quickly into France. The Commander-in-Chief of Fighter Command, Air Marshal Dowding, had been ordered to reinforce the fighter squadrons in France and this he did by rotating a very limited number of squadrons, such as 17 Squadron, in and out of France on a daily basis. Briefings on arrival in France were very sketchy. When we scrambled it was often for defense and we usually had only a limited or vague idea of the location of the enemy and where we might intercept him.

"There were five Hurricane Squadrons, 17, 87, 111, 253 and 615, at Lille Marcq that day. They were dispersed to the north, west and south sides of the rectangular grass field and fighters were being scrambled throughout the day. Tension began to rise in mid-afternoon as reports came in that the Germans were advancing towards Lille. Orders were received that if a green rocket went up in the sky east of the field, all aircraft were to scramble. The rocket was soon seen by all the pilots at the same time. Their main aim now was to get airborne in the quickest time possible and not be caught on the ground. Hurricanes could be seen taking off in all directions regardless of the wind. There were many near misses but miraculously no accidents. The Hurricanes rising from Lille Marcq were like bees leaving a hive.

"Somehow 17 Squadron managed to form up and set course back to Hawkinge. Intelligence debriefed us on our arrival, about our combats. Our spirits were effervescent but we were somewhat tired. We were also greeted on our arrival by our new C.O., Squadron Leader Edwards-Jones, who was to lead us back to France early next day and into combat against Me.109s, when we were to lose two of our pilots. Our squadron carried out several sorties daily for the remainder of the Battle of France, moving at one time to Le Mans. The squadron was one of the last to leave France, on the final day of resistance. Before the summer and the Battle of Britain were over the squadron had had five commanding officers."

In the Battle of Britain Bird-Wilson added to his score and in September was awarded the D.F.C. for six victories and five shared victories plus several probables. Later that month, however, he was shot down and wounded and did not see combat again until early 1941. However, he managed to stay in the war until the end, completing four tours of operations and flying 600 missions. He commanded his first Spitfire Wing in early 1943, during which time he was awarded a bar to the D.F.C. He had a break from operations attending the Command and General Staff School at Fort Leavenworth, Kansas. He then returned to England to lead another Spitfire Wing in mid-1944. Later the Wing converted to P.51 Mustangs and flew bomber escort missions deep into Germany. In January 1945 he was awarded the D.S.O. and in May of that year took command of the first jet unit of Meteors.

Bird-Wilson has flown 198 different aircraft—and is still flying. He has held various R.A.F. commands in several countries since the Second World War. He went to Korea to study fighter tactics, a description of which is given in Chapter Thirty-one, and flew missions there in the Meteor with 77 Royal Australian Squadron from Kimpo.

"The future of air fighting? There will always be fighters. After every war it's said changed conditions outdate the fighter. It was said after the First World War and after the Second. The principles are generally the same. They're much faster, of course, speed always having been of vital importance. Of paramount importance to a fighter force is the need to keep its doctrine and tactics up to date."

It was, of course, superior speed plus an advantage in numbers which enabled the Hurricanes of 17 Squadron to be victorious on 18 May 1940. But taking place in French skies at that time was a different overall trend in the air war; 17 Squadron's experience was an exception to the rule. The squadron's victories on that sortie came eight days after the German attack had begun. In those eight days the Luftwaffe had achieved what it had set out to do. If the Do.215s and Me.110s were usually unable to cope successfully with Hurricanes, it should be pointed out, to maintain perspective, that British Battles and Blenheims were thrown against advancing German armor that week and were even more harshly treated by flak and German fighters. The Luftwaffe had destroyed most of the Belgian and Dutch air forces on home fields and attacked many other targets—some German pilots flying as many as nine missions a day. Effective resistance from the air to the German Army's advance was in this way prevented. In a desperate bid to check the panzers the French and British sent their bombers against them, sometimes unescorted. They were usually very badly handled by the Me.109s, and even when additional Hurricanes were sent to protect them the German concentration of fighter strength at the breakthrough point (Sedan) was so great, and the flak so concentrated and accurate, that some R.A.F. formations were wiped out. On the 10th, the first day of the attack, of thirty-five Battles sent out thirteen were lost and all the rest damaged. On the next day eight attacked German armor; one returned. The next day five attacked two bridges near Maastricht and none returned. Blenheims flying from England fared no better. Me.109s shot down five out of six on one raid at this time and eleven out of twelve on another. The trend became crystal clear on the 14th, with strong German armored units across the Meuse at Sedan, posing a mortal threat to France. Every Allied bomber was ordered to attack the spearhead, but some French units refused to take such losses and their missions were not flown. Of seventy-one light bombers sent against the spearhead that day by the R.A.F. only thirty-one returned, many damaged. The Luftwaffe was winning its war by using its 109s to devastate enemy bombers and to keep the Hurricanes assigned to protect them away from Sedan.

Bird-Wilson's combat of the 18th, and Beamont's of the

11th, were victorious but were exceptions to the general trend in the air. Of the Allied aircraft then involved only the Hurricanes were proving successful, and that usually only against enemy Stukas, destroyers or bombers. It looked as though nothing could check the Luftwaffe in the air. But the Spitfire was being held in reserve in England, to be committed at the proper moment. Five days after Bird-Wilson flew from Merville two Spitfires flew from England to France and, though heavily outnumbered by a gaggle of Me.109s they encountered, took them on and emerged victorious, flying back to England. This was one of the first hints all was not lost in the air for the Allied cause. It is to this day, on which the first 109 was destroyed by a Spitfire, that we turn our attention in the following chapter.

16

SPITFIRE DEBUT

The R.A.F. refused to send Spitfires to France in the crisis
of 1940. They were still few in number, facilities in
France were inadequate and the front was moving backward so rapidly they might have been overrun and captured. When the B.E.F. was trapped in a coastal pocket
surrounding Dunkirk and hundreds of thousand of British
soldiers desperately needed air cover to escape, Spitfires
were finally committed in numbers for the first time—and
the Dunkirk story is also widely known. Less widely
known is that before Dunkirk a few Spitfires, flying from
English bases, engaged the 109 over the coasts of
France. The pilot who is thought to have shot down the
first Me.109 of the war in a Spit was a New Zealand
sheep-farmer who had come to England in 1937 to join
the R.A.F. He first served with 74 Squadron, and was
then transferred to 54 Squadron, which received Spits in
1939. Alan Christopher Deere, D.S.O., O.B.E., D.F.C., had
thus flown Spits for a number of months when the time
came for him to meet the famous 109 in one of them, in
May 1940.

I visited him in England more than twenty years after
the end of the war. Somewhat large for a fighter pilot,
blond, easy-going and soft-spoken, he was still serving in
the R.A.F. as an Air Commodore, and had recently
served as Aide-de-Camp to H.M. the Queen. The historic
encounters he experienced on 23 May 1940 provided eagerly awaited proof that the Spitfire IA, at lower altitudes
at least, was the match or master of the Me.109E then in
use. He participated in two weeks of combat over the evac-
uation beaches at Dunkirk following the sortie of 23

May and in those two weeks he shot down five aircraft
and was himself shot down, but managed to get back to
England with evacuating Army troops! His story, even in
the modest manner he tells it, is obviously that of one of
the R.A.F.'s most aggressive fighter pilots.

"In New Zealand I always wanted to fly. I was one of
the first twenty-four accepted there as a pilot trainee.
Nineteen of us arrived in England in 1937 to begin training. I soloed in Berkshire and later served at Hornchurch,
with some of the best R.A.F. pilots defending the London
approaches. Squadrons 54, 65 and 74 were stationed
there. Sailor Malan and Stanford Tuck were at
Hornchurch. In my opinion, Malan was the greatest
fighter pilot of the war.

"We had Gloster Gladiators then—in 1938. The Germans had Me.109s. Chamberlain gave us a year to get
most of our squadrons equipped with Hurricanes and
Spitfires, a year we badly needed. When the war began in
1939 I was at Hornchurch with 54 and we had Spits but
didn't see much action. We dispersed and put sandbags
about but there was only limited flying. We were holding
back, getting ready."

The day he had years been getting ready for came two
weeks after the beginning of the German offensive against
France and the Low Countries. His account of the action
demonstrates the advantage of the Spitfire's shorter turning radius and higher speed. Deere proved to himself that
day that his Spit, Kiwi I, could outclimb the Me.109,
though technical and statistical comparisons showed the
109 could then both outdive and outclimb the Spit. The
reason for this might have been that 54 Squadron was
then experimenting with the Rotol constant-speed propeller, which other Spitfire squadrons did not yet have, which
meant better climbing performance.

"I flew my first patrol over France on 15 May 1940,
and on the 23rd Johnny Allen and I, patrolling above
Calais Marck airfield on the coast of France, engaged in
the first recorded combat between Spits flying from bases
in the United Kingdom and 109s. That day I had already
been on one patrol over the beach and came back without

seeing action. Squadron Leader White of 74 Squadron had been forced down at Calais Marck across the Channel, however, in the first clash with 109s (no kills) shortly afterward. Flight Leader James Leathart, A Flight, volunteered to fly a Miles Master across the Channel to fetch him back to Hornchurch, though we didn't know who would control the field when we got there. 'Prof' Leathart and Johnny Allen and I always flew together, so naturally I took Allen on my wing as escort. Officially, it was to be a training mission; the station commander suggested it and authorized the use of two Spitfires. We took off abreast at about eleven a.m. It was warm and I had on a blue cotton shirt and service trousers, black slippers and the yellow Mae West. I wore a brown helmet but no goggles. Our heading was 110 degrees. The Master was fast enough for a throttled-back Spit and we stayed low, at 1,500 feet, and maintained radio silence. The Master was leading. We crossed the Channel in thirty minutes. I turned on the gun switches for the eight .30-caliber Brownings when we saw the French coast. The gunsight was a reflected orange ring and bead. There was about five-eighths broken cloud at five thousand feet. Visibility was good below. We saw the field and flew over it. A Spit was parked there, almost certainly the Squadron Commander's.

"Leathart had said he would waggle his wings when he was ready to go down and now he signalled he was going down to pick up White. I told Johnny to climb up above the clouds to about 8,000 feet and circle and patrol, and he pulled away from me. I would cover the field while staying low. Leathart landed safely and I circled above. Everything was going well and he was taxiing to the small hangar when Johnny suddenly yelled from above that 109s were approaching the field! By now the Master was taxiing out for takeoff. An Me.109 suddenly came down and out through the broken clouds south of the field. He was obviously going for the Master. Leathart was practically helpless. I was off to Leathart's right, behind, just north of the field and immediately turned sharply left and pointed the Spit at the oncoming 109. My purpose was to startle or frighten him away from the Master. He came on fast and I had the Spit at full throttle to intercept and just as he turned in behind the Master, left, I fired a burst and he caught sight of me. He took a quick shot at the Master, then pulled up quickly, surprised. I racked the Spit around as tight as I could turn to get on his tail. The radio sounded just then and it was Johnny, above: 'I'm surrounded and being attacked by 109s. Come and help me!' All I could do was say, 'When I've dealt with this chap.' I rolled out of my turn below him but on his tail and though he was fast I gained. When he saw me behind he turned right but I could turn tighter and closed in. I approached to about 300 yards—the guns at this time were unfortunately set to converge at 450 yards, too far we found out later. He tried to avoid my fire by pulling almost vertically upward; I opened fire. I could see the De Wildes striking him almost immediately. The strikes continued and then smoke poured from his engine, he tipped over and down, and plunged earthward. I watched him go straight in and hit the sand at the water's edge. He had helped me by turning. By that time I was at 2,000 feet and banked left into a climbing turn and called to Johnny: 'I'm coming up.'

"I was at full throttle climbing as fast as I could—these were the first constant-speed Rotol props in the IA—and reached the cloud layer at 5,000 and pulled up through them. As I came out, directly in front of me were two 109s. I pulled in behind number two easily. The leader had seen me and they began to turn. Number two skidded one way and then the other, to distort my aim. I easily stayed behind him and closed to about 100 yards and opened fire. It took only one good burst and he turned on his back and was soon falling out of control. He went straight into the ground below but at the time I was turning after the leader. He dived groundward and initially gained on me. But when we flattened out above the tops of the trees I began to close. He tried every maneuver to escape, even a sustained climb, after I fired a burst. After another burst, he headed east and I was out of ammunition. I stayed behind him—this had been a perfect opportunity to see if the Spit would stay with him—and then I pulled back on the stick, looped up into the clouds and rolled out and headed homeward! Johnny had shot down an Me.109 above me. Leathart, who had stopped his takeoff, saw one of the Me.109s hit the ground and hurriedly jumped in a ditch, where he found himself next to White! I called Johnny who was crossing out north of Calais, worried about his Spit. He had been hit in his fight with the 109s. I found him and joined him and flew him back. About ten minutes later Leathart and White scrambled into the Master and took off and made it safely back to the field."

Deere was credited with a victory and a probable, and with Allen's victory the score for the two Spits against a number of the enemy was 3–0. In addition, they had accomplished their mission, to protect the Miles Master. More than that, the combat had demonstrated the superiority of the R.A.F.'s Spitfire over the Luftwaffe's 109 at low altitude. Deere is quite clear in his mind about the Spit's overall superiority at that height.

"In these fights the enemy pilots tried about everything, including a sustained climb, and the Spit outclimbed them."

He used the lesson learned in this historic encounter to change the aiming pattern of his guns. Whereas the eight guns had been set to converge for a concentrated pattern at 450 yards, Deere had his gunners change his Spitfire's pattern to a converging concentration at 250 yards. It should be noted that he hit his first victim on the 23rd at 250 yards and the second at 100 yards. The war would soon show that the more successful fighter pilots fired from very close behind whenever they could, and achieved most of their success from this close-in position. Other R.A.F. pilots, following Deere's example, changed the firing pattern of their guns also, and this change was helpful in the combat over Dunkirk a few days later and in the Battle of Britain three months later.

This encounter with Spitfire IAs impressed the Luftwaffe pilots; those who saw what two Spitfires did that day, in the face of odds, knew they were up against a very fine fighter flown by capable pilots. The Me.109s would do better on many occasions that year, especially in utilizing the dive and high-altitude combat (and the climb against other Spits), but the days of easy victories over enemy fighters, which Luftwaffe pilots had achieved in Spain, Poland, Holland, Belgium and France, were clearly at an end in the war against the Spitfire.

Deere, Leathart and Allen scored twenty-five victories between them by 17 June and Deere was awarded the D.F.C. that month. (He had flown two more sorties on the 23rd, destroying another 109 in a long dogfight.) By 8 August he had eleven confirmed victories and several shared with others. Though shot down at Dunkirk, from which he crossed back to England by sea, he continued to fly and was shot down several more times while increasing his score. On 31 August he was taking off when a bombing raid on his field began and one of the bombs burst almost directly beneath him and completely destroyed his Spitfire. He again escaped. By this time he had seventeen victories and had been shot down seven times. Higher authorities ordered him off combat duty.

He returned on several occasions during the remainder of the war, rising to Squadron Commander in 1943, in charge of 403 Squadron, and then to Wing Commander. At the end of the war he was officially credited with twenty-two aerial victories and was widely recognized as one of the leading Allied fighter pilots of the war. In all his contributions to the Allied cause no single mission was more worthwhile than his performance on 23 May 1940, when all seemed to be going wrong for England and the democracies and everything right for the Luftwaffe and the German Army. Deere's aggressive spirit, combined with his flying ability and marksmanship, demonstrated to other R.A.F. pilots what the Spitfire could do in combat against the Me.109, and the success he and Allen scored that day was a definite boost to other R.A.F. fighter pilots.

17

THE NORWEGIAN LESSON

Some of the most challenging operating conditions faced by Allied fighter pilots in the first part of the war were encountered by R.A.F. pilots in Norway in 1940 in their effort to repel the German invader. Because the Germans occupied most of the cities before the British arrived, few airfields were available, but the British Navy steamed into Narvik, in the far north, destroyed a German fleet, bombarded the town, landed troops and captured the harbor. The R.A.F. acquired Skånland and Bardufoss; the former field was too soft for fighters but Bardufoss could accommodate them, and so it was that, on 26 May, 46 Squadron, with sixteen Hurricanes, flew to Bardufoss from the aircraft carrier *Glorious* to begin operations. The leader of this ill-fated group of pilots was Squadron Commander (now Air Chief Marshal Sir) Kenneth Cross, K.C.B., C.B.E., D.S.O., D.F.C., and he remembers clearly to this day the strange combat conditions in this northerly theater. The Germans had been pushed out of Narvik but they had air bases nearby and also control of practically all of the country. They quickly responded to the British capture of the port (and the sinking of the German destroyer force in the harbor) with bombing attacks against ships in the harbor and anchorage.

Cross's Hurricanes were assigned the task of protecting British forces and ships from the German bombers, and since the Germans began their attacks the second night after the city's capture, fighter attacks on German bombers began almost immediately. In the brief combat period before 46 was withdrawn from Norway, the squadron claimed fourteen He.111s and Ju.88s for a loss of six Hurricanes. Three of the R.A.F. fighters lost were shot down by rear gunners in the German bombers, two were lost because of unknown causes and one was entrapped in a bog. In this combat the Germans were handicapped by not having Me.109s with which to escort the bombers, and the lesson the French and British learned the month before in France, that bombers could not be sent safely against fighter-defended targets without fighter protection, the Luftwaffe glimpsed briefly in this theater. But the Luftwaffe did not pay the price long, for things went so badly in France for the British and French, and the German threat to England became so imminent, that in early June the Hurricanes of 46 Squadron were ordered to return to England.

Some believe the R.A.F. fighter campaign in Norway, if it had been continued, would have been a success, and it seems the Luftwaffe would eventually have been compelled, at the least, to make an effort to establish fighter bases in the area. This would not have been easy. Whatever the outcome would have been, fighter operations this far north were certainly novel. R.A.F. fighters sometimes managed to destroy enemy bombers before the fighters were detected. In the fjords the mountain shadows played tricks with the light. Often the Germans flew up the coast, as the easiest means of navigation, then turned inland to strike at targets. R.A.F. interceptors, as a result, were sometimes able to predict which targets were to be hit, and to carry out successful interceptions.

Cross's 46 Squadron was equipped with Hurricane Is with two-pitch screws, and Cross and other pilots of the squadron were keen on them. The other squadron—263—was equipped with Gladiators.

One could hear great distances in this country and it was possible on some occasions to hear enemy aircraft approaching from many miles away. Pilots would often arise at two or three in the morning—it was already getting light—and make interceptions at that hour. Cross once managed to catch four He.111s at an early morning hour even though they immediately turned and fled when they caught sight of several Hurricanes taking off to intercept. The German pilots by now knew they couldn't outrun Hurricanes; the fighters gained steadily as the 111s attempted to escape climbing up the fjord. But rear gunners hit Cross as he hit one of the fleeing He.111s, a probable, and he flew back to Bardufoss (the top of a plateau surrounded by mountains) with a windscreen covered with oil. Nevertheless, the bombing attack had been prevented, which was the decisive consideration, and German bombers in this theater found it practically impossible to catch the R.A.F. fighter base unprepared.

On the day Cross overtook the He.111s, 46 Squadron began evacuating Norway. Pat Jameson, one of 46's flight leaders, led the first three Hurricanes to attempt a landing on the aircraft carrier *Glorious*. Twenty-pound sandbags were placed in the rear-most bay of the fuselages so that pilots could stand on brakes as soon as the fighters touched deck. (None had ever landed on a carrier prior to this time. Cross had flown out to the carrier in a Walrus the day before to arrange with the captain for the attempt.)

Jameson and his two companions landed successfully that day and Cross and the rest of the pilots landed successfully on the 8th. A stiff wind, *Glorious*'s 30 knots and skillful handling had seemingly combined to extract the squadron safely from Norway, but on the afternoon of the 8th the British carrier was intercepted at sea (heading for Scapa Flow, south-west, because of a shortage of fuel) by a German naval force including the battleships *Scharnhorst* and *Gneisnau* and sunk with heavy loss of life.

The tragedy of 46 Squadron was probably the grimmest for any Allied fighter unit in the war, in suddenness and completeness. Only Sir Kenneth and Jameson of 46's fighter pilots survived the sinking of *Glorious*.

Though Cross's experience in Norway was brief, it emphasizes the vital importance of fighter escorts for bombers striking targets protected by fighters and illustrates the growing importance of air power in general. (Had the

R.A.F. possessed the P.51 Mustang at that time, which with extra tanks could easily fly a thousand miles, 46's aircraft could have flown from Bardufoss to the Faeroe or Shetland Islands, and the pilots would have survived.) The strategic lesson of the Norwegian campaign in 1940—the clearest lesson in history up to that time—was that air power properly installed and employed could force even the most powerful ships and navies from waters within aerial bombing range. Air reconnaissance, which the Germans maintained over much of Norway and the Norwegian Sea, enabled the Luftwaffe and the German Navy to sink many British, including a number of warships. The Luftwaffe's transport capability enabled the Germans to hold on in the Narvik area, according to Werner Baumbach, commander of its bomber forces.[1]

Control of Norway's air bases enabled the Germans to turn back British forces landed in the Trondheim area (a direct seaborne attack on Trondheim was called off because the fleet would have been exposed to air attack) and this meant defeat also for the other British counter-invasion of Norway.

The landing at Narvik in the north has been criticized as having had no worthwhile military purpose;[2] avoiding that debate, it seems clear that where the British had an air base and fighter support, they did not do badly, and indeed Cross came away still convinced the northern operation could have succeeded, whatever its value. The enemy held the Trondheim air base (in the central Norway operation) and the Royal Navy demurred from a direct attack on Trondheim. Two forces of troops were landed ashore under General Carton de Wiart and General B. C. T. Paget but were subjected to merciless air attack from the Luftwaffe for some ten days until they were withdrawn, a withdrawal completed at heavy cost.

Because the Germans had control of the air they were

---

[1] Werner Baumbach, *The Life and Death of The Lufwaffe,* Chapter Four.

[2] J. F. C. Fuller, *The Second World War*, p. 61.

able to supply their forces, and to inflict serious losses on British ships supporting the British Army. Thus air power proved dominant in Norway, both tactically and strategically, for the first time in a major land–sea campaign.

18

THE AIR WAR BY NIGHT

The growing role of air power, tactically and strategically, was demonstrated in Norway, in the German attack on France, Holland and Belgium and in the Battle of Britain in 1940. Stukas, fighter bombers and medium bombers joined panzers to deliver an integrated assault of such effectiveness that Allied defenses were overwhelmed in the Battle of France. The air effort was tactical co-ordination of a new degree of intensity, and proved decisive. Desperate appeals for British air power from the French—their last hope to blunt the armored spearheads which broke through at Sedan—showed that military leaders now recognized the new, key role of air power.

Two months later in the Battle of Britain R.A.F. fighters once again demonstrated the decisive nature of air power. To the astonishment of much of the world, British fighters turned back the best-equipped and best-trained bomber force in existence (though not a strategic force) even though that air armada was escorted by modern fighters. The margin was narrow, but the Luftwaffe couldn't sustain the losses inflicted on its bombers by the British fighters and Operation Sealion (the invasion of Britain) was cancelled.

The consequent turn in the development of air warfare was inevitable—expanded night operations. The Luftwaffe, stung by the tenacious daylight fighter defense of the R.A.F., turned to night bombing and initial attacks were highly successful. In neither Germany nor Britain (France had now fallen) had night fighters been totally neglected, but because targets were more easily located and accurately bombed in daylight, and also because in both countries it was assumed by many that bombers could get through regardless of fighter defenses, daylight bombing had been stressed. Now Germany would try bombing at night in an effort to achieve what it could not achieve, with acceptable losses, in daylight. Just when the R.A.F.'s fighters had finally discarded vulnerable vic formations and set patterns of attack and had adopted the finger-four formation of two-section (the Americans were to call them elements) flights, just as its fighters were getting reflector sights superior to the old types, in other words, just as day-fighter defense was perfected, the Luftwaffe turned to night attacks, which required an entirely different defense.

On the night of 14 November 1940—about two months after the Luftwaffe realized the Battle of Britain was lost—a new air campaign began that is the least understood of the great aerial engagements of the Second World War. It would not end until it had established night bombing and night-fighter interception on a par in intensity with daylight operations and until fleets of bombers and fighters of roughly the same size as the day armadas were streaming in and out of hostile skies. It would continue until the war's end in 1945.

On that night of 14 November the Luftwaffe utilized a radio beam to guide twelve He.111s to Coventry. They also utilized crossing beams from German-controlled transmitters, which enabled them to calculate wind, speed and distance. The twelve lead bombers (the British called them pathfinders, and were later to use this tactic for night bombing on a far greater scale) dropped flares on the target, Coventry, and then over 400 German bombers each unloaded more than a ton of high explosive, incendiary or parachute mine bombs on the city in the next few hours. The attack, on a moonlight night, caused devastation and industrial damage which shocked the British public, partly because of the realization that the R.A.F. could do little about such attacks, that the country now lay open and vulnerable to such night terror. At this time the R.A.F. was using Blenheims, primarily, for night defense. They had proved highly vulnerable in daylight operations and were not to be the answer in night-fighter defense either, though they were useful for training pilots and crew who later became highly proficient in Beaufighters, Mosquitoes and other aircraft.

The German onslaught against Coventry was followed in the ensuing days and weeks by heavy (by that day's standards) night bombings of London, Southampton, Birmingham and many other cities. The R.A.F. was unable to inflict much damage on the attackers. In the raid on Coventry, for example, night fighters probably failed to bring down a single bomber; anti-aircraft gunners claimed two destroyed.

The Germans, of course, had bombed London by mistake early in the Battle of Britain and the R.A.F. had retaliated by striking at Berlin. The R.A.F. had also struck at German targets in May. The German claim is sometimes made that the British began deliberate area bombing of cities, of civilian populations, before London's ordeal. But the Luftwaffe had used such bombing attacks in Spain (Göring admitted as much in Nürnberg), had bombed Warsaw, Rotterdam and other cities, and argument over the question is thus pointless. In night bombing it is impossible to limit the fall of bombs to military targets and neither side seriously thought it could be done. As Air Marshal Sir Arthur Harris admitted,[1] those bombs which missed specific targets at night were looked upon as weapons to damage enemy morale. The U.S. Army Air Force is often given credit in German accounts for its policy of precision bombing—carried out in daylight. In the war against Japan, however, the United States resorted to area bombing of Japanese cities and finally to the dropping of atomic bombs on cities.

The night war in the air found both England and Germany relatively unprepared. Fighter Command not only lacked effective night fighters and trained crews but lacked fields, ground crews, modern detection equipment inland from the coast and guns and searchlights capable of bringing down invading bombers. Only one thing saved England from a terrible ordeal at night spanning a period of

[1] Arthur Harris, *Bomber Offensive*, p. 77.

years—Hitler's decision to attack Russia. Had not two-thirds of the Luftwaffe been transferred to the East in May 1941, the assault on England's cities would have continued and expanded, and no one can say with certainty how great the damage would have been and what the final effect on English resistance would have been.

In 1940, for example, both searchlights and anti-aircraft guns in England were ranged by sound devices. The German bombers were so fast there was a considerable time-lag in the sound reaching these ground hearing devices. The ill-equipped, under-trained night-fighter crews made heroic efforts from November 1940 until the pressure lessened but progress had only been modest by the time that the German assault slowed because of the attack on Russia. The worst enemy of the night-fighter crew was bad weather and darkness, and when night fighters were unlucky enough to be shut off from their home airfields by foul weather closing in, tragedy often overtook them.

Night fighting requires steadiness, patience and an ability to stalk one's foe, in addition to flying and navigational talent of a high degree. That is because locating an enemy bomber in the night sky is almost impossible without the help of radar (the radar operator was the other crew member besides the pilot in the night fighters) and ground control. The English found that, while their coastal radar stations had been sufficient to warn of the approach of German formations in the daylight Battle of Britain, enabling fighters to intercept, finally, by visual identification, this was not enough at night and that unless night fighters were carefully guided up to the last minute or second there was little chance of success. Thus a whole new defense system had to be organized, in which an operator on the ground was able to control only one or two fighters in the air above at a time, limiting the number of night defenders which could be employed until a vast ground organization was in existence.

In the beginning of the night war radar was primitive and its perfection was the most important single element in the steady progress and success of night fighters. With better radar and aircraft, better-trained pilots and a better ground organization, night defense finally became fearsome indeed. The German defense, for instance, began to exact such a heavy toll of R.A.F. heavy bombers that in 1944, when the Germans were primarily on the defensive, new bomber tactics were ordered in an effort to decrease rising losses, tactics which included the sending out of hundreds of bombers on a decoy mission, two attacks on the same target the same night, at different times, and so on. British Bomber Command at this time also abandoned its practice of dropping route markers along the bomber route into Germany because German night fighters were using them to find the bomber stream.

In the first major night campaign of the war, the German offensive which began in 1940, the British defense technique began with a plot of the tracks of incoming German bombers at sector operating rooms, the sector controller assigning various incoming groups to other controllers (at what were called ground-controlled interception stations, G.C.I. stations). These were the new radar stations which were being built as fast as possible. At these stations the G.C.I. controller called in a night fighter from an aerial patrol line nearby and attempted to vector him to a position about three miles behind an enemy bomber. If everything went right, the fighter could then pick up the enemy bomber on his own radar detection set and continue the pursuit from this point. The G.C.I. operator was scanning blips on a screen, and when the radar operator aboard a night fighter, who sat facing the tail, picked up the enemy's blip he took over and talked his pilot into the position astern of the bomber. The idea was to get astern and below, in the bomber's blind spot, usually. The land mass below was dark and helped hide the approaching fighter, while the sky above was light. The night-fighter pilot, of course, could more easily see the bomber's silhouette against the background of the sky above. When the fighter had slowly closed the distance to firing range (if he overshot the bomber his prey was usually lost), the pilot eased his aircraft upward with added power and when the bomber was squarely in his sights pressed the firing button on the wheel and hoped his aim was true—the distance usually being 200 feet or less.

In the autumn of 1940 the R.A.F. had about a dozen night-fighter squadrons, which could have caused respectable losses had they been equipped with modern radar, manned by well-trained crews and effectively directed by an adequate ground organization. But this was not the situation. Half the squadrons were equipped with Blenheims, three with Defiants, which like the Blenheim had proved inadequate for day fighting, and three with Hurricanes. These squadrons made valiant efforts under trying conditions, flying from grass fields with primitive, often malfunctioning, radar sets and guided by less than efficient ground control. If they accomplished little, the enemy's night assault in the autumn of 1940 nevertheless started the R.A.F. on the road to building an effective night-fighter defense force.

The German experience was somewhat similar. Basing their defense plan on lessons of the First World War, the Germans attempted to protect likely targets with anti-aircraft guns, searchlights and barrage balloons (which the English also used), plus a very limited number of night fighters. The Me.109 was the Luftwaffe night fighter at the outbreak of the war and quickly proved unsuitable when the British launched their first night assaults in 1940. (A small number of pilots had been training for night operations in this aircraft before the war.) The initial German defense relied partially on what was called the Air Defense Zone West, a concentration of anti-aircraft guns in the Siegfried Line system which theoretically would be able to bring any enemy bomber flying from or to the west at 23,000 feet or lower under fire for three or four minutes. (To avoid such fixed defenses the R.A.F. would often approach Germany from the sea.) When the war began, although the A.D.Z.W. belt was not completed, it comprised some 197 heavy flak battery positions and 44 light flak positions and though it was short of searchlights a program to form a continuous searchlight belt across the defense zone was undertaken. (Copper was required in large amounts in the construction of searchlights, and copper was especially scarce in Germany during the war; this was a constant problem, especially when Hitler later demanded high priority be given to searchlight construction. The amount of copper required to build a searchlight was approximately equal to that needed to produce an aircraft.) Next came the Kammhuber line (belts of searchlights named after the first night-fighter division commander in the Luftwaffe) and in 1941 radar-equipped ground control stations and zones, which enabled fighters to be vectored to enemy bombers, as in England. Finally, in the latter part of the war German night fighters were allowed free pursuit with their own improved radar sets.

When it was realized that Me.109s could not do the job, the Luftwaffe had formed—in 1940—night-fighter units of twin-engine Me.110s and Ju.88s. Progress at first came slowly, as in Britain, but by the time of the first massive R.A.F. night bombing of a German city, the 30 May 1942 attack on Cologne, Luftwaffe night fighters and flak accounted for forty bombers. This was a 1,000-plane raid, so the loss of forty bombers did not represent a catastrophic loss, but it was a serious loss and pointed to heavier losses to come as the German night-fighter force expanded and became more efficient. The British were still expanding their night-bomber offensive in the summer of 1943 when they subjected Hamburg to enormous destruction from the air in a solid week of night bombing. (Losses in this raid were held to a minimum by the use of technical devices to confuse German radar.) The fire raid which opened that awful July week claimed 60,000 lives. Such R.A.F. attacks stunned the leaders of the Third Reich and Luftwaffe into urgent efforts to improve the night-fighter force. But as the Luftwaffe's bombing of civilians in England had not broken British morale, the R.A.F. night-bombing offensive against Germany failed to break German civilian morale.

German night-fighter pilots grew steadily more effective until by 1944 they were sometimes shooting down sixty, seventy, eighty, or ninety heavy bombers a night. Considering the total loss of trained crew, plus the damage sustained by other bombers which managed to return home, it can be seen that such losses actually constituted victories for the Luftwaffe's night fighters. Various Luftwaffe night-fighter pilots shot down a number of Allied bombers; the greatest, who scored more night victories than any other, was Heinz-Wolfgang Schnaufer, with the astonishing record of 121 confirmed night victories. He became a night-fighter pilot in the spring of 1942 and scored his first victory in June of that year. By August 1943 he had shot down twenty-one victims. On 16 December 1943 he shot down four Lancasters and he scored his fiftieth victory in March 1944. On 25 May of that year he shot down five Lancasters in one night and at the end of 1944 had scored 106 night victories and was Germany's leading night-fighter ace. His most successful twenty-four hour period came on 21 February 1945, when he brought down two Lancasters in the morning, then seven more that night, in seventeen minutes. (The tail fin of his night fighter, with its record of kills, can be seen today at the Imperial War Museum in London.) Schnaufer's radar–radio operator was Fritz Rumpelhardt. It is an amazing record, made possible in part because of the very large number of heavies being sent over Germany almost nightly, providing night fighters with an ample supply of targets, but that fact in no way detracts from the performance. What Schnaufer's record, and that of many other good German night pilots, shows, is that from a meagre beginning, when German pilots in 1940 even doubted whether a bomber could be shot down by a fighter at night, the night-fighter arm of the Luftwaffe had come a long way. (It was not until the night of 20 July 1940 that Werner Streib, in an Me.110, became the first Luftwaffe night-fighter pilot to shoot down an R.A.F. bomber—a Whitley. Two days later Streib scored again.)

Another remarkable record is that of Helmut Lent. He had been a 110 pilot (with five victories in the Norwegian campaign), transferred to night fighters and scored his first victory in December 1941. By the time of his death in a crash in October 1944 he had scored 102 night victories, which gave him a total of 110 victories in all. He was the first German night-fighter pilot to receive the Oak Leaves with Swords and Diamonds to the Knight's Cross of the Iron Cross. And indicative of the importance attached to night fighters in the Third Reich is the fact that two of the nine Luftwaffe pilots to receive the Diamonds to the Knight's Cross were night-fighter pilots, Lent and Schnaufer.

In the early years (1940–1) Luftwaffe night fighters scored greater success in what Colonel Josef Kammhuber termed long-distance intruder operations against the British bombers' home bases than in defensive attacks on the bombers over Germany. Kammhuber, in the post-war years Inspector of the new Luftwaffe, had first projected this two-part night-fighter defense, and in 1940 and up to 1942 twice as many R.A.F. bombers were shot down over their own bases or near them by long-range night intruders (Ju.88s and Do.17s) than over Germany.[1] The long-distance night-fighter Gruppe which did so much damage for a time was based in Holland (between Tilburg and Breda). It was assisted by some remarkable radio intercept service intelligence. Special operators listening in Holland could tell when R.A.F. crews turned on their aircraft radios to check them and so detected that early that a raid was in the making. Frequently it could be discerned how many bombers would be taking off from what bases and because the Germans knew what bomber types were based at various bases the identity of the aircraft was also known. There were three different attack waves: the first hit the bombers just after they had taken off from fields in England, the second interception was over the North Sea as they approached the continent, and the third was an attack as the bombers were on their way home, often over England.

These intruder attacks, quite successful considering the small number of aircraft employed, were suddenly called off by Hitler in 1941. He didn't want German crews captured by the English. Post-war studies of the air war (including an official Air Ministry publication, *The Rise and Fall of the German Air Force*) agree that this was a major

---

[1] Cajus Bekker, *The Luftwaffe War Diaries*, p. 207.

error on the German side. Kammhuber, now a General, persevered and extended and enlarged the belt of night-fighter zones (called *Himmelbett* zones), which had been begun in the summer of 1941. Late that year he began to receive the first German radar (Lichtenstein sets) for his fighters. The great limitation of zones, which vectored the better-equipped fighters, as had been found in the defense of England, was that only one aircraft could be controlled in a zone at a time. But since R.A.F. bombers were still, at this time, flying singly, good defensive results were possible.

When the R.A.F. shocked all Germany with its fire raid on Hamburg in July 1943, the Luftwaffe's night fighters were just beginning to achieve impressive results (though the defense failed at Hamburg). In the Battle of the Ruhr, which began that spring, and with deeper penetrations into Germany, R.A.F. losses were inching upward and on some raids totalled ten per cent of the attacking force shot down or damaged. This was still not costly enough to check the bomber offensive but it was a marked increase over the meagre defense of 1940–1. Hamburg spurred the night-defense effort on, and what were called *Wilde Sau* ("Wild Boar") attacks were authorized—attacks by night fighters flying in areas hitherto barred to them because of German flak. Because of the gravity of the situation, even single-engine fighters were now once again ordered into night interceptions, though now with new devices to enable them to land more easily.

What happened at Hamburg, to defeat German defenses, was that R.A.F. bombers dropped millions of small pieces of silver paper ("Window"), which registered on German radar sets and confused operators. That greatly complicated the process of detecting the bombers and it was some months before new radar sets and counter measures enabled the German defense to cope with the situation. With the introduction of the Lichtenstein SN2 airborne radar sets, however, the Luftwaffe's night-fighter arm resumed its steady rate of progress and by December 1943 had once again become a major threat to the

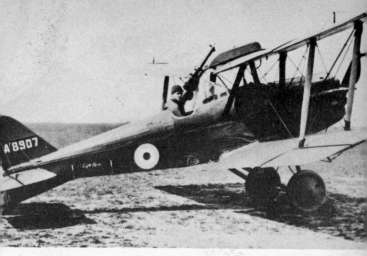

Captain Albert Ball, the first great British fighter pilot, in the cockpit of his S.E.5

The first Fokker, with a 110-horsepower engine, at the Front in 1915

The famous French Nieuport, seen in 1917 in France; note the gun mounted on the upper wing

A British De Havilland, 4, shot down by the Germans in 1918. Carl August von Schoenebeck, who flew with the Richthofen Geschwader, is the figure on the right

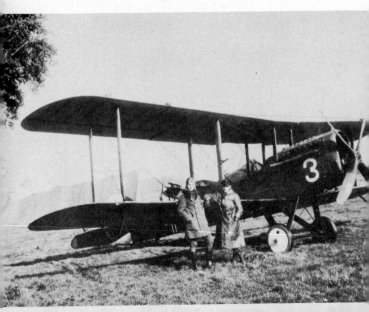

Arthur Gould Lee as Air Vice-Marshal during the Second World War

A squadron of Sopwith Camels in 1918

Manfred von Richthofen (the 'Red Baron'), wounded in 1917

Manfred von Richthofen in his all-red Fokker Dr. 1. Triplane

Captain L. H. Rochford (right) with Lieutenant R. Stone in front of his Sopwith Camel in 1918

Elliott White Springs, fifth-ranking U.S. ace of World War I, stands before Sopwith Camel he nosed up landing. Springs served in 85th Aero Squadron of R.A.F. and in U.S. 148th Aero Squadron in France. Photo taken in 1918

Theo Osterkamp as the commander of the German fighters in the Battle of Britain

Hermann Göring in his Fokker D. VII in the First World War

Hurricane Mark IICs over the Western Desert in 1942

The Spitfire I, the R.A.F. fighter which first successfully opposed the Me.109 in 1940

Air Commodore A. C. Deere (retired) as a fighter pilot in 1940

Wing Commander R. P. Beamont, now a Director of the British Aircraft Corporation, in the late 1960s

Günther Rall, now Inspector of the Luftwaffe, as a Second World War fighter pilot

Georg Peter Eder, famous Luftwaffe fighter pilot, pictured during the war in front of his Me. 109

The Messerschmitt 109, mainstay of the Luftwaffe fighter arm in the Second World War

General John C. Meyer, now
Vice Chief of Staff, United
States Air Force; P.51 fighter
pilot during the Second
World War

The United States P.51 Mustang fighter

The Messerschmitt 262, the first jet fighter, of the type flown by Erich Rudorffer and seen by General Meyer

Major Erich Rudorffer, who in service with the Luftwaffe on all three of Germany's fronts scored 222 victories during the Second World War

The United States P.47 Thunderbolt high-altitude fighter

Erich Hartmann, highest-scoring fighter ace in the history of aviation, meets Ginger Lacey, top-scoring British fighter pilot in the Battle of Britain, for the first time at a publication party for the author's *The Fighter Pilots* in London in 1967

Colonel Frank Gabreski, as the leading United States scorer in Europe in the Second World War with 38 air victories

in the Korean War

The F.86E Sabre Jet, one of the first United States jet fighters, which played a vital role in the Korean War

A Russian-built MiG.15, with North Korean insignia, which was flown to South Korea by a defector during the war

The Russian MiG.21 all-weather fighter of the Soviet Air Force, as used in Vietnam

General Robin Olds, U.S.A.F., high-scoring
fighter pilot in the Second World War and
leading U.S. fighter pilot in Vietnam, flying
the F.4, over twenty years later

The F.4E (Phantom II), used as an air-to-air fighter by the U.S.A.F.
in Vietnam

Top fighter pilots, English and German, meet at a party in 1968 to celebrate the publication in Germany of *Die Jagdflieger:* (left to right) the author, Johannes Steinhof, Wing Commander Stanford Tuck, Adolf Galland and Erich Hartmann

R.A.F.'s night offensive. (This set enabled night-fighter pilots to pick up bombers three miles distant.)

German sources claim major victories for the night fighters the next three months; the record shows that in 1944 the R.A.F. lost 78 bombers on a raid on Leipzig (19–20 February), 72 on a Berlin raid (24–5 March), and 95 plus 71 damaged (twelve of which were scrapped) on a Nürnberg raid (30–1 March). Thus night-fighter defense had come a long way since the feeble efforts in England in November 1940 when the Luftwaffe shattered Coventry. On the Nürnberg raid the British dispatched 795 bombers; those lost or damaged on the night's attack were twenty per cent of the force. Such a loss rate could not, of course, be accepted and Bomber Command was forced to alter its tactics.

Thus the German night-fighter defense which began with a few Me.109s had expanded to six Geschwader, with a defense zone from northern Jutland almost to the Alps and numerous underground defense control centers, by 1944. Fighters had demonstrated that bombers could be turned back at night—radar detection being the key.

On the British side, night-fighter operations had also developed at a steady pace. The R.A.F.'s night fighters had continued to improve their techniques, and were equipped with better aircraft and radar sets. They were flying long-range escort missions with bombers into Germany—to counter German night-fighter defense. And German bombers continued to bomb England at night, though attacking forces were small in number. The R.A.F. pilot who did more to inspire British night fighters than any other and who shot down the second greatest number of enemy aircraft at night in the war was John "Cat Eyes" Cunningham, whom we shall meet in the next chapter.

The famous Hawker Siddeley Aviation works is located near Hatfield, some twenty miles north of London, and there the Executive Director and Chief Test Pilot is the famous night-fighter pilot of the Second World War, John Cunningham. He was so good as a night pilot the press and public nicknamed him "Cat Eyes" (though neither he nor his comrades ever accepted the name). From the Hawker Siddeley main gate I was directed to a red and white checkered building at the side of a hangar. A concrete runway and a grass field stretched into the distance. Cunningham, still youthful more than twenty-five years after he brought down his first German bomber, welcomed me to his third-floor office and we launched into a discussion of the night air war in 1939–45.

Cunningham was a test pilot for De Havilland before the war, and returned to them after it was over. He is still an active test pilot with Hawker Siddeley, who took over De Havilland. Thus he has kept his hand in flying over a span of more than thirty years and also, he emphasized, has faith in fighters as a key weapon in the jet age.

I asked him to tell me how he managed to shoot down his first bomber in 1940 and something of night-fighter tactics at that early period of the war.

"My first kill was a bloody miracle," he said, and slipped easily back into the past:

"It was at Middle Wallop. We arrived there in the summer of 1940, during the Battle of Britain. I was a Flight Commander and we flew Blenheims. Then, in September, we got Beaufighters, with the new radar. We hadn't had much success but the Beaufighters were an improvement over Blenheims and we all hoped to score at any time. The form was to fly practice missions in the afternoons, often to act as a target while others checked the range of their sets and made sure it was giving the correct positions of the target. Rain or bent aerials on the wings, you know, could produce squint, an off reading. We tested bearing and elevation until the pilot satisfied himself the set was working properly. Then one would ask the pilot ahead, if he had a target plane out front, to take evasive action, and we would try to follow. These afternoon flights were after lunch, usually at about two or two thirty in the afternoon. When we landed we'd have some tea and were ready from about four on—ready to go. Of course, before lunch, on a normal day, we went down to one of the hangars and found out if we were on the program for that evening. We had two nights on and two off in those days. Then we'd go down to the dispersal area, the hut, where the flight commander would arrange who would fly the test flights that afternoon. The squadron was two flights, six to eight in a flight, and I was commander of B Flight. For the test flights we took off in pairs, one alongside the other. We wore great long-sleeved jerseys, and fur-lined brown trousers and fur boots for it was cold at night, especially at altitude.

"On 19 November 1940, I remember I had flown about an hour and a half in the afternoon, and then came down and had tea and changed clothes. Early that evening I was back at readiness at the hut. The first patrol aircraft always took off at a definite time, to get out on a line across the track of incoming German bombers. Group Operations rang up shortly after the first two had gone and said they wanted two more aircraft off, and so on. We normally just sat around playing cards or chess, or reading, waiting for the black telephone to ring. Operations for 10 Group was at Colerne, near Bath. They rang straight in and gave the orders. At Sopley near Bournemouth there was an elementary radar control station, with a generator and a caravan tent, where a man turned an early radar detector by hand. The controller there would take over from Middle Wallop—his name was Brown. His call name was 'Starlight.'

"That night I was one of the first three off. When the call came I went out and spoke to the fitter and rigger, oldtimers who had been with the squadron for years, then climbed in through the door in the bottom of the fuselage, almost directly between the undercarriage; I had to put my feet forward over the collapsed back of my seat to get in. The rigger followed me in and strapped on my parachute and then pulled the lever that opened the door for parachuting out, got out through it and closed it with a bang. That told me it was secured. My radar operator on this flight was John Phillipson, very good indeed. His mother was from the Midlands, his father from Ireland. John was young, blond, ruddy-complexioned with a fine face and straight pointed nose. He sat fifteen feet behind, with the ammunition drums, guns, breeches and his radar set. The Beaufighter was armed with four twenty-millimeter cannon, two on each side, under the feet.

"Phillipson got in after me, checking the door outside to see it was properly closed and then checking the racks of ammunition. Most guns were loaded with a small proportion of high explosive incendiaries but I refused the incendiaries; I had some explosive on contact. I made the cockpit check, checked with Phillipson, and then contacted the tower—my call name was 'Fearsome 24'. I made a last check of the fuel, pressing a selector for the reading. Then I primed the Birstol Hercules sleeve-valve radials, which were air-cooled. There was a big exhaust collector ring around the front, two great pipes extending out and down beneath, which made them very quiet. (The Japanese later called the Beaufighter 'Whispering Death.') The props were big three-bladers, the electric starting was good; the pilot just pressed a button after selecting which engine he would start first. I always started the left first and they were quick starters, each of the two producing about 1,500 horsepower. I made sure of the oil pressure, and checked with Phillipson, who reported 'All Set,' then we were off.

"The Hercules engines at full power lifted us quickly off the field. I cut back on the throttle after we were off. Phillipson checked his set. We climbed into the darkness, the earth below largely blacked out and only stars twinkling. After a short time Middle Wallop Control came in on the radio: 'I'm going to hand you over to Starlight.' That was Brown and we were now at about 10,000 feet, and he told us he was putting us on a coded patrol line. He reported: 'There's activity east of you,' and that raised our hopes. There was a good chance we were in the path of bombers about to come our way. We continued on a patrol for a time and then Starlight's voice came in again. He had picked up something, and gave us a heading designed to bring us into contact with the unidentified aircraft he had on his screen. He was watching the bogey's blip as well as ours and we were near enough to intercept—our patrol line location had been good. 'Steer One One Zero,' he said and I banked the Beaufighter onto the new heading. Now it seemed hours as we approached the unseen aircraft in the darkness. He was higher and we were climbing to reach his altitude. It was important not to overtake too quickly, that was one of the most common errors, coming in too fast, going under and ahead, with no way to stop. Brown called again and gave us a course correction and we continued to climb higher. It was a long climb, then Brown said we were getting close, but we weren't close enough to see him. At most, you see an aircraft at about 300 feet on a dark night.

"Phillipson was concentrating with all his power on the black box, waiting for the moment a blip would appear and he could call it out. Ahead I could see searchlights fingering the sky. This might be our quarry. We were getting closer and Brown reported we were nearing radar range. It was almost certainly an enemy bomber. I continued climbing steadily and Phillipson suddenly came in over the intercom: 'We've got a contact.' He gave the range estimate, and added: 'It's still above us.' I pulled the nose up slightly and continued on course, looking ahead into the night to catch sight of a slim dark silhouette which would mean the chase was coming to an end. Phillipson called out, 'Closing slightly but still above.' He was gazing so intently at the cathode ray tubes he didn't realize for a moment that his microphone had frozen up but he soon had it working again.

"It took four or five minutes from the time we picked up the contact until I sighted him. I was staring out front and one cluster of stars seemed to move differently from the rest. I took my eyes off them and looked back and in doing this the faint outline of a wing ahead registered. I made out his exhausts, and he was still above us ahead. I called Phillipson: 'I think I can see some exhausts.' He was desperately clinging to his set, speechless. Remember, none of us night fighters had ever brought one down up to this time, and we had lost several good contacts in recent days and didn't want to lose this one. I increased the throttles with my left hand quickly, keeping my eyes fixed on those exhausts above. I was uncertain as to the type. There were four exhausts—could it be a four-engine plane? I was probably closer than I realized then, I was new, and I was probably only about 200 feet behind him. I called Phillipson again: 'It's still above.' I hung on to the fiery exhaust gases and got below him in the relatively blind area. I slowly climbed from there and as I came up to his level brought the nose up and the guns to bear. It was a two-engine enemy bomber. The moment had arrived and I pressed the firing button. There was a hell of a noise. The shells streaked into him, ten a second, and there was a blinding flash. To my astonishment, I could smell all sorts of fumes.

"I didn't see anything else. It wasn't very satisfying. I wasn't sure what had happened. On later flights I got in closer and saw many blow-ups, one when a whole wing came off, and often collected bits of aircraft and smelled that same filthy smell but I didn't see anything this time. I called Phillipson: 'I've lost it. Can you see it?'

" 'I've got something. It's going away.'

"I called Brown, reported that I had had combat and asked for further instructions. He had no other trade in the area and I was told to return to Middle Wallop and land; Brown gave me a course to steer. I soon reached the field; there were dim lamps on the approach (there was no enemy activity about) and a beacon light down the grass runway. The path was laid out according to the wind. There was always a flashing beacon a few miles from the airport and we knew the signals of the code, which told us which field it was. The beacon would be moved from time to time and the code changed. We approached the field at 100 miles an hour from about 800 feet, made our approach and touched down and slowed in the grass. We still didn't know anything definitely. I parked and the fitter and rigger immediately asked what luck we had had. 'I'm not sure but I think we hit something,' I said. But the Intelligence officer was waiting outside for me, and greeted me with the exciting words: 'We've got one down. I think it's yours! The Observer Corps people heard your cannon fire and discovered the wreckage.'

"It was exciting news. We had been trying so hard for so long. It had been a long wait and a lot of people were on the spot. Then 10 Group Commander-in-Chief called, Air Vice-Marshal Sir Quinton Brand. He was frequently at Middle Wallop in those days. I was to report to him. He wanted to hear all about it, how we had done it. I told him the set had worked well, that Phillipson had operated it efficiently. The news went to Fighter Command and the Air Ministry but the public wasn't told anything about our secret black box. They were told my eyes were so good that I could see in darkness like a cat, and that's how I became known, unfortunately, as Cat Eyes. Soon after that someone shot down another bomber in the Tangmere sector. Toward the end of December or in January a few more fell. We were all learning. My victim had been a Ju.88—the two engines had twin exhausts."

Some time had passed since Cunningham had begun. We adjourned the interview at the hangar to resume at one of Hatfield's more famous pubs (rare sketches adorn the walls) and continued the discussion. I asked about night-fighting tactics.

"You should be within two hundred feet before firing, or closer. The great mistake is to lose speed as you pull up to open fire at the last moment, then you lose distance and can also lose your view. Firing too far away like this gives you away, the tracers are seen and the enemy often gets away. In the Beaufighter the sight was set higher than the guns so sometimes I fired under the target. One of the great errors of night fighters is coming in too fast and not being able to stop before you are sliding out in front of your intended victim. A stable aircraft is also important. The Beaufighter, with a small tail, would dive or climb with a full load of ammunition. It was difficult to trim— and we didn't have much instrument training in those days. It was a trying job to fly it on a poor night with no visual horizon, with only a few instruments. Today's aircraft are far more stable."

Though Cunningham shot down his first victim flying with John Phillipson, he flew more sorties with Jimmie Rawnsley than with any other operator, and Rawnsley after the war joined with Robert Wright to produce one of the best books on night fighting ever published, *Night Fighter*.

Cunningham went on from this first success to shoot down a second victim three weeks afterward and another ten days later. He shot down another in February 1941 and then, between 3 April and 23 May, destroyed twelve more bombers. Targets were never so plentiful after the German attack on Russia (June 1941) but by the second half of 1941 he was a squadron commander wearing both the D.S.O. and D.F.C. He took command of a Mosquito squadron in early 1943 and by January 1944 had been credited with twenty confirmed night victories. None of the twenty were as important as his first, which did so much to encourage scientists striving to give the R.A.F. a lead in the vital field of radar detection, an edge which contributed greatly, in 1943, to turning back the challenge of the German U-boats.

20

AN ME.109 INTERCEPTION

North-east from Wiesbaden on the Rhine fifty miles into Hessen hills lies the town of Nidda—on the Nidda river. On an autumn day, rain pounding, trees turning yellow, I drove from Wiesbaden, crossed the busy Frankfurt–Cologne autobahn, then the Frankfurt–Kassel autobahn, in Nidda, and arrived at midday. I was there to interview one of the great German fighter aces of the Second World War, Kurt Buehligen, third-highest scoring German fighter pilot on the Western Front with 112 victories.[1] He was one of those rare fliers who was in the fighting from the beginning and remained in it throughout the war. He had been a pilot of skill and experience when the war began in 1939.

Born in Grandchütz, Thüringen, in 1917, he attended flying school at fifteen in Lutzen, where he learned to fly gliders. He worked at that school four years, logging many hours sail flying. He volunteered for a technical flying school in the new Luftwaffe, training at various flying schools in the late thirties and graduated early in 1940. In July of that year, just before the Battle of Britain, he was posted to a fighter unit soon to be well known to all British and American fliers who fought against Germany from English bases, Jagdgeschwader 2 (Richthofen). Buehligen began as a non-commissioned officer; by the end of the war he had become the Geschwader's Commodore, its last.

---

[1] Buehligen's 112 total was surpassed by two other fighter pilots who flew against the West. Hans-Joachim Marseille's 158 victories included 151 in Africa. Heinz Bär's 220 victories included 96 in the East and 45 in Africa. Marseille died in the war, Bär in 1957.

I found the famous pilot at his place of business, a serious, friendly man with a forceful personality. His hand shook slightly at times when he talked—he was only fifty—and his hair is graying but he still laughs readily and clearly remembers the war years. I asked for his evaluation of the fighters he flew in the war, and those he flew against, because having served throughout the war he is uniquely qualified to discuss practically all of them; I also asked about flying tactics which best suited various fighters.

"I flew the Me.109 and then the F.W.190 and the 109 again later in the war. The 190 was better at low altitude. I liked the 190. But late in the war I had a special 109; it was very light and wonderful to fly.

"We could out-turn the P.51 and the other American fighters in either one. The turn rate of the 109 and 190 was about the same. The Spitfire was the best in turns, of course. I didn't turn with Spits. The P.51 was faster than us but our munitions and cannon were better. The P.47 was very heavy, too heavy for some maneuvers. We would see it coming from behind, and pull up fast and the P.47 couldn't follow and we came around and got on its tail in this way.

"As for American heavy bombers, the B.17s were harder to shoot down. The B.24 and the P.38 fighter were easy to burn. Once in Africa we were six and met eight P.38s and shot down seven. One sees a great distance in Africa and our observers and flak people called in sightings and we could get altitude first and they were low and slow.

"Combat formation? We flew four-abreast, not in the finger four. The four-abreast pattern was better than the finger four. I never lost a wingman during the war and always used it. Behind the Schwarm would fly the Staffel, higher, and these pilots weaved and searched the sky from behind and above." To be certain I understood his description of the formation, Buehligen took a piece of writing paper from the top of his desk and drew in the position of the four aircraft in the Stab Schwarm in the lead and the three fours of the Staffel which followed behind, each grouping of four in abreast formation. I asked how he had achieved such a remarkable record and he finally admitted that he had enjoyed exceptional eyesight as a pilot. Perhaps that is why he was never shot down by another aircraft, though he experienced several forced landings because of flak damage. I asked the types of aircraft he had fought against and he recalled having shot down Hurricanes and Spits in 1940 and 1941, P.38s and P.40s in Africa, B.25s, B.26s, B.24s and B.17s. He volunteered the opinion that the fighter war against the western democracies, on the Western Front in Europe and in Africa, was more difficult than the war in the East against Russia.

"All the pilots who came to me from the Eastern Front fell on the Western Front," he said. Returning to tactics, he stressed the importance of gunnery and explained the method he used to shoot down a very fast fighter like a Spitfire.

"The best shooting distance was from 300 feet to 150 or less. We often used the head-on pass, especially against bombers, and I always went under on the head-on pass. We had to shoot under a fast aircraft like the Spitfire— which would fly into the shells. Our sights were such that the ring filled when the Spit was 1,100 feet away. That was too far. From a good behind position the wing stuck out far on both sides of the sight ring when it was time to shoot." (British fighter pilots had found the same to be true; see Chapter Sixteen.)

One of the secrets of some German fighter pilots was to fly with the 109 trimmed slightly to climb, Buehligen revealed. The nose was held down by constant forward pressure on the stick, and then when the pilot wanted to pull up quickly, he pulled back and the nose came up more quickly and the aircraft didn't mush.

Ironically, though Buehligen didn't fly against the Russians during the war he was imprisoned by them afterwards. He was captured and freed by the Americans when they overran his unit on the Cheimsee in Bavaria in 1945; when he went home to Tollwitz the Russians made him a prisoner of war and sent him to Russia, where he was kept for five years. After his release, he has made his home in the small town of Nidda, in which he had been stationed in 1944. The Stab and II Gruppe of Jagdgeschwader 2, of which he was the Kommandeur, was stationed at Nidda that year. Three months before the end he married Elle Schirmer and they are now back where he had lived as a wartime pilot many years ago, with a son of eleven and a daughter of twenty-four.

I asked Buehligen to describe a combat action against Allied fighters which stood out in his mind, recalling the tactics used, and whatever details he could remember. He clearly remembered a most successful mission over France in 1941. He believes it was flown on 13 June 1941, after the Luftwaffe's fighter strength in France had been greatly reduced in preparation for the assault on Russia, to begin a week later, when German fighter pilots in the West were often flying five times daily to give an impression of strength.

"At the time I was an Oberfeldwebel with II Gruppe, flying in the Gruppe Stab, as wingman for the Kommandeur, Heini Greisert. I had begun as a Korporal with Kommandeur Schellman; at that time Helmut Wick was flying with us. We had been at Beaumont le Roger then, not far from Evreux, but when Kommandeur Greisert moved to Abbeville I went with him as his wingman. We lived in an old three-story house about three miles from the airfield. We were up an hour before sunrise and after breakfast with the Kommandeur drove in his PKV to the base. The field was grass, with the various Staffels (squadrons) located around the edges. There were loudspeakers in and around the buildings where the pilots waited and we would get orders over them or by the firing of a green rocket, which meant a command to take off.

"That day we had flown in the morning. It was just after lunch when we were told the English were assembling south of London and along the south coast—in huge numbers! We were to take off in five minutes. We had to take off at exactly the right time, so we would have enough fuel for combat after interception. If the timing was off, we were often called back to land. The Stab, in Me.109Fs, was off first; we took off together. The Staffel took off next and flew behind, higher. As I recall, it was about two in the afternoon.

"We headed in the direction of the incoming raid, toward Boulogne, and everyone watched the sky ahead. We were climbing fast. It had only been a few minutes when a voice broke the silence: *'Achtung! Achtung! Rechts voraus! Möbelwagen! Viele Indianer!'* [German pilots called bombers furniture trucks and fighters Indians, among other things.] The English bomber stream was about 15,000 feet high, and there were about 100 Spits guarding the bombers—which were Blenheims. We were approaching the front of the enemy formation above all of them, still gaining altitude. When we were about a thousand yards distant, still to the left of the approach column—they were about to cross inland almost directly over Boulogne—we winged over into a dive and started down—we would come up very fast from the dive. At this time our 109s were equipped with two 7.9 machine-guns and one cannon. Later we had two cannons. We were higher than both bombers and escorting Spits and dived on the Spits. They would have dived on us had we gone for the bombers.

"I came down and then up fast with the Kommandeur and we each selected a Spit. I watched my sight ring fill with the wing-span and came on still closer. I aimed below, the Spitfire was fast, and when I was very close opened fire. The Kommandeur was doing the same. A big dogfight now developed but I managed to stay behind this one and my shells poured into him. Pieces began to fly backward, then there was black smoke. He started down. There was no chute. The Kommandeur, I think, got a Spitfire also, but we had by then become separated. I saw my victim go down and then looked around. I saw the Kommandeur trying a pass on another Spitfire. He was closing too fast and instead of going under the Spit he pulled up and passed over his tail and continued up to the left, as if to come around for another pass. But the Spitfire pilot turned left, too, to come up and around behind him. I was in position to curve in from behind and follow the Spit and I turned as sharply as I could on his tail. He was intent on shooting down the Kommandeur. I managed to gain and hung on in the turn. When very close I opened fire again and almost immediately saw hits. White smoke began to trail backward and I kept firing. Then half his tail came off. It had been fast and again there was no parachute. Greisert had seen what happened and yelled to me over the microphone: *'Prima! Gratulieren!'*

"The planes had scattered and we pulled up together to gain altitude. We turned to a north-west heading and had flown only a short distance when the radio burst out again, *'Achtung! Hurris!'* I looked and there they were— two Hurricanes almost straight ahead of us. The Kommandeur headed for them and when we were just high enough, and near enough, behind, we dived. Our pass took us down below them and we came up from behind—in the blind spot. I was to the left of Greisert and we were now coming up on them for the firing pass—and his guns jammed. My guns still worked and I opened on the Hurricane to the left when I was almost on him and hit him at once. I remember seeing the same black smoke from this one, too, as had come from the Spitfire. I kept firing until all my ammunition was gone. The Hurricane was badly hit and plunged straight down as I pulled up after the pass.

"It had been an exceptional mission for me—three fighter kills! I was now out of fuel and out of ammunition and it was time to head back to Abbeville. The flight had lasted about an hour and we landed at about three that afternoon. The Kommandeur had another *'Prima!'* for me when we landed. I wasn't sure I would be credited with three victories at the time but all three of the victims were found and so that day is one which stands out clearly in my memory. I got credit for three kills, two of them Spitfires."

Buehligen's tactics, as he describes them, are interesting in several respects. He turned briefly with a Spitfire in his second victory, though he acknowledges that the Spit could out-turn him; it was fortunate for him his shooting was accurate. Also interesting in this engagement is the use of the dive from superior height and then the pass from below, behind the intended victim. In this the 109s had speed, were shooting in a blind spot and could get away (with the speed) climbing up again or diving if they missed. These tactics were used almost throughout the war, the German pilot seeking to use his higher ceiling for diving altitude, his resulting speed from the dive, greater initial diving velocity and better climbing rate, when he had it, to go on by or prepare for another pass if he missed. (In late 1944 and 1945 Luftwaffe pilots in Me.262 jets would use the same tactics. The American fighter pilot in the Pacific, in the first part of the war when U.S. fighters were outclassed in many ways by the Zero, employed the same tactics.)

Buehligen remembered another day, in 1944, during the Battle of Germany, when he shot down two B.17 Flying Fortresses and a B.25 Liberator: three heavy bombers. He brought down thirty American airmen on that day.

He flew, in all, 700 missions during the war and his 112 victories included 24 four-engined bombers. He is proud that he lost only two pilots in his Staffel in operations in Africa. He was transferred to that theater in November 1942 (II Gruppe of J.G. 2 served in Africa), and between then and March 1943, when he escaped capture in Africa by flying out, scored forty victories. It was in Africa that he flew F.W.190s.

I asked Buehligen, as one of the three highest scorers against the West, with almost three times the number of confirmed victories of any Allied fighter pilot flying against Germany, if he had any explanation of the wide difference in scores—which in the immediate post-war years led some to claim German confirmations were exaggerated.

"The difference in scores was that the R.A.F. and Americans took their pilots out of combat, rotated them, and we stayed in the fighting throughout the war", he answered. He also noted that German pilots, especially in the later years of the war, had many more targets to shoot at. But, of course, even when one accepts this, one still is left with impressive records of many German fighter pilots. One point of interest which Luftwaffe historian Hans

Ring has noted is that the very able and successful fighter pilots tended to survive the war. When an unusually able pilot had survived a break-in period of learning and became what the Germans called an *Experte,* he often survived a very long period of operations.

It was the youngster with inadequate training who so often failed to get through the baptismal of fire. This was very noticeable in the Luftwaffe in the last year or two of the war, when flying schools were unable to give trainees enough flying time (partly because of the shortage of fuel). Many of these new pilots fell on an early mission. Buehligen was a seasoned pilot when the war began and his experience, flying and shooting ability served him so well he won the Knight's Cross to the Iron Cross in 1941, the Oak Leaves in 1944 and the Swords in August of that same year. He is still sure of his tactics in the Second World War.

21

FRANCE: MAY 1940; AFRICA

One fast-moving day in the interviewing of pilots for this book began with a pre-dawn flight from Hamburg to London. A train to Bentley Priory in Middlesex enabled me to keep an appointment with the Air Officer Commanding-in-Chief of Fighter Command, Sir Frederick Rosier, K.C.B., C.B.E., D.S.O., the last Commander-in-Chief of Fighter Command, which had been arranged a month earlier.

I reached the entrance to Bentley Priory, Stanmore, about two in the afternoon; inside the two-hundred-year-old building in the reception room were two large glass cases filled with model aircraft, lighted. On the walls there was a painting of "Stuffy" Dowding at his desk in 1940 and one could read the names of all Fighter Command commanders-in-chief—thirteen. There was a plaque containing the list of fighter squadrons which served under Fighter Command in the Second World War—Czech, Dutch, Belgian, Norwegian, Polish, French and American squadrons among them.

Squadron Leader John Pugh briefed me on the things of special significance, reminding me that Queen Adelaide once slept in one of the rooms. When Pugh (or perhaps Flight Lieutenant John Graham) ushered me into Sir Frederick's office, the atmosphere was even more heavy with the ring of nostalgia and history. The view from the desk Dowding used in the Battle of Britain, over the beautiful downs, the painting of bombers and fighters in combat on the wall, the trophy case, a famous, framed letter Dowding sent the Air Ministry in 1940, added to the impact, especially if one remembers those days in 1940, or was a fighter pilot. Sir Frederick quickly exhibited a re-markable memory of events which had taken place thirty years ago. Rosier was not a great fighter ace and was quick to tell me that, but he was a great fighter leader, both in Europe and Africa, and the number of unusual adventures he survived is truly remarkable.

Concerning aerial combat and the talents of the out-standing pilots, his candid analysis was: "Very few pilots in combat have the ability to scan the sky and to take it all in." Comparing the Second World War fighters he be-lieves the Spitfire was the best at the beginning of the war. "It had the speed, a fine rate of climb, and good maneuver-ability. However, throughout 1940 both in France and dur-ing the Battle of Britain we almost had no alternative but to remain on the defensive—we had to react to the en-emy's initiative. Thank goodness we had the performance of the Spitfire. At the same time it would be wrong to give the impression that the Hurricane was much inferior. It was a rugged aircraft, extremely maneuverable and it formed the backbone of our fighter forces. Thank good-ness we had both the Spitfire and the Hurricane."

Rosier's experiences in the first days of the German at-tack in the West in 1940 are interesting in that they illus-trate clearly the disproportionate advantage of concentra-tion of superior numbers in fighter combat. They also demonstrate (again) how German fighter pilots effectively used superior altitude and a diving pass out of the sun to surprise adversaries, as they had done in the First World War. The conditions he encountered and describe in France are an indication of the confusion and fear which did so much to weaken French resistance. Having to oper-ate under such conditions on the ground, faced with an enemy outnumbering them in the air, usually sighted at a higher altitude, it is remarkable that quite a number of the pilots in his group survived the grim weeks in May, begin-ning with the attack on the 10th. (The R.A.F. lost ap-proximately 300 fighters in the French collapse.)

"In the evening of 16 May my flight of six Hurricanes, together with a flight from No. 56 Squadron, flew to Vitry en Artois, near Douai in northeast France. As we were taxiing in a chap dashed up and asked if we had any fuel left as forty plus enemy planes were approaching. After remaining at stand-by for some time, during which no enemy aircraft materialized, I sent one of my pilots to find out what was happening. Apart from us, he found the airfield deserted. Such was the confusion and panic that not only had the chap who had told me about the enemy aircraft forgotten to release us from stand-by but it required a show of force, in the way of brandishing pistols, before we found billets for the night.

"We were a mixed bag of 56 and 229 Squadrons, flying Hurricanes. We were up at three in the morning to go on our first patrol. It was to be our first combat. I led the patrol that morning, 17 May. We were only six Hurris. Taking off in the near-darkness we climbed immediately and continued climbing until we had reached good height. Our orders were to patrol between Brussels and Antwerp and we wanted to begin as high as possible. We reached the area at 25,000 feet and began our patrol. On the very first leg, down they came from above, a whole mass of 109s, I would say forty or fifty, and we were suddenly in a series of dogfights, our first. I had shots at several of them and one of the 109 pilots scored hits which smashed my instrument panel. I managed to land safely at Lille, part of the way back—we had lost a couple—and found that the French weren't flying! Yet we did six sorties this day. We were, of course, very tired.

"But next day we were ordered to escort some Fairey Battles which were to bomb a strategic bridge over which the Germans were pouring. It was in the afternoon of the 18th and I was to lead the escort. Just as we were taking off the 109s dived on us and, of course, we were at a disadvantage. The sky was immediately full of dogfights. I got on the tail of one but just then I was hit by another. My Hurri caught fire. I found I couldn't open the cockpit. I couldn't get out!

"Burning fuel began to come into the cockpit and my flying-suit started to burn but I still could not open the hood. Then the aircraft must have blown up for the next thing I remember was falling through the air. After pulling the parachute release, I saw that my trousers were on fire. I attempted to extinguish the flames with my hands and can still remember vividly how surprised I was when I saw some of my skin coming away. The next thing I remember was being in an Army hospital. Incidentally, an old friend of mine, Squadron Leader Teddy Donaldson, now Air Correspondent of the *Daily Telegraph,* stopped some French soldiers shooting at me as I was coming down in my parachute. Obviously they thought I was a German.

"In France it was a shambles. We had only Hurricanes and there were so many 109s, numbers were against us."

This hopeless, against-odds battle in France was a hard beginning, but Rosier's fighting did not end with the burns received on 18 May. After spending that summer in a hospital he was pronounced fit in time to participate in the latter part of the Battle of Britain, this time as a Squadron Leader commanding 229 Hurricane Squadron.

In May 1941 he took his squadron to the Middle East, flying off an aircraft carrier in the Mediterranean and then on to the Western Desert via Malta.

At that time Tobruk was besieged by German and Italian forces and was kept supplied by small ships which docked in darkness and got away before dawn. Their protection from air attack, particularly when in the proximity of the German airfields, was of high priority. During one of these missions, when attacking Ju.87 (Stukas) at a very low level, a bomb burst so close to Rosier's fighter that it flipped him over on his back and tore off the outer covering of the right wing and tail. But he somehow managed to right the aircraft and land it safely.

Although Rosier rated the Spitfire the best English figher he had praise for the Hurricane in Africa. In particular, the long-range version of the Hurricane was specially well suited for certain operations. He had great praise for the spirit of the Allied and German pilots. Individually, some of the Italians were first class but in general they seemed to lack thrust and doggedness. To illustrate this lack of "press-on" spirit on the part of some Italian air force units he recalled a trick he pulled off success-

fully in the spring of 1942. At that time he was based at
El Adem, just south of Tobruk and had a small forward
radar unit at El Gazala, close to the German lines.

"Throughout that period we had a very good tactical
intercept unit attached to my headquarters. They constantly monitored what was happening on the other side
and were able to provide me with very good Intelligence
as to what the enemy air forces were up to. The Germans
also had an intercept unit which was able to monitor our
own wireless traffic. One morning when all our fighters at
Gambut were unable to operate because heavy rains had
turned their airstrips into seas of mud, I was told there
was a strong possibility of an enemy Stuka raid against
Tobruk. I decided to try to hoodwink the enemy. I told
my chap at the radar station at Gazala that I was going to
pass radio orders to an imaginary airborne unit and that
he was to briefly acknowledge the orders, just as an aircraft commander would do. Sure enough it was not long
before our radar picked up some plots coming in. They
were Stukas from an Italian unit escorted by both German
and Italian fighters. I scrambled my imaginary fighters
and started vectoring them towards the raid. It was not
long before I heard from my own intercept unit that the
commander of the enemy raid had been told he could expect to be intercepted by British fighters. I continued to
give directions to my mythical fighters, eventually saying
that they could expect to see the enemy within the next
minute or so. As the incoming raid got closer I thought
that my trick had not worked, but all at once there was a
shout of joy from our intercept people: the enemy raiders
had jettisoned their bombs and were returning. To put it
mildly there was a certain amount of altercation between
the escorting fighters and the bomber leader. Whilst this
was amusing the great thing was that the trick had
worked, and an unopposed bomber force had not dropped
its bombs on Tobruk. But I doubt whether it could have
worked twice."

Rosier smiled as he recalled the episode, one of the
war's happier ones; he still remembered names and dates
and had taken a pen and drawn a map of the towns and

bases mentioned in our discussion. Young in appearance, as are so many fighter pilots, even some from the First World War, he has an open mind about air combat of the future, though convinced that manned aircraft will play a major role in any future conflict.

He was, of course, sentimental about the end of Fighter Command, which in the spring following this visit was to be combined (with Bomber Command) into Strike Command. Looking out over the beautiful downs, and appreciating the history in this building, from which the Battle of Britain had been directed, it seemed a shame.

22

RUSSIA: RALL'S 275 KILLS

One of the most accomplished German fighter pilots in the Second World War was Günther Rall, now Inspector General of the German Air Force. I had discussed Rall's almost incredible record of 275 victories with other German pilots and with German historian Hans Ring in Munich in the early sixties during preparation of *The Fighter Pilots*. In that book I devoted a paragraph or two to him in a chapter concerning the top Luftwaffe fighter pilots. More recently I wrote to him from Switzerland asking for an interview. Some days later I received a card from his wife, Dr. Hertha Rall, in Salam in Baden, and we arranged an appointment.

And so one October morning I approached a long, pale-green stucco building on Manfred-von-Richthofen-Strasse in Munster. There were rose gardens and a green weeping willow to the right of a stone-columned entrance and just inside stood the flags of all NATO nations, the Stars and Stripes on the far right. There were models of aircraft in glass cases—as one sees at Fighter Command. Other than the fact that German was spoken, and the uniforms a bit different, the atmosphere was about the same as at an American or British headquarters.

General Rall's office was on the second floor and after his orderly brought me a cup of tea he emerged from his office and took me inside. Blue-eyed, handsome, spirited, speaking excellent English, he said: "We now speak only English in the airfield towers. Even when I fly to France I request an English-speaking controller—they have to have one. All our Air Force people learn English. Some of them don't even know the German word for some of the English expressions."

I asked what was included in the Third Air Division, which he commanded at that time. "We have all types of aircraft, fighter-bomber wings, a reconnaissance wing, a Pershing missile wing, and so on. I was the project officer for the F.104, did all the testing at the factory—Edwards Air Force Base. The Air Force is now happy with it. It was the first highly complicated weapons system the new Air Force acquired. Now it's under control. We were in a production pool with Holland, Italy and other countries, and couldn't make decisions alone." (Rall probably mentioned the 104 because many have crashed on training flights in Germany, giving the public the impression they're unsafe. A joke then making the rounds in Germany was an imaginary conversation between two West Germans. One asked how he might obtain an F.104. "Buy some land and get a chair and go out and sit on it. In time you'll have one.")

"What many people don't know," Rall said, "is that for the past year the German Air Force was tops in the accident rate in NATO. So our accident rate is not as bad as some think."

Rall began military service as a cadet in 1936 and attended the Army War College, officers' school and then in 1938 transferred to the Luftwaffe. He finished at the famous fighter pilots' school at Werneuchen, northeast of Berlin, and was posted to Jagdgeschwader 52 just before Hitler launched the Second World War. His flying career began in the West, in the German attack on France and the Low Countries, and later he flew in the East against the Russians. So he had been in the fighter war from the beginning and had fought on the two main fronts, and was well qualified to discuss aircraft and tactics.

"In the Battle of Britain we in 52 were very inexperienced and in two months our strength went from thirty-six pilots to four. We really wasted our fighters. We didn't have enough to begin with and we used them the wrong way. I mean in using them for direct, close escort we lost the advantages we had. We were tied to the bombers, flying slowly—sometimes with flaps down—over England.

"My first kill was a P.36 Curtiss over France. I was at Calais for the attack on Britain. The British were sporting. They would accept a fight under almost all conditions. We were at a disadvantage in being tied to the bombers and couldn't then use our altitude advantage, nor could we properly utilize our advantage in a dive. Of course, the Spitfire was very good and had a marvelous rate of turn, and when we were tied to the bombers and had to dogfight them that rate of turn was very important. The Hurricane also had a fine turn rate.

"Tactics were different in Russia. The Russian pilots liked to fly in large masses. And at the beginning of that war we had experience, and it was easy. Later it became much more difficult. They didn't have the individual initiative of pilots we fought on the Western Front. But the Red Banner Guard regiments were very good. Their fighters were painted red up to the cockpit and they liked dogfighting. Our 109s were much better at high altitude, especially in the first part of the war. We could shoot down fifty planes in a day and the next day the same number would come again."

Was the air fighting in the West more difficult than that in the East? ˙

"I really can't say it was. I can't say the East was easier because, psychologically, flying over Russia was pretty bad. It was a heavy mental burden. If you flew against the West and were shot down and captured, you would spend the rest of the war in Canada. You could bail out and live a good life afterward. But the Russians killed many of our pilots. Our people bellied in or bailed out when badly hit, and we watched. Many never came back. It wasn't an easy war on either front. I was shot down eight times, bellied in several times in addition to that, was wounded three times. Basically, I flew almost the entire war in the East, between Orel and the Caucasus—in this area the Russians kept two-thirds of their aircraft. Soon after the beginning of the war at least fifty per cent of the Russian aircraft were American or British planes—P.40s, P.39s, Mitchells, Bostons. I shot down my first Spitfire in Russia. It was at Krymskai and when I reported having shot down a Spitfire there was a lot of static about it but next day there they were—we saw many of them.

"We could have beaten the Russians if so much Anglo-American equipment hadn't been given them—planes, tanks, lorries and so on. Their numbers constantly increased with the years. We flew three and four times a day, sometimes more often, and some days a pilot would shoot down four or five, perhaps including a long-nosed Yak or a Lagg with that big air-cooled engine. They were good aircraft. We were opposed by a tremendous number of fighters as the war progressed.

"Our farthest penetration in Russia was down to the Caucasus Mountains. The Stalingrad battle moved us back and we were used for ground attacks. There were heavy tank battles. We lost many aircraft, a large number on the ground. At that time we stayed in action continuously. Finally we had only a few planes left. In early 1943 we were re-equipped and came back to Kerch. From Kerch we flew in some really big battles in 1943."

I asked Rall to describe combat on the Eastern Front, and the tactics he used against Russian aircraft.

"We switched to Me.109Es before the Russian war. In June 1941 I was transferred to Constanza, on the Black Sea. The Rumanians had refineries there and the Russians were expected to attack them. I landed—I think it was about 25 June—late in the evening. It was a grass field in flat country and we lived in tents. There was only my Staffel, the 8th of III Gruppe, J.G.52. Our twelve 109s were each armed with a cannon and two machine-guns. I took a car and went to Constanza, and rode on the sandy beach to a flak regiment to find out what they knew. We felt certain the Russians were coming next day and very early in the morning I put all pilots in their aircraft and sent two out over the Black Sea. It wasn't long before the two on patrol called: *'Sie kommen!'*

"We scrambled as fast as we could. The Russian bombers were at 15,000 feet, two-engine DB-3s, and we flew northeast to intercept them. Only six or seven of us took off, for we were without spare parts—later they came by Ju.52. The Russians were about twenty miles away when we took off and, climbing fast, it wasn't long before we saw them straight ahead. They had come from the Crimea, I think, and the two patrol 109s had already attacked and shot down some of them. When they saw us coming out to meet them—we were still below them climbing—they turned back east, some dropping their bombs. They were silver-colored or white, and now the chase was on. We attacked from below and behind and shot many of them down. I aimed at the right engine of one and set him afire. He went into a spin. We continued our attacks until we were about out of fuel, and had to turn back toward the base. Since they had no fighter escort it was simple. You can see how easy it was then. It was our first attack after we had been rushed down to Rumania and was quite successful. We all returned safely—one at a time—though some of our aircraft had been hit. The mission had begun at six in the morning. I had been up before dawn. In attacking them we had come very fast from underneath and behind. In this way we achieved excellent results. When I returned to the base the sun was just lighting up the two metal hangars at the field.

"I went to Constanza and phoned Gruppe headquarters. Next day another Staffel came down. A week later we went back to Mizil in Rumania, then were sent to Russia, our first base being near Bjelaia Cerkow I think, and from there we took part in the battles around Kiev."

Rall's description of the early fighting in Russia reaffirms that bombers without escorts were cold meat for fighters—in the East as well as the West. Allied fighter pilots in the West, of course, didn't have things quite as easy, for German bombers—at least in the opening weeks and months—often hit or shot down fighters closing from the rear and were probably faster. Rall's Staffel attacked from below the Russian bombers, where it was more difficult for the Russian gunners to hit them. Rall now turned to perhaps the most memorable encounter of the war:

"The mission on 28 November 1941 resulted in a big dogfight between Rostov and Taganrog. I survived the air fight but shortly afterward flak hit my engine and I began to lose power. I managed to get back to German lines but had to crash-land and it was rough country for a forced landing. I tried a belly-landing but crashed into a canyon and broke my back—in three places. It left me paralyzed. I was taken to a hospital, but being badly hurt was sent back to Vienna, to the more elaborate hospital there. They put me in a cast to stretch me and a woman doctor took an interest in me. She thought I could recover, cut off my cast and began to work regularly with me. She tried many things and encouraged me—and finally I began to move again after four months. During this period of convalescence my father died—it was January 1942. I was called to the telephone and couldn't move. She took the call and talked to my mother and told me about it and that's how we began talking and how I got to know Hertha, who's been my wife for over twenty-five years. We were married later that year, in 1942. She got me flying again, playing tennis, skiing and so on—but I still get cramps. We have two daughters and lost two in the war. One we lost when Hertha was aboard a train that was attacked from the air while leaving Venice—she was pregnant. The other was born too early right after the war. But the two who lived are now seventeen and twelve.

"When I was shot down I had thirty-six victories. I returned to flying in August 1942 and was quite eager. I had led my wing when shot down and felt I had lost much time. By 1 November that year I had my 100th victory and received the Knight's Cross with Oak Leaves. I got my 200th victory in August 1943 and shot down forty aircraft in October of that year, reaching my 250th victory in November." (In recognition Rall became the thirty-fourth German flier awarded the Knight's Cross to the Iron Cross with Oak Leaves and Swords.)

Rall believes fighters will be an important part of any conflict involving NATO. He therefore seeks for Germany combat fighters with superior performance—manned by well-trained pilots. If today's German fighter pilots become as formidable in the air as he was over twenty-five years ago, the German Air Force of which he is the ranking officer will be in good hands.

Part Four

THE SECOND WORLD WAR: SECOND PHASE

23

1943: WIDENING AIR WAR

From 1939 until early or middle 1943, generally speaking, the Luftwaffe enjoyed a technological advantage over its opponents in the fighter war. The F.W.190 appeared in 1941 and maintained the edge provided earlier by the Me.109. While the Spitfire was a match for the 109 in 1940, the majority of British fighters in the Battle of Britain had been Hurricanes, and when the F.W.190s arrived in 1941 they had a performance edge over the Spitfires then operating which lasted approximately two years. But then the tide began to turn against the Luftwaffe. In 1942, the United States' first full year of participation, American factories were getting into production to provide a growing advantage in numbers, to be felt in the Pacific in 1943 and in Europe by late 1943 and 1944. In 1943 itself a new Spitfire began to appear—the Spitfire IX—which could equal or outperform the F.W.190. In late 1943 and especially in 1944 the P.51 Mustang appeared over Germany. It more than any other fighter signalled the defeat of the Luftwaffe—because its range enabled American pilots to search out German fighters deep inside Germany, at their bases; it forced them into fighter-ver-sus-fighter combat, and the Mustang was faster than all but a few of the 109s and F.W.190s. The British were now turning out the Tempest and the remarkable Mosquito, and these and other new, fast aircraft were too much for the Luftwaffe—even though Hitler finally awoke to the need for more fighters and German factories were, in 1944, turning out record numbers of them. (The Germans "souped up" the engines of some of their fighters to deal with the Mosquito, but the Mosquito was too fast for even these special units.) The Americans had first sent to Africa and Europe the P.38, the P.39, and the P.40, but they were no match for the best German fighters. Now came the P.47, a huge, formidable fighter, though it lacked the range of the P.51. It, with the P.51, was one of the two standard U.S. Army fighters in the last years of the war.

From 1943 onward the air war in Europe turned into the Battle of Germany. The R.A.F. had won the 1940 Battle of Britain and the Luftwaffe had won the 1941–2 fighter war (both on the defensive). Faced with a strengthening Russia in the East, a major front in the South, and the Americans and English in the West, the Luftwaffe by 1943 was up against tremendous odds.

In the Pacific the tide turned at about the same time, perhaps earlier. Whereas the Mitsubishi Zero-Sen had reigned supreme in December 1941 and in much of 1942, by 1943 new U.S. fighter types were superior and the number of U.S. Army, Navy and Marine fighter squadrons began to multiply at a rapid pace. The various Zero types, however, remained unequalled in maneuverability.

Even British pilots flying Spitfires in the Far East found themselves out-turned by the Japanese fighters. But most Japanese fighters lacked self-sealing fuel tanks, which made them highly vulnerable, and the new U.S. Corsairs, Hellcats, Thunderbolts and Mustangs, arriving in 1943 and 1944 in an increasing stream, were faster than most of the enemy's fighters and had greater firepower. They were also capable of taking greater punishment. As the Allied superiority in numbers increased, Japanese pilots were often tempted to adopt defensive tactics. The great U.S. Navy ace of the war, David McCampbell, took advantage of this defensive mood when Japanese fighters resorted to a First World War Lufbery maneuver in the Battle of Leyte Gulf in 1944. Coolly standing aside, waiting until one broke out of the circle, McCampbell shot down nine and possibly destroyed two more in one mission—an unprecedented achievement, and one never equalled by any other fighter pilot in the Pacific. He, his wingman Roy Rushing, and five other Hellcats (F.6F) pilots took off from the aircraft carrier *Essex* on 24 October and encountered an incoming Japanese strike force of sixty planes—forty fighters (Zekes, Oscars and Tonys) above twenty bombers (Bettys and Vals).

The five intercepted the bombers and McCampbell and Rushing attacked the fighters, though confronting them initially from a lower altitude. They were able to gain a height advantage—the Jap pilots didn't see them—and then dived on the forty enemy fighters from behind, approaching the three V-formations from astern at their altitude. They began to pick them off one by one.

The Japanese pilots then went into a Lufbery, and, though in Africa Hans-Joachim Marseille had developed a technique for diving in and out of that defensive formation scoring quick kills, the F.6F was a bigger target and after two head-on passes at the Jap circle, in which he sustained hits, McCampbell pulled up above the enemy gaggle and waited. (He was near the *Essex,* which the Japs had just missed finding, and they were far from their bases in Luzon.) His strategy worked. After a short time the Japanese broke the defensive circle and headed back west for Luzon.

In the ensuing chase McCampbell and Rushing shot down fifteen, using altitude for speed in passes from behind, pulling up after firing, translating speed back into altitude.

Speaking of this, his greatest day in combat, McCampbell summarizes his tactics:

"It must be remembered that this opportunity of a lifetime came to me after I had had five months of rather active combat, involving actual enemy combat on sixty-one missions. During this period I had learned much through bitter experience, as to what my capabilities and limitations were. Also, I had gained that confidence which is so necessary to overcome any sense of timidity or uncertainty which might cause one to tense up in a situation like this.

"The big decision came when I recognized the defensive mental attitude personified by the Lufbery circle and disengaged from further attacks at that time. Otherwise, Roy and I would simply have expended all our ammo, making difficult overhead runs, with probably only limited results. With only slight modifications the above-rear type pass was the same tactic I had used training my pilots to defend themselves by using the Thatch weave, so in vogue in the training commands in 1943.

"I had long been of the belief that aggressiveness was fundamental to success in air-to-air combat and if you ever caught a fighter pilot in a defensive mood you had him licked before you started shooting. I must admit that, on occasion, it would have been foolhardy to stand on principle; such occasions occurred to me but in the end I broke even. Of the four head-on-approach experiences I had, I pulled out first twice and I made the other guy break first twice. I got three of them but the other damn near got me, with twenty-one holes in my plane. I remember each of these three incidents more vividly than almost any other in my combat career—I've dreamt about them more often than others. . . ."

McCampbell knew how to exploit the considerable advantage of his higher-performing fighter, appreciated the approach from behind as a safer attack than a head-on pass and, most important of all in his encounter on 24 October, realized the advantage of deliberate or careful aggressive tactics. What he doesn't mention, is that he was one of the war's great marksmen. To bring down nine enemy planes (to say nothing of the two more probables) most pilots would have had to reload several times. McCampbell proved that, as in the First World War, shooting was the key, and that getting close, from behind, the easiest, surest gunnery pass.

A tactic which came into its own in the last part of the Second World War was deflection shooting. The difference between the really good fighter pilots and the average was often the ability of the former to bring down an enemy by shooting from the side—deflection shooting. Deflection passes were more productive in the 1939–45 war because firepower was greater and gunsights more efficient. To bring down an aircraft with a deflection burst required an ability to judge accurately "lead" ("forward allowance" in R.A.F. terminology). In other words, the pilot was shooting ahead of his adversary because of his great speed; distance from target, its speed and other factors entered into such calculations, which had to be made in seconds. The best marksmen were able to bring down their foes from behind or with a deflection shot from the side, above or below. A lesser shot merely hose-piped his adversary from behind. He sometimes registered enough hits—if he hung on in that position long enough—to bring him down. Because of this, Johnnie Johnson, the great R.A.F. ace, notes that in early air combat, before gunnery training was properly stressed in the R.A.F., "the kills in any squadron always seemed to fall to the same few pilots while the others usually scored a probable or a damaged."

American fighter pilots were to undergo the same break-in period, in Asia, Africa and Europe, before gunnery was properly appreciated and mastered. Even the highest-scoring American ace of the war, Dick Bong, who died in an air crash just after the war, felt he had scored his first twenty-eight victories against the enemy as a poor marksman. (He expressed that view to General George Kenny, his commanding officer in what was then Dutch New Guinea, after returning from gunnery training in the U.S.A. in the summer of 1944.)

Bong was ashamed of the ammunition he had wasted in his first victories. He felt he had learned so much about gunnery at Matagorda—on the Gulf coast in Texas—that every fighter pilot should attend such a school, if possible. Before Bong returned to Asia that year I was among those in a group he lectured on gunnery, a group departing shortly for overseas combat. The most important single factor in dogfighting, he repeatedly stressed, was good shooting. But in saying that he insisted that he was not a good shot, having scored so many of his kills from dead astern. (On that trip home in 1944 he and an ace from the First World War, Eddie Rickenbacker, agreed at a Pentagon discussion that better gunnery training and better gunsights were badly needed at U.S. training schools, and that the surest method of scoring a kill was getting close. This principle had not changed from war to war.)

In 1943 the first of the really high performance U.S. fighters in Europe, the P.47, was available in force. But it could often be out-turned by German pilots. At the end of the year the P.51 appeared and boasted a superior turn rate and great speed.

Jim Goodson, who flew a P.47 in 1943, recalls the introduction of this fighter into the European air war. This American ace had flown Spitfires with the R.A.F. and, at first, shared the skepticism of other pilots for their "seven-ton milk-bottles." But Goodson learned to appreciate the P.47's potential. It was fortunate that he did, for on one of his first missions in the new fighter he engaged the Germans whom Allied pilots called "the Abbeville boys." On this day the enemy pilots, who flew from Abbeville, were in F.W.190s, which Goodson says had in 1941 and 1942 "flown circles around us." The Spitfire he was then flying could out-turn the 190 but that was about all. (The Spitfire IX, which became operational in 1943, was a much better performer.)

It was in the summer of 1943. Goodson was flying under Colonel Don Blakeslee in the 4th U.S. Fighter Group, and Blakeslee dived after several 190s. Blakeslee called for him to follow, saying there were numerous enemy fighters below, and Goodson followed with his wingman, Bob Wehrman. Two 190s dived when Blakeslee approached but after their initial gain didn't pull farther ahead. Blakeslee gave chase. Goodson reached Blakeslee's level in time to see three other 190s closing in on him from behind. He yelled for Blakeslee to break and the 4th Group leader banked hard left immediately. But he couldn't out-turn the 190s. (Goodson is convinced the 190s could out-turn the Thunderbolt; he recalls that they also rolled very easily, which explains why German pilots so often rolled over and split-S to get away from an opponent on their tail.)

Goodson was nevertheless able to cut inside the 190s with speed and good position and shoot two of them off

Blakeslee's tail and hit the third before running out of ammunition. As he charged to the rescue Goodson shouted over the radio, "I've got 'em," and Blakeslee called back, "The hell you've got 'em; he's got me!" After shooting two down, Goodson cut in front of the last 190 and managed to shake him off Blakeslee's tail, to save his commander, whose P.47 was by now badly holed.

This is one of the early encounters which introduced the P.47s into combat and to the Germans. If the P.47 couldn't out-turn the 190, nevertheless the 190 couldn't dive away from it, as it could from most other Allied fighters. And the P.47 was probably as fast as the 190s it flew against in 1943. In addition, it was a very rugged aircraft and could return home after absorbing heavy damage.

After flying the P.47 for a time the 4th Group switched again—to the P.51 Mustang. Goodson liked the P.51 but never depreciated the P.47. When the Group had changed to the 47 from the Spit, Goodson had been one of those selected to get special training in it and he realized its possibilities. Speaking about the day he saved his commanding officer, and the first few days the Group flew P.47s, he says: "I was probably the only one at that time who felt we really had a good chance in the Thunderbolt." Goodson remembers the power of the 47's eight 50-caliber machine-guns that day. "The first 190 I shot down from about a hundred yards . . . his wing broke off. The 190, being air-cooled, didn't smoke as much when hit as the 109."

The Americans on this occasion were engaged in a fighter sweep and at this stage of the war, the summer of 1943, the fighter battle hadn't been finally decided. Stiff opposition was usually just across the English Channel and, as Goodson notes, the Germans up to that time had been able to fly "rings around us." There were many U.S. pilots who preferred the P.47 to anything else; they do not agree that the 190 held an overall edge against it. What is certain is that, as these tough and formidable fighters, the P.47s and P.51s, and new British fighters, began to appear, the tide turned against the Luftwaffe.

As the American fighter pilots received indoctrination in air war, they—like the British before them—discarded peacetime formations. Flying escort to heavy bombers going into Germany U.S. fighter squadrons were sometimes jumped by enemy fighters while still in relatively close formation. On some occasions squadron commanders frowned on individual pilots turning quickly out of formation without orders—even to avoid being caught from behind when enemy fighters were seen approaching. After a few hard-earned lessons, U.S. formations spread out and the finger-four and sometimes four-abreast formation became generally accepted as the best combat formation to fly. And the pilot who first spotted enemy fighters making a bounce turned into them at once, calling them out, and the others formed on him.

It should be remembered, in analyzing the arrival of higher-performing U.S. fighters and the development of the U.S. fighter offensive in 1943 and 1944, that in the first months of this struggle U.S. pilots were engaging veterans who had an edge in experience. The Germans had lost a surprisingly small number of fighter pilots in the West in 1941–2. A year later, or by the end of 1944, many of the German veterans had been shot down and the average number of training and flying hours for the new German pilots was far less. That is when the better U.S. fighters, flown by pilots who had gained experience, really began to take a heavy toll. It was in 1944 that long-range U.S. fighters broke the Luftwaffe fighter arm's strength and devastated the remaining fighter strength of the Japanese Army and Navy in most of the Pacific.

There was also a tremendous expansion of the nightfighter war. The R.A.F. strategic bombing offensive, consuming a major portion of total British production, had forced the Luftwaffe to expand and improve its nightfighter forces and, just as in the daylight battle, high-scoring night aces were emerging, radar techniques improving, and bomber losses increasing. To protect their heavy bombers, which began to suffer sometimes intolerable losses at the hands of Germany's fast-improving night-fighter defense, the R.A.F. began to send night fighters with them. These night fighters hunted German night fighters in a sustained campaign for the first time in the history of air war. Escort fighters, feints to confuse German defenses, Window to confuse radar and other devices enabled the R.A.F. to continue its assault, but R.A.F. losses at night in the 1943–4 winter were often heavier than U.S.A.A.F. bomber losses by day and on the grimmest nights greater than the U.S. Eighth Air Force ever sustained by day, forcing Bomber Command to limit the depth of its penetrations into Germany. The pressure on German defenses was round-the-clock, and Germany's defense was requiring an increasing fighter effort by both day and night. But the Luftwaffe's night fighters were probably achieving more, at less cost, at this time than its day fighters.

In the Pacific the Japanese were now facing Hellcats, Corsairs, Mustangs and Thunderbolts. In some of the carrier and land battles the Japanese loss ratio was as high as twenty to one. The Japanese (and Germans) were making some very advanced piston-engine fighters, but they were too few. The Germans equipped their 109 with a Daimler-Benz 605 AS engine in a last bid to check the daylight onslaught against Berlin and Germany. But though these 109s were able to fly higher than U.S. fighters, and accelerate faster, as the Germans claim, they were too few, the flying time too short, firepower too reduced, to be the answer to the heavy bomber offensive. In theory, these high-altitude 109s were to draw off the U.S. fighters while armor-plated and more heavily armed F.W.190s took on the bombers. But there were too many U.S. fighters to be drawn off, stretched out over too many miles, and not enough Luftwaffe *Experten* to accomplish the goal.

In the last part of 1944, of course, the Luftwaffe began to receive the Me.262 jet fighter, unquestionably the most advanced fighter of the war. The 262s had, as everyone now knows, been delayed in arrival by Hitler's order that they were to be built as bombers. The Me.262 was faster than any other fighter in the war, could fly higher, and had the Germans been able to put several thousand into the air as late as 1944 they might have turned the air tide back in their favor. Dr. Willi Messerschmitt, the designer of the Me.109, Me.110 and Me.262, thinks that this jet fighter, if produced in time, might have changed the course of the war, though he prefers to quote Allied experts who hold that view. He is certain, however, that the Luftwaffe could have had the jet long before it finally received it. In an interview on that subject Dr. Messerschmitt told me: "Berlin thought we would win the war before we needed the Me.262. We could have had it two years earlier than we did."

The 262 was the one fighter which might have changed the air situation drastically. But it could not have won the war for Germany; it might have made the invasion of Normandy very much more difficult and it might have made the U.S. bomber offensive so costly it would have been called off. However, it could not have stopped the Russian Army in the East. And it might not have been capable of stopping the Allied air offensive, if only because of the sheer weight of numbers on the Allied side. I asked General Theo Osterkamp, the famous German fighter pilot in the First World War and a high-ranking officer in the Luftwaffe in the Second World War, whether, if the Luftwaffe had had more fighters in 1943 and 1944, it could have defeated the Allied bombing attack. He thought not. But no one will ever finally know what two thousand 262s would have been able to accomplish had they been available in 1943; it was the one fighter ahead of all the rest in performance. Only about a thousand were built and many of these were destroyed on the ground. All who flew against them in the final days of the war in Europe knew how good they were—and the Germans claim a forty-to-one victory ratio for them in 1944–5.

Likewise, the Japanese built several excellent fighters in the last two years of the war. The best was probably the Frank, on which there was a most interesting report in the June 1970 issue of *Rendezvous* (American Fighter Pilots

Association) by Edward Maloney, followed by a comment by Bud Mahurin, who test-flew the one remaining Frank in existence. Maloney says the Nakajima-built Frank had a top speed of 427 m.p.h., was powered by a 2,000-horsepower engine, mounted two 12.7-mm. machine-guns and two 20-mm. cannon and had the quite impressive range of 1,800 miles! The Frank, which was first delivered to the Japanese Army in the spring of 1944, would outclimb any Allied fighter (including the P.51D), and would out-turn all of them (including the Spitfire). The Frank was known in the Japanese Army as the Ki-84, and tests showed it to be faster than the Zeke 52. These, plus the Tony and George, were certainly advanced fighters but they were not jets, and by that time the weight of Allied superioriy in numbers was so overwhelming, and Japanese training and production facilities so disorganized, that they have never been properly acclaimed for their excellent performance.

The Axis powers, in short, were overwhelmed by a greater number of capable Allied fighter pilots, especially American, flying very good fighters, in the last two years of the war. And in the Japanese theater, U.S. pilots showed a decidedly better aptitude to think for themselves in combat. Italy having been knocked out of the war in 1943, and its fighters having been obsolete even then—or for that matter when Italy joined the war in 1940—this turning of the tide in the fighter war in its last two years relates primarily to only Germany and its satellites and Japan. But in Japan, as in Germany, individual fighter pilots compiled incredible records. German pilots shot down Russian aircraft in wholesale numbers (the top German ace, Erich Hartmann, bagged 352!) and some Japanese pilots scored over 100 victories against Allied fighters. But, as we saw in the opening phases of the war in 1939 and 1940, superior numbers confer a tremendous advantage in fighter combat. And the Allies had this advantage in the last part of the war, plus ample supplies, replacements, fuel, and other essentials.

These last two years of the fighter war produced air

fighting on a scale which dwarfed anything yet seen in the air, just as the last year of the First World War produced air combat on a scale vaster than anyone had conceived at its outbreak. The fighter war in Europe reached all the way to Berlin. Thus Jim Goodson suspects it was he who on one occasion chased the German ace, General Adolf Galland, over the rooftops of the German capital—a chase with symbolic significance, as P.51s were beginning to turn the tide. Goodson recalls: "He was at 25,000 feet and we were at 30,000. He was flying an Me.109G with a direct injection carburetor and that 109 was better than the Mustang at 30,000 feet. But I dived on him and had the height advantage and we went down to the treetops. He went low over housetops and even ticked several trees. He went over a clump of them and disappeared."

Galland recognized the problem facing the Luftwaffe, with such dogfights now occurring regularly, even directly over the German capital. He felt that the Luftwaffe's last chance lay in building technically superior fighters (Me.262s) as fast as possible and in gathering a massive fighter force with which to strike a surprise overwhelming blow against the invading bombers, which would shake the morale of Allied airmen. But it was too late, and Hitler committed the 262s piecemeal in the invasion crisis of June of 1944, with little effect and with heavy loss of aircraft.

As for fighter combat, Galland says that speed was more important in the Second World War, while maneuverability was of primary importance in the First. "But you must break this down," Galland said. "For escorting bombers maneuverability is important; otherwise, speed, acceleration and rate of climb are very important. Acceleration is of key importance and often overlooked." Our discussion took place in Galland's home. The distinguished R.A.F. ace, Stanford Tuck, also participated. Galland and Tuck agreed that the day when fighters will not be needed in armed conflict is not foreseeable. "You must have them," Galland said. "But you are far behind the Russians." And he warned: "In case of a new war the critical question would be whether NATO could stop the Warsaw Powers from overrunning Germany in the first few days. NATO must have that clear goal, and training and armament should be designed to achieve it."

24

NEW STRATEGY AND TACTICS

The Battle of Germany involved greater numbers of aerial gladiators than had ever been engaged before. It led to the development of a new overall fighter strategy and new combat tactics.

The daylight struggle was largely between American bombers and fighters and German fighters. U.S. fighter squadrons were usually composed of sixteen aircraft (compared to twelve in the normal R.A.F. squadron) in four flights of four. Their primary task, of course, was to protect the heavy bombers. U.S.A.A.F. leaders profited from German and British trial and error in escort work and from hard-earned experience of their own and extended fighter units a good distance from bomber boxes. Fighters were not cramped for time and space in defending the bombers and were free to attack enemy gaggles seen rising at some distance to intercept. The U.S. command also decided to send fighter units on broad sweeps on both sides of the bomber stream, and in front, to harass fighter fields from which German fighters were assembling. Since the P.51 Mustang could outdive the 109 and the 190, being faster than all but the souped-up versions, German fighters, for the first time in the war, could no longer break off combat at will with the familiar split-S and dive. They were forced to fight, and were often followed to their bases. The Luftwaffe was thus confronted with a foe who now appeared over its airfields, and if there was no air opposition strafed German aircraft on the ground. U.S. fighters also confounded radar defenses by roaming over Germany at low altitude and although flak sometimes took a toll of these invaders they caused heavy damage at airfields and to the German transport system, especially to trains.

In 1944 U.S. fighters on one occasion crossed Germany from England to land at Russian bases, from which they flew to Italy and then returned to England. From island bases in the Pacific this same year U.S. fighters began to escort bombers almost a thousand miles to attack Japanese targets. But the fighter opposition in Japan was nothing like that encountered over Germany, nor was the flak comparable. Thus fighters, for the first time, began to roam the world as much as bombers.

Fighter tactics naturally were adapted to such long-range tasks. Escorts were often assigned in relays, those relieved usually dropping to the deck to strafe as opportunities appeared. When such marauding fighter units caught German aircraft either taking off or landing a slaughter sometimes ensued. This, of course, disrupted training and normal flying operations of all kinds. And when German fighters arose in great numbers to do battle with the invading host they had not only to contend with the massed boxes of ten-gun bombers but with a numerically greater force of superior defending fighters. Cajus Bekker in *The Luftwaffe War Diaries* suggests that this war of attrition reached the "mortal" phase for Germany in March 1944. In bitter air battles on 6 March defending Luftwaffe fighters achieved the feat of shooting down sixty-nine bombers and eleven fighters. But eighty German fighters were lost and many others damaged. This was about half the defending force employed, and losses approaching fifty per cent were, of course, unacceptable. Later that month, when U.S. heavy bombers attacked Berlin, German fighters failed to shoot down a single bomber. And so it seems reasonable to argue that this might well have been the decisive turning-point. There were to be other days when heavy losses would be inflicted on the bombers, but after March 1944, there was never any question whether the daylight bombing offensive would be interrupted.

New fighter tactics developed in this long-range escort battle were nicely summarized by one of the great U.S. aces of the war, who some feel might well have been the highest-scoring American fighter pilot of the war had not his own ground gunners shot him down by mistake on Christmas Day, 1944. Captain George Preddy's P.51 disintegrated and he was killed almost instantly when hit by ground fire while he was chasing an F.W.190 over the treetops. He had, a little earlier, been asked by the Assistant Chief of Staff to summarize his concept of successful escort fighter tactics. Through the courtesy of John Beaman, Joseph Noah and Sam Sox, Jr., a copy of the third-ranking (Europe) U.S. ace's analysis follows:

In reply to your letter dated 3 March 1944, I am writing down a few principles of operational flying. All of these facts or ideas are based upon experience in this theater while flying the P.47 on fighter sweeps and escort missions.

To begin with, it is an old story that the pilot who doesn't get across the Channel will not see any action. One of the big problems in this theater is weather and since a good 50% of our flying is done in instrument conditions, it is necessary that all pilots be proficient at instrument and close formation flying. The formation used going through an overcast is as follows: In the flight the No. 2 man flies on the leader's left wing with 3 and 4 on the right. In the squadron the flights fly line astern stacked down. The whole outfit is in very close, and if each man flies a steady position it is possible to take 16 or 20 ships through an overcast. If visibility in the soup is very bad or turbulence exists, it becomes necessary to split the squadron into two or more sections.

On the climb out, the flights and individual ships fly close formation as this reduces throttle-jockeying and saves gas. When we approach the enemy coast, everybody moves out into battle formation; i.e., line abreast and 5 or 6 ships length apart for individual ships and line abreast for each two flights. This is an easy formation to fly when flying a straight course and offers excellent cross-cover.

When escorting several large boxes of bombers it is impossible to keep the group together, so squadrons and sections of squadrons are assigned a particular section of the task force. We usually fly two flights of 4 planes each. The flights fly line abreast to offer cross-cover, but if the lead ship is turning a lot, it is necessary to fall in string. Normally, the flight leaders and element leaders look for bounces with the wing men on the defensive. This doesn't mean that leaders look back or wing men never look down. It is impossible to see everything, but each pilot must keep his head moving and look to find.

When a member of the flight sees something suspicious, he calls it in and the leader takes the section to investigate. When it is identified as enemy, we notice the number and formation and try to make a surprise. The first flight of four goes down and the second flight stays up for top cover. It is necessary to have this protection as a decent bounce cannot be made when trying to protect your own tail. If only one flight is in the vicinity, the second element acts as top cover. If a surprise can be made on several enemy aircraft, all ships in the flight can pick one out and drive up behind them and shoot them down. If the Hun sees you coming from above he usually starts diving and turning. It is necessary for the wing man to stay with his leader as the leader cannot follow the Hun through evasive action and do a good job of shooting unless the wing man is there to guard against attack by another enemy aircraft. Should the attacking flight or element get bounced, the wing man turns into the attack immediately and calls the leader.

When the leader is preparing to make a bounce he should inform his squadron of his intentions. If a wing man sees an enemy plane which would get away if he didn't act immediately, he goes down on the bounce calling in as he does so. In this case the leader becomes the wing man.

When being bounced the first thing is always turn into the attack. The flight does not follow the leader into the turn, but each ship turns into the attackers.

If a pilot sees an enemy aircraft behind him in firing range he must take evasive action immediately. He slips and skids the ship as much as possible giving the Hun maximum deflection. It is a good idea to turn in the direction of friendly planes, so they can shoot or scare Jerry off your tail.

There will be times after a combat that you are down on the deck. If you are alone and can't find a friend to join with, the best thing to do is head for home taking advantage of clouds for cover. If there are two or more they should climb back up providing they still have speed and gas. They should push everything to the firewall and keep speed in the climb, the leader must do a lot of turning in order to keep the man behind him up. Each man must be on the lookout for a bounce and watch each other's tail. If there are only two or three of you, you should find friends and join them.

As a conclusion, in escorting bombers it is a good idea to range out to the sides, front and rear and hit enemy fighters before they can get to the bomber formation, but do not run off on a wild-goose chase and leave the bombers unprotected.

Adolf Galland, former General of the German Fighter Arm, agrees that the fatal turn in the war for the Luftwaffe was the switch by U.S. fighters from close bomber defense to the offensive, following the tactics developed by leaders like George Preddy. This success by long-range U.S. fighters proved again the old and accepted principle of fighter combat: aggressiveness is the best defense, of bombers being protected or fighters themselves.

U.S. fighter leaders learned in the long-range Battle of Germany that it was impractical to attempt to control more than a limited number of fighters. On one mission the outstanding Don Blakeslee, 4th Fighter Group Leader, was given radio control of all the hundreds of fighters flying a Berlin escort mission. But even Blakeslee had no way of controlling, or even keeping abreast of, the activities of so many squadrons, strung out over a hundred miles.

Defending German fighters, meanwhile, grouped in larger formations as the battle grew more desperate, and these required gaggles of fighters, as Allied pilots called them, could be an intimidating sight and were sometimes effective in executing systematic attacks on bomber boxes. It will be remembered that Douglas Bader of the R.A.F. had championed this same defensive tactic in 1940 in the Battle of Britain and achieved success when demonstrating it in an attack with several combined squadrons against invading German bombers.

These large gaggles of German fighters were sometimes

composed of heavily armored, four-cannon F.W.190s, which were to attack the bombers from behind, and more lightly armored 109s which were either to engage the U.S. fighters or to attack the bombers head-on. (By this late stage of the war the Me.110 was recognized as highly vulnerable against U.S. fighters, and it and the Ju.88 were used extensively for night-fighter work.) The German fighters' aim was to scatter the bombers, which were more easily attacked when separated. German fighter pilots were taught that head-on attacks on heavy bombers were preferable to stern attacks, where defensive gunfire was heavier. They were instructed to pass above the bombers, to be in position for another attack rather quickly and because by diving they were exposed to heavier defensive fire. But German fighters suffered heavy losses both to bomber gunners (though not nearly as heavy as these gunners claimed) and to U.S. fighters.

German interceptors in the night struggle were more successful. By early 1944 they had achieved such proficiency in finding R.A.F. bombers by night that they forced Bomber Command to restrict the distance of its missions. German night fighters attacked from behind and from below, some of the Ju.88s being equipped to shoot almost straight up into the bellies of the heavy bombers. In the 1943–4 winter R.A.F. bomber losses to defending fighters and flak averaged more than five per cent per mission.

But if the Luftwaffe had won something of a victory in this night-fighter war, it had lost the day-fighter war, and General Osterkamp recently described the sending of German fighters against the U.S. bomber stream in 1944 as "criminal."

In numbers, the Battle of Germany on some days involved over four thousand aircraft. The U.S. Eighth Air Force would dispatch 1,300 bombers and 800 fighters over Germany. Hundreds of German fighters rose to intercept. The U.S. Ninth Air Force in France would strike at targets on Germany's border with hundreds of medium bombers and fighter bombers. From Italy the U.S. Fifteenth Air Force would send hundreds of bombers and fighters against southern Germany. The R.A.F., in addition to extensive shorter range daylight operations, would send perhaps nine hundred bombers and escort fighters into the struggle at night, and German night fighters would intercept them. There had never been an air battle on such a scale, and probably will never again be one involving so many aircraft, because of the great increase in destructive power of today's modern bombers.

The Eighth Air Force's fighter strategy, an assault on all parts of Germany from low and high altitude, had never before been employed on such a scale and at such a distance. It is not the purpose of this book to attempt to analyze the strategic bombing offensive, but it is clear that this fighter strategy enabled that offensive to be carried on. In post-war analyses a number of eminent historians impressively question the rate of return on the Royal Air Force's long and costly night-bomber offensive, which absorbed so much of the total British war effort. Even U.S. daylight bombing achieved less than enthusiastic wartime supporters claimed. But the daylight, so-called precision bombing effort of the U.S.A.A.F. was more effective in inflicting serious industrial damage on the German war effort, especially in the field of ball-bearings and fuel, than the night offensive, which however carried with it a far greater tonnage of bombs.

The advantage of darkness, thought to have been with attacking bombers at the beginning of the war, turned into an advantage for defending fighters toward the last year of the war. The defending night fighter, being faster than the bomber, often found the bigger bomber more easily than it could be detected and destroyed the invader before being seen. The obvious answer to this radar approach was for bombers to be equipped with better radar, which is already the case today. But because of missiles and the expanded role of today's fast jet fighter-bomber, designed to streak to its target alone or in formation, fire or drop a nuclear weapon of enormous destructive power, and return to base, the bomber stream of the Second World War, which enabled so many day and night fighters to down several victims in a short period of time, is almost, certainly a thing of the past.

In succeeding chapters we visit German fighter aces who fought to check the aerial offensive against Germany in the last two years of the war, and American pilots who carried the air war to the farthest corners of Germany.

25

RUDORFFER'S 222 VICTORIES

One of the more remarkable records compiled by a fighter pilot in the Second World War was that of Major Erich Rudorffer. Born in Sachsen in November 1917, the year Russia surrendered to Germany during the First World War and the United States entered it against Germany, Rudorffer began his flying career in 1936 at the age of nineteen. In 1939 he joined the Luftwaffe and in service on all three of Germany's fronts during the war, from beginning to the end, shot down 222 aircraft. While this is not the highest total of any German fighter pilot, it is especially notable because Rudorffer shot down 48 Allied pilots in the West, 26 in Africa, 136 on the Russian front and then 12 more in the Me.262 jet, in the last months of the war. He stayed in combat for five years, flew over 1,000 missions, and shot down just about every type of aircraft the Allied forces employed against Germany. He was shot down himself sixteen times and baled out nine times, which must be close to a record. Only six German fighter pilots shot down more aircraft than he did, and all of them claimed their victims on the Eastern Front. There are German students of the air war who consider his record, and that of the late Oberstleutnant Heinrich Bär, unsurpassed. Bär shot down 124 aircraft in the West (45 in North Africa), 96 in the East and 16 more with the Me.262 jet, only to die in an air crash in 1957 at Brunswick. Among those who knew him, his personal charm and wit are hard to forget.

In the Atlantic Hotel in Hamburg one evening Rudorffer came with wife and daughter to keep an appointment for a long-awaited interview. He was then a flying teacher at Lübeck, dark-haired, slightly graying, with the obvious sincerity of a conscientious man. He is taller than some fighter pilots, still trim, with large, piercing, light-blue eyes. He was modest about his accomplishments. Among them were such feats as having shot down eight aircraft in one day (9 February 1943), seven in one day six days later and eleven on 11 November of the same year!

Since Rudorffer had flown the Me.262 I asked him how effective it was against Allied fighters in the daylight bombing of Germany.

"It was very good, and very fast, but there were too many Allied fighters in the air at that late stage of the war for the number of Me.262s we had," he said. German pilots experienced many technical bugs in the new jets, he explained, which was perhaps to be expected, the jets being a revolutionary innovation at this time. But most of all it was the tremendous numerical odds that the German pilots faced which made their task hopeless. "One day in 1944 I saw about 2,000 Allied aircraft over Germany. On that day I had fourteen Me.262s. We attacked B.17 bombers and also P.51s. We shot down seven and lost two pilots. I got two Fortresses that day—I think it was in April—but my plane was badly damaged.

"We always flew the Me.262s at about 620 m.p.h., never much under that. There were too many aircraft around. We climbed at about 465 m.p.h. I was Kommandeur of Gruppe II, J.G. 7, the first real 262 Geschwader, based at Kaltenkirchen near Hamburg. An extra Staffel was composed of famous pilots with many victories. That was in January 1945. I had learned to fly the 262 first at Lechfeld. We could only fly about fifty-five minutes in the 262 at full power, maybe an hour and a half or a little more at cruising speed. Once I managed to stay aloft for an hour and fifty minutes—that was my longest flight.

We knew the American bombers and fighters came in over Dümmersee and often used that lake as a rendezvous point. Therefore we assembled over the Steinhuder Meer, a lake near Hanover. I recall one flight in which we assembled there, carried out our attack, flew to Prague, then to Munich-Rosenheim and finally landed in Dresden. It was very difficult in those days to find a safe place to land—because there were so many U.S. fighters roaming the skies. That was one of the difficulties for German pilots in the Battle of Germany at this stage of the war. German aircraft were often shot up on the ground or trying to land, and the short flying time of the 262 made coming in for a landing a serious concern almost from the beginning of a mission.

"The great numbers of U.S. aircraft didn't surprise me, really. When I heard Germany had declared war on America in 1941, I knew the war was lost then ... we in Jagdgeschwader 2 knew what it meant, many of us did."

I asked Rudorffer to evalute the fighters he fought against in the West. He felt the German Me.109 and F.W.190 were superior to the P.40s and P.38s he flew against in Africa. He considered the Spitfire and the P.51 very good fighters. I asked him if he thought the Spitfire was more dangerous in a dogfight. He didn't think so; he had a high respect for the Mustang, which he said on some occasions had shot down Me.262s. From machines we changed the subject to Allied pilots and the code of ethics which prevailed for most of the war among most of the fighter pilots fighting it.

"Once I saw a German pilot strafed in his parachute, an Me.262 pilot, and he was shot at by P.51s. It was a shock. In the fighter war against Britain I had never seen this and in Africa I never saw it. I think this must have been an ex-soldier who had become a pilot and didn't know any better." Rudorffer related the incident without bitterness. He continued: "It was different in the Battle of Britain. Once—I think it was 31 August 1940—I was in a fight with four Hurricanes over Dover. I was back over the Channel when I saw another Hurricane coming from Calais, trailing white smoke, obviously in a bad way. I flew up alongside him and escorted him all the way to England and then waved good-bye. A few weeks later the same thing happened to me. That would never have happened in Russia—never."

At that time Rudorffer was flying the 109; later he switched to the 190. Asked about the two fighters and his tactics, he said: "The F.W.190 was very good up to 24,-000 feet and the Me.109 was better above that. But I never had a special machine. I flew the same machine as my men. . . . I would never have had a better one. As to gunnery passes, the best was when you dived with speed, made one pass, shot an opponent down quickly, and pulled back up. Hans-Joachim Marseille was an expert at this in Africa, of course, and when I was in Tunisia I developed the same technique. You could come from above or below at speed, with timing and marksmanship. The secret was to do the job in one pass; it could be from the side or from behind and I usually tried to open fire at about 150 feet. I practiced swooping in and out of defensive formations with my comrades. In Africa Allied fighter pilots often used the Lufbery and in this circle it was often possible to slip in and out and shoot many of them down.

"On one day—it was 9 February 1943—I got eight in about fifteen minutes in this way—six P.40s and two P.38s. It was south of Tunis, about 120 miles. I was in an F.W.190, Kommandeur of II Gruppe, J.G. 2. We got word—we were based at Kairouan—that bombers and fighters were on the way. One Staffel was already sitting in their aircraft and I ordered them off. I was always the last to take off and I waited to get the latest information on the enemy's course and speed. Then I took off with my Schwarm of four and we assembled with the others in the air and headed toward the *"dicke Autos und Indianer."* They were coming from the west, about twenty-four B.17s, eighteen P.40s, twenty P.38s and some twenty Spits. Some of them may have been Hurricanes because when the dogfight began I thought I saw some Hurricanes also. We were at about 21,500 feet and the bombers were below us, the P.40s above. When we started for the bombers the Curtiss fighters came down on us and that's when the dogfight began. After a time the P.40s, which were not as fast as us, went into a Lufbery circle and I began to slip in from low and high and shoot them down. I managed to shoot down six in about seven minutes. As I recall the combat report, I got one at 13.59, another at 14.00, a second within the minute, another at 14.02, one at 14.05 and the last at 14.06. By that time the fight had broken up and everyone had scattered. Then I saw some P.38s strafing below us and though I had only about four 190s with me at this time I went down on them and surprised them. I got one coming from above and then went up again and came down on another and shot him down. That gave me eight for the day—I remember it because it was one of the best days I ever had."

From Rudorffer's account of the tactics he used in Africa it would appear that he and Werner Schroer were two of the few German fighter pilots to master what is called the Marseille technique in that theater. Rudorffer's description of that technique of attack against fighters in a Lufbery is almost exactly the same as that of Marseille, as described to me some years ago by Marseille's wingman, Reiner Pöttgen, and his commanding officer, Eduard Neumann. Those who are skeptical about Marseille's achievement are now faced with combat performances by Rudorffer and Schroer, who used Marseille's tactics, and were also successful with them. Rudorffer shot down seven aircraft six days after the day he got eight.

His comrades remained silent during his eight triumphs on 9 February 1943. "I forbade congratulatory talk on the radio. But, of course, when we had landed—and we all landed together—they all came over to my plane. Later I got a telegram from General Christiansen in Bari congratulating me. The celebration that night was mild, however, because I was not a drinker. I smoked much but there was no wine."

The Luftwaffe had sent some of its best fighter pilots to Tunisia in November and December 1942 to blood the Americans and Rudorffer was one of those who apparently did just that. He and his fellow pilots were experienced veterans in superior aircraft, but they were unable to save Germany's foothold in Africa. The Allies had too much support on land and sea; American troops closed in from the west and General Sir Bernard Montgomery's Eighth Army approached from the south. As the German-Italian-held area in Africa shrunk in size so, of course, did the number of airfields from which the Luftwaffe could operate. This was one of the biggest handicaps faced by German fighter pilots in the closing days in Africa.

."We lost many of our aircraft to bombers in the last days in Africa, at Tunis and later at Bizerte and the flak was very dangerous at the last. I remember that the enemy flak at Tebessa was very good. We flew our planes out at the end [May 1943]."

Rudorffer shot down over a hundred Russian aircraft and flew extensively on all fronts, so is well qualified to discuss a question still argued by German fighters of the Second World War. Was it easier to score a victory in the East?

"When I was sent to Russia—in August 1943—the Russian pilots were no longer so bad. But it was always tougher in the West."

Rudorffer had brought along to the interview one of his log books and we went over the various entries. (He had given the late Hans Otto Boehm his larger log book and at this time it still had not been returned.) He enjoyed recalling his flying record. Flying is still his profession; he often flies seven hours a day in a Piper as an instructor at the flying school in Lübeck. And in spite of the fact that he had scored 222 victories, many of them against Western pilots, and is unquestionably one of the world's greatest fliers, Rudorffer remains modest and soft-spoken. In that trait he closely resembles the highest-scoring fighter pilot of all time, Erich Hartmann. Tactically they thought and fought alike. Rudorffer tended to have bigger days in combat. In addition to shooting down eight U.S. aircraft on 9 February 1943 and seven on the 15th of that month in Africa, he was credited with eleven Russian machines on two occasions in the East, on 6 November 1943 and 28 October 1944. (He may have got as many as thirteen Russians on 6 November—six Yak IXs and seven Yak VIIs.)

Perhaps this tendency to stay in aerial combat longer explains why he was shot down sixteen times and forced to bale out nine times. One would never guess that this soft-voiced, friendly, gentle man had been so aggressive and successful in the Second World War or that he is one of the world's greatest pilots.

26

MEYER; THE PHANTOM JET

In the intensified air fighting towards the end of the Second World War it is significant that the most successful pilots generally avoided the classic dogfight. Instead, they developed specialized attack patterns, usually a fast pass from above taking opponents by surprise, a close-in burst, then disengagement by diving or climbing out of range with a speed advantage. The classic dogfight, featuring turns and just about every maneuver, which thousands of pilots had believed standard combat procedure, was rejected by these fighter leaders as excessively dangerous. Some of the aces using these tactics taught replacement pilots their philosophy of fighter combat, though many flew to the end of the war without being aware of the trend. It was not, of course, a new approach. Richthofen, in the First World War, and others had adopted similar, cautious tactics and had been highly successful pursuing them.

The fourth highest-scoring American fighter pilot in the European Theater of Operations (the highest scoring when ground kills are added to the total) was one of those who arrived at the same conclusions as Hartmann and others, at about the same time. John C. Meyer, Vice Chief of Staff of the U.S. Air Force as this book is written, was then (1944) Deputy Commander of the 352nd Fighter Group. He appreciated the risks a fighter pilot ran when entering a disorganized dogfight involving a number of planes, many of them in a turning contest. At a recent interview in the Pentagon recalling the tactics he used successfully in 1944 and 1945, General Meyer explained his reasoning:

"I didn't turn with enemy pilots as a rule. I might make

one turn—to see what the situation was—but not often. It was too risky, not because the Me.109s and F.W.190s could out-turn me. I was flying a P.51 and it could do anything better than both, except perhaps at about 21,000 or 22,000 feet, where the super-charger cut in.

"My approach was to attack from above if possible in a fast pass, and to pull back up after firing. I could quickly move out of the other fellow's gun range and wait until he stopped doing whatever he was doing. If he had gone into a turn he would have lost speed and I was in good position to come back down on him with speed. I should mention that in those days most German pilots I met were not up to snuff. Only seldom at this stage of the war did I meet a really proficient enemy pilot—most of them were probably just out of training schools. And, of course, part of turning a fighter is who is turning it. This might have made the P.51 seem to have an even greater edge over the 109 and the 190 than it actually had."

(In a letter of protest to Luftwaffe commander Herman Göring, Germany's leading ace, Erich Hartmann, pointed out the inexperience of German pilots sent into combat at this time, as he also did in a conversation with Hitler—in which Hitler, interestingly, admitted the war was all but lost.[1])

During that year, however, Meyer became one of the first American pilots to encounter a very different enemy fighter, the Me.262, and his experience was enlightening. Erich Rudorffer, subject of the preceding chapter, was one of those who flew the 262—in the area where Meyer made contact. Meyer assessed the performance of the 262 very accurately after that encounter in the summer of 1944:

"On one mission that summer we were north of the Friesian Islands not far from the coast of Denmark. I saw three aircraft at a distance and since they were lower I thought we might overtake them without dropping wing tanks. I took two flights—eight Mustangs—and turned

---

[1] Raymond Toliver and Trevor Constable, *The Blond Knight of Germany*, pp. 9 and 145.

toward them. At that time Intelligence had told us nothing about the possibility of encountering a jet. And so we went after them, with a slight altitude advantage and began to close the distance. We were on an escort mission, I believe, and hadn't yet rendezvoused with the bombers, so we had only a limited time for the attack. At first we closed the distance. Then suddenly we were not gaining. I pushed the throttle to the firewall but still we didn't gain. Then they began to climb easily away from us. They were very quickly far above us and in a very short time out of sight. We had never seen anything like it.

"At the end of the mission that day, when we were back at the base, we naturally gathered to talk about it. I felt as if I hadn't really seen it, that it was unbelievable. We looked at each other and asked if the others had seen the same thing. We even doubted our own experience because it was irrational. But what we had almost surely seen was the Me.262 jet. It was our first experience of a quantum jump in aviation science. But we still didn't learn anything much from our own people, though we reported what had happened.

"The second experience I had with these new fighters was on the return from another escort mission. We were coming out of Germany after escorting the heavies and in the vicinity of Dümmersee. In response to a Mayday distress call we found a lone B.17 bomber far below, one engine out and badly damaged, trying to make it out of Germany. An Me.262 was making a pass at him—they were at about 12,000 feet—and I led my eight Mustangs down to defend him. We were eight against one but the 262 didn't break off the attack. Instead, he would turn away and we would turn away after him and he would break back and we found that he could fly the circumference of the circle around the crippled Fortress in the time it took us to fly the diameter to cut him off. Thus if we followed him he was so much faster he could fly around to the other side and cut back in without allowing us an opportunity to use our guns. I then positioned four Mustangs on each side of the B.17, which left us in a position to turn into him from almost any approach. From this experience

I came to the conclusion that eight P. 51s were the equal of one Me.262 if each knew of the other's presence."

In response to the question whether the 262 was able to turn with the Mustang, in other words, what its capability in a turning dogfight was, Meyer answered:

"The 262 couldn't out-turn the Mustang. But it didn't need to. Think of it in this way. If one was starting with these two fighters from the same point on the outside of an apple, for a theoretical analogy, the 262 couldn't out-turn the Mustang but it was so much faster that it could fly the outside of it about as fast as the P.51 could fly the line cutting straight through it. He had the initiative and could go around and get into position for a pass while staying well outside our gun range. The Mustang pilot could break sharply to prevent the 262 from staying on his tail but that is, of course, a defensive maneuver, and the 262 had the speed and initiative and could come around and get in position again and make another pass, and its pilot could also break off the action when he so desired."

Asked about the comparative value of speed and maneuverability in the Second World War, Meyer said it depended upon whom he was fighting.

"If it was the Germans, in Europe, I'd take speed above maneuverability. One can always translate altitude or potential energy into speed."

Though Meyer was and is an expert in the field of tactics, the last major Luftwaffe effort of the war caught him in a situation in which all his knowledge and skill might not have saved him—emphasizing the role of luck, or fate, in war. As it turned out, he was good enough as a flier and gunner to shoot down his twenty-third and twenty-fourth German aircraft that day but he also came close to being shot down just as Richthofen probably was in 1918, near the end of the First World War—by ground fire. It was one of those situations no pilot can avoid, however careful and prudent he may be.

He was flying from a field near Asch, in Belgium. The 352nd Fighter Group had been rushed there in December to help check the German offensive in the Ardennes, the

Battle of the Bulge. On the morning of 1 January 1945 he was at the end of the runway when the Luftwaffe's last bid to inflict a really smashing blow unfolded above him. Hitler had high hopes for his last great military gamble in the Ardennes and, to a small degree, for the Luftwaffe strike. Albert Speer, in his memoirs,[1] reports on Hitler's mood in his underground headquarters near Ziegenberg the night before this early morning effort. Speer reached the bunker at two o'clock that morning. The circle around the dictator was drinking champagne. Only Hitler himself was abstaining, yet he was, as Speer puts it, the only one in the crowd in the grip of a permanent euphoria. He made optimistic forecasts for the new year. At first this unrealistic tone failed to convince the others—adjutants, doctors, secretaries, and other staff—but after two hours Speer says Hitler had converted everyone to a more optimistic frame of mind. On this night Hitler certainly knew of the planned strike by over five hundred Luftwaffe fighters and bombers for dawn—a few hours later.

The morning of the 1st was foggy at Asch, as at airfields all over Europe, and so it was not until 9:43 that morning that Meyer was at last at the end of the runway preparing to take off. As he began to roll down the runway he was puzzled by bursts of flak at the far end of the field. While inquiring by radio he noticed the low-wing front silhouette of a descending, approaching aircraft. (The tower had told him nothing was in the area.) A heavy barrage of anti-aircraft shells began bursting at the end of the field and now he recognized the oncoming aircraft as an F.W.190. The field—as were many others all along and behind the front—is under attack by many German aircraft.

Meyer doesn't turn off the runway or interrupt his take-off but gives his Mustang full throttle and just as he gets its wheels off the ground the F.W.190 is in his sights—beginning to strafe a transport plane parked to one side. As the two fighters close rapidly, Meyer fires a quick burst head-on and the 190 flashes by and dives into the ground

---

[1] Albert Speer, *Inside The Third Reich*, p. 418.

even before Meyer has turned out of the traffic pattern. As soon as he is airborne he finds himself in the company of German fighters. He fastens onto the tail of another 190 as an Me.109 begins to turn in behind him, but fortunately another Mustang which had scrambled turns in behind the 109. Meyer turns his attention back to the 190, which now—at 3,000 feet—rolls over on his back, does a split-S, and dives straight downward. Meyer feels he will go into the trees below and, incredulously, watches the German pilot pull the nose up desperately, just in time. The 190 takes tops out of some trees pulling out and is now racing off over the treetops. Meyer dives after him. Soon he is closing behind, as the German, seeing him, turns back and forth. Ground fire streaks up from below. Meyer stays behind his foe even though his plane is holed several times and finally gets him in his sights, opens fire and brings him down, his second victory of the morning.

When he tries to return to the field the tower tells him it's still under attack. Every field at which he seeks to land in the next hour is under attack. He sees enemy formations on many occasions and, having no more ammunition, manages to avoid them, once after a hard chase. After an hour and a half he is able to get back into the field. Hundreds of U.S. and British aircraft have been destroyed and hundreds badly damaged. But the Luftwaffe has also lost hundreds in this hour and a half, largely because of the inexperience of its pilots.

That morning Meyer was hit by ground fire, as his friend Major George Preddy also of the 352nd had been, with fatal results, only six days earlier, and as were so many fighter pilots who descended to low altitude to chase an opponent over the trees. Richthofen, less than one hundred miles away, near Amiens, twenty-seven years earlier, had probably met his death this way. It was a day on which Meyer was unable to exercise the prudence he employed so effectively in fighter combat.

Chance and circumstances thus sometimes overwhelmed even the best tacticians and the coolest thinkers. With good luck, however, those pilots who worked out their own patterns of attack and exercised patience, caution and keen intelligence enjoyed better odds for survival, and as they achieved victories they became more proficient in flying and gunnery. Meyer was, in 1944, recognized as one of the U.S.A.A.F.'s best and, with Preddy and Virgil Meroney, was asked to summarize successful air fighting and tactics for the War Department. Here is his description of the air-fighting philosophy he believed in, as submitted to Washington in response to that official request:[1]

In every case when attacked by enemy aircraft I have turned into the attack. We have found that the turning characteristics of the P.47 as against the Me.109 and F.W.190 are very nearly equal. Since, when we are attacked, the enemy aircraft has almost always come from above, he has excessive speed and turning inside him is a simple matter. If the enemy aircraft is sighted in time, it is often possible to turn into him for a frontal attack. On two occasions I was able to do this and the enemy aircraft was reluctant to trade a head-on pass and broke for the deck. Thus I was able to turn a defensive situation into an offensive one.

The sun is a most effective offensive weapon and the enemy loves to use it. Whenever possible I always try to make all turns into the sun and try never to fly with it at my back. Clouds are very effective for evasive action if there is eight-tenths coverage or better. They're a good way to get home when you're alone.

When attacked by much superior numbers I get the hell out of there using speed, or clouds (there are usually plenty around in this theater) and only as a last resort by diving to the deck. An aggressive act in the initial phases of the attack will very often give you a breather and a head start home.

I had one experience which supports this last statement and also shows what teamwork can do. My wingman and I, attacking a pair of 109s, were in turn attacked by superior numbers of enemy aircraft. In spite of this (the enemy aircraft attacking us were still out of range for effective shooting) we continued our attack, each of us destroying one of the enemy aircraft, and then turned into

---

[1] John C. Meyer, "The Long Reach," *T.A.C. Attack.*

our attackers. Our attackers broke off and regained the tactical advantage of altitude but during this brief interval we were able to effect our escape in the clouds. Showing a willingness to fight often discourages the enemy even when he outnumbers us, while on the other hand I have, by immediately breaking for the deck on other occasions, giving the enemy a "shot in the arm," turning his half-hearted attack into an aggressive one.

I do not like the deck. This is especially true in the Pas-de-Calais area. I believe that it may be used effectively to avoid an area of numerically superior enemy aircraft because of the difficulty in seeing an aircraft on the deck from above. With all-silver planes even this excuse is doubtful. The danger from small-arms ground fire is great, especially near the coast. I realize that I differ from some of my contemporaries in this respect, but two-thirds of our Squadron losses have been from enemy small-arms fire. Just recently I led a 12-ship squadron on a fifty-mile penetration of the Pas-de-Calais area on the deck. We were under fire along the entire route. We lost one pilot, three airplanes, and three others damaged. I repeat I don't like the deck and can see little advantage in being there. Caught on the deck by three 190s I was able to outrun them by using water injection.

Mainly it's my wingman's eyes that I want. One man cannot see enough. When attacked I want first for him to warn me, then for him to think. Every situation is different and the wingman must have initiative and ability to size up the situation properly and act accordingly. There is no rule of thumb for a wingman.

I attempt to attack out of the sun. If the enemy aircraft is surprised, he's duck soup, but time is an important factor and it should not be wasted in securing position. I like to attack quickly and at high speed. This gives the enemy aircraft less time to see you and less time to act. Also speed can be converted to altitude on the break-away. The wingman's primary duty is protection of his element leader. It takes the leader's entire attention to destroy an enemy aircraft. If he takes time to cover his own tail, he may find the enemy has "flown the coop." Effective gunnery takes maximum mental and physical concentration. The wingman flies directly in trail on the attack. This provides maneuverability and he is there to follow up the attack if his leader misses. Once, however, the wingman has cleared himself and is certain his element is not under attack he may move out and take one of the other enemy aircraft under attack if more than one target is available. Good wingmen, smart wingmen, are the answer to a leader's prayers.

If surprise is not effected the enemy aircraft generally turns into the attack and down, thus causing the attacker to overshoot. When this happens I like to break off the attack and resume the tactical advantage of altitude. Often the enemy aircraft will pull out of his dive and attempt to climb back up. Then another attack can be made. A less experienced enemy pilot will often just break straight down. Then it is possible and often fairly easy to follow him. Usually on the way down he will kick, skid, and roll his aircraft in violent evasive action for which the only answer is point blank range. Compressibility is a problem which must be taken into consideration when following an enemy aircraft in a dive.

The effect of superior numbers in a decision to attack is small. The tactical advantage of position—altitude—sun—and direction of attack are the influencing factors. With these factors in my favor the number of enemy aircraft is irrelevant.

It is not wise to attack when the enemy has the advantage of altitude, and as long as he maintains it. If you're closing fast enough to overshoot, you're closing fast enough to get point blank range. At point blank range you can't miss.

I am not a good shot. Few of us are. To make up for this I hold my fire until I have a shot of less than 20° deflection and until I'm within 300 yards. Good discipline on this score can make up for a great deal.

I like to attack at high speeds and break up into the sun, making the break hard just in case his friend is around. Then I like to get back that precious altitude.

Enroute to rendezvous we fly a formation which has for its basis mutual protection rather than flexibility or maneuverability. The group is broken down into three Squadrons of sixteen ships each. The Squadrons are stepped up with the second Squadron about 1,000 feet higher, into the sun and line abreast; and the third Squadron 2,500 feet higher than the lead Squadron on the down-sun side and line abreast. This alignment makes it impossible for any one Squadron to be bounced out of the sun by an attacker who is not clear of the sun to one of the other Squadrons. The flights fly in line abreast providing mutual cross cover between individual planes and flights within the Squadron.

Upon rendezvous with the bombers the group generally breaks down into eight-ship sections of two flights each operating independently and at various ranges from the main bomber force. One flight of this section remains in close support of the other on bounces. This method has been the most successful one tried by this organization. It has certain disadvantages in that they may run into superior forces in which case considerably more would have been achieved by keeping a larger portion of our force intact. However, our main problem to date has been in seeking out the enemy, rather than his destruction once found. This method of deployment has been the best answer to that problem. These eight ships are under orders to remain within supporting distance of each other at all times. These sections operate above, below, around, ahead, behind, and well out to the sides of the main bomber force. The extent of ranging is dependent upon many factors such as weather, number of friendly fighters in the vicinity, and what formation we may have as to enemy disposition; the decision on this is left up to the section leaders.

There is no rule of thumb limitation on who makes bounces. The primary job of the flight leaders is that of seeking out bounces while that of the other members of the flight is flight protection. If any member of a flight sees a bounce and time permits, he notifies his flight leader and the flight leader leads the engagement. However, if the flight leader is unable to see the enemy the one who spotted him takes over the lead, or in those cases, of which there are many, when the time element is precious, the man who sees the enemy acts immediately, calling in the bounce as he goes.

Usually if the combat is of any size or duration, flights become separated. The element of two becoming separated however is a cardinal and costly sin. We find it almost impossible for elements to rejoin their Squadrons or flights after any prolonged combat. However, there are generally friendly fighters in the vicinity all with the same intention and we join any of them. A friendly fighter is a friend indeed no matter what outfit he's from.

Recently we have tried imitating enemy formations but have not had any particular success with it.

On the defensive the eight-ship section turns into them presenting a 64-gun array which the enemy is reluctant to face. If we are hopelessly outnumbered or low on gas after the initial turn, the individual ships keep increasing their bank until in a vertical dive using the superor diving speed of the P.47 for escape. On one occasion when we were extremely low on gas one of our flights of eight was bounced by three 190s. That flight broke for the deck with the 190s following. We crossed over following the 190s down. They immediately broke off their attack and zoomed back up. We continued our dive and effected our escape.

We drop belly tanks when empty. Gas consumption is a primary tactical consideration in this theater and we don't like to use it to drag empty belly tanks around.

The number of aircraft to go down on a bounce is influenced purely by the number of enemy aircraft. In any case at least one flight stays several thousand feet above until the situation is carefully sized up, at which time the leader of that flight makes the decision on whether to join the fray or stay aloft.

We pursue all attacks to conclusion if a favorable conclusion seems possible. In other words, if by continuing the pursuit it seems reasonable the enemy may be destroyed. There are exceptions to this however, as for instance, the enemy sometimes will send a single aircraft across our nose to draw us away from the bombers while their main force attacks. This must be watched for and the decision made by the flight leaders.

Every effort is made to hit the enemy while he is forming for the bomber attack. Generally he forms ahead and well to the up-sun side of the bomber force. A large part of our group force is deployed in that area.

Our group was the first to attempt a penetration in force on the deck for a strafing mission. Out of this experiment I have these recommendations to make: That penetration to within ten miles of the coast be made on the deck, then the force to zoom to 8,000–12,000 feet, navigating at that altitude, penetrate beyond the target, hit the deck at some prominent point a short distance from their target, and then proceed to it. This, rather than penetration all the way on the deck where the enemy small-arms fire is intense and pin-point navigation impossible. That when an aircraft is below 8,000 feet over enemy territory, it be just as low as possible. Twenty feet above the ground is too high.

Such tactics summaries are still valuable guides in the jet-fighter age. Meyer has been a student of fighter tactics in both Korea and Vietnam. "In modern conditions to get superior speed one must go supersonic. But most of the air fighting done now is at high subsonic speed. Speed is and always has been tremendously important for conversion into altitude. The big difference today is supersonic speed. But this great speed is used mostly for the initial attack and to leave an area.

"In Vietnam there has been little air fighting since we halted the bombing—since about 1968—but before that the enemy was using principally hit-and-run tactics. He was in his own Ground-Controlled Interception environment and he came in fast and got out fast. That has been Vietnam's equivalent of dogfighting."

27

ATTACKING BOMBERS: A GERMAN ACCOUNT

One of the outstanding Luftwaffe fighter pilots of the Second World War was Georg-Peter Eder, son of a Kaiser's Guards Regiment veteran of the First World War, who is now a successful businessman in Wiesbaden. He was unusually effective against four-engine bombers (he was credited with shooting down thirty-six and with forty-two other aircraft, and probably brought down eighteen others), was shot down seventeen times, and wounded thirteen times. Practically all of his victories, moreover, were scored in the West, a good indication of his skill. One afternoon recently I drove to his home in Wiesbaden to hear him describe how German fighters opposed the U.S. heavy bomber offensive in the last years of the war.

Eder served under the famous Egon Mayer, the first German pilot to achieve one hundred victories on the English Channel and a specialist in attacking four-engine bombers. They were in Jagdgeschwader 2 (Richthofen), perhaps, the best-known German fighter wing in the war. Eder served from the beginning to the end of the war (the end found him recuperating from a crash at Holzkirchen near Munich which had broken both his legs). He was born at Ansbach, near Nürnberg, in 1921 and thus at the outbreak of the war was only eighteen, an air cadet. In 1940, the second year of the war for Germany, after graduating from the fighter school at Werneuchen near Berlin, he was promoted to Leutnant and in October joined J.G. 51 (Mölders) near Calais. By then the Battle of Britain had been lost and Eder fretted about how much action he would see. He was to see plenty, and was wounded so severely in August 1941, that he was sent to Germany and remained there until 1942. Then he had to attend fighter school again (as a teacher) because he had suffered a concussion. He "had to start over again."

In March 1942, he was again posted to the West, this time with J.G. 2. Later he would serve in the famous J.G. 26 and also in Walther Nowotny's famous Erprobongs Kommando Wing of Me.262s at Achmer, near Osnabruck. (Nowotny's death is often referred to as a mystery; Eder says he saw four R.A.F. Tempests shoot him down.) Eder himself scored seven victories in the jet, which he describes as an excellent fighter. "It was safer than the other fighters, especially at that time, becuase it was so fast. But in combat it closed very fast!" At the great speed the Me.262s had to be flown, for safety in skies crowded with Allied fighters, the time for aligning an enemy aircraft in its sights and firing was greatly reduced. Thus the pilot had to open fire at longer range and have the sight squarely on the target to register hits; the firing pass lasted only a few seconds. Eder was shot down for the last time by P.51s, and he gives them much of the credit for decimating Germany's fighter defense in 1944 and 1945. He says he out-turned P.47s in the air fighting before that.

When I asked him to describe tactics in a typical Luftwaffe interception of heavy bombers he selected a successful day in 1943, 14 July, when he was flying an Me.109G6 from Evreux (near Rouen) in Normandy.

"We slept in the town, the pilots. The sixteen of us in the Staffel lived in a big, grey, brick house. There were sixty-four fighters, plus the Stab of four, in II Gruppe. I was 12th Staffel Kapitän (squadron commander). At this time there were four Staffeln to a Gruppe, four Gruppen in a Geschwader. I had a bedroom and a living-room, with a field telephone in my bedroom. At about three in the morning this day there was a knock at the door. *'Guten Morgen, Herr Hauptman. Es ist drei Uhr. Aufstehen.'* I washed and shaved in about fifteen minutes, dressed and strapped my pistol to the right calf, my knife—to cut off my chute if I fell in the sea—on the right upper leg, map on the upper left leg and a belt of cartridges just atop the left boot. We dressed in blue with black tie. I drove to the field, about two miles away, about twenty minutes past three. I had a Citroën and the other pilots had two French Metfords and a truck. We ate breakfast at the squadron ready room. The doctor advised us to eat white bread rather than black, because the heavier bread might expand the stomach at altitude. Each pilot got one litre of milk and twenty grams of coffee each day. We also got chocolate with dextrose and chocolate with caffein, which I carried in my left breast pocket. After breakfast I went out and looked over the aircraft. When I came back to the ready room I called Ops and reported: *'Zwölfte Staffel ist einsatzbereit, mit sechszehn Maschinen und vierzehn Flugzeugfuhrern.'* (Number Twelve Staffel ready for action, with sixteen aircraft and fourteen pilots.)

"I would always ask, *'Wie ist die Feindlage?'* and on that morning the reply was that radar showed three bomber divisions assembling in England. We usually had a long wait after that. We knew which bomber divisions were assembling and just waited and rested. I inspected my aircraft and signed the *'Klarmeldung.'* At about 5:30, we got the first alert: *'Achtung! Fünfzehn Minutenbereitschaft!'* Then we had to be ready to go in fifteen minutes. We smoked, went to the toilets, checked our swim vests and so on. That morning we waited until 6:30, a full hour, before we got the *'Fünf Minutenbereitschaft'* and at that time Operations told us where the enemy force was coming from and its strength and we went out and waited by our planes.

"We were told that a large number were coming and were given the exact course. In about five minutes the *'Sitzebereitschaft'* was announced and we climbed into our machines. This morning some of the bombers were flying to Rouen and some to Paris. We waited in the fighters a long time. It wasn't until 7:23 that three green rockets went up over the field—the signal to take off. Each Schwarm reported ready and we all took off into the north. In two minutes all fifty planes in the Gruppe were airborne and then the four Gruppen assembled.

"Mayer's Gruppe led and I was slightly back, left, another Gruppe back on the right and the last Gruppe centered, behind us, higher. It wasn't long before ground control warned us: *'Achtung! Möbelwagen in Gustav Paula eins! Sechstausend Meter. Begleitet von vielen Indianern!'* (Attention! Bombers in square G P One! Eighteen thousand feet! Protected by many fighters!) Our radar had sent us off at just the right time and just after that I sighted the bombers: *'Achtung! Dicke Autos in zwei Uhr!'*

"Mayer came right back: *'Fliegen Sie 45 Grad.'* We took up that course and followed him—he had led an attack on heavies in January and shot down eighteen. We were now at twenty-one thousand feet and, as we approached, turned to fly ahead of them, well above. From that position, about two miles in front, we banked right and turned to come head-on at them, Mayer giving directions. The bombers, about two hundred of them, were in three groups, the fighters above them, and Mayer called for me to attack one of the bomber boxes. When I replied 'Victor' he knew I had received the order. There was no radio talk after that. On the radio he was Buzzard Eins and I was Buzzard Zwei. I pushed the black button on the right of the panel and the three yellow rings and cross flicked on on the sight glass. I was leading the first four of the Gruppen, with one on the left and one on the right, just back, and the fourth behind them in the center, higher—the same formation with our Schwarms in the Gruppe as was flown by the Gruppen in the Geschwader. We were doing about 280 m.p.h. now and were coming down slightly, aiming for the noses of the B.17s. The 109sG6 had four 20-mm. cannon and two 30-mm. cannon, each of the latter with seventy shells per gun, so we were heavily armed. There were about two hundred of us attacking the two hundred bombers but there was also the fighter escort above them. We were going for the bombers. When we made our move, the P.47s began to dive on us and it was a race to get to the bombers before being intercepted. I was already close and about six hundred feet above and coming straight on; I opened fire with the twenties at five hundred yards. At three hundred yards I opened fire with the thirties. It was a short burst, maybe ten shells from each cannon, but I saw the bomber explode and begin to burn. I flashed over him at about fifty feet and then did a Chandelle [a climbing turn and then a course reversal]. When I had turned around I was about a thousand feet above and behind them, and was suddenly mixed in with American fighters.

"Straight in front was a Thunderbolt, as I completed the turn, and I opened fire on him immediately, and hit his propwash. My fire was so heavy his left wing came off almost at once and I watched him go down. By now I had only three fighters with me—my lead Schwarm—the others had split away in the attack. We flew south, ahead, for a few seconds, preparing for another strike at the bombers and then, coming from above, I saw them. I called a warning: *'Indianer über uns!'* and as they came in behind us we banked hard left. There were ten P.47s and four of us and we were all turning as hard as we could, as in a Lufbery. I was able to turn tighter and was gaining. I pulled within eighty yards of the 47 ahead of me and opened fire. I hit him quickly and two of the others got one each, so that in a minute and a half three of the P.47s went down. The pilot of the one I hit baled out and I saw his chute open. But one of my men had been shot down and there were now three against seven and I called on the radio for an emergency dive to get away: *'Nach unten vereisen!'* and we all rolled over and did a split-S and dived with full throttle. We were at about fifteen thousand feet then and the full-throttle dive at emergency power naturally made a lot of smoke. Many Americans thought the smoke was a trick, to make it appear the 109 was hit, but it was really only emergency boost. And it usually got us out of trouble, as it did this time. We pulled away from the P.47s, which either couldn't follow us or stayed near the bombers. As we pulled out and saw no fighters behind us we began to head southward and toward the bombers again, gradually climbing. We were soon in sight of them again, one of the boxes coming back from Paris probably. It was just in front of Paris and I called over the radio: *'Dicke Wagen vor uns!'* and we began to dive slowly, for they were at about twelve thousand feet, and no longer in close formation. There were about twelve of them and we headed straight into them for a head-on pass, diving not too fast. On the first pass the three of us got one of them smoking and he started down. We turned back and went after him and from about three hundred yards opened fire at this straggler and he burst into flame. But he was firing with all ten guns and just before his wing went up and he flopped over on fire I heard thumps and my engine and cabin was hit, hard hit. The engine immediately began to knock loudly and I put the prop in fine pitch. I went into a long dive and looked around as I headed down. There was a field ahead—Le Bourget.

"I didn't have any power and knew I would have to belly-land it. I managed to reach the field, pulled the electric landing gear lever on the right of the panel but nothing happened. I reached for the hand lever and got the wheels down in time. I was only a thousand feet off the grass field when the wheels came down. I hit going very fast, about 110 m.p.h. I was wondering who had hit me; I think it was one of the bombers above, not a fighter and not the bomber going down. The other two landed with me and we were taken in an ambulance to a telephone and connected to the base. I remember they asked me how the fight had gone and I reported having shot down two P.47s and two B.17s and having lost one of my 109s. Ops offered 'Gratulieren' on my victories and told me to send one of the pilots back by car. When I landed at the base I learned the Geschwader had lost six or seven fighters but had shot down about twenty, most of them bombers. We all met with Mayer in the Ops center to discuss the mission and then I went back to the Staffel and made out my combat report."

During the description of that interception Eder had taken me down to his *"Fliegerkeller"* in which there were pictures of many Second World War aircraft on the walls, and of Galland and Mölders and other comrades. He showed me a yellow lifejacket he had worn when flying from Evreux and maps such as those he had carried on flights. Eder remembered practically every detail of the war days. He showed no outward ill effects from his thirteen wounds and appeared in excellent health. His dark brown hair was once blonder, he is high-strung though not over-nervous and volunteered much information and made telephone calls to get other answers.

In his garage was one of a few B.M.W. sports models of its kind manufactured, a car which could attain over 150 m.p.h. I told him that was too fast and recalled how many top wartime fighter pilots had been killed since the war in car accidents. Speaking of speed in the air, he was of the opinion that late-model Me.109s would fly as fast as the Mustang P.51s, and he was not the first German fighter pilot to make this claim, though some believe the Mustang was faster. The later model 109s were indeed fast. Erich Hartmann, of whom we will learn more, liked the 109 so much he chose to fly it throughout the war, and said later models, such as those with the Daimler–Benz 605 AS engine, could do better than hold their own at high altitude.

Certainly the armament of the 109 flown by Eder was impressive and one notes how quickly aircraft as big as the B.17, which was not an easy bomber to shoot down—not as easy as the B.24 in the opinion of German fighter pilots—exploded under its direct, close-in fire. Eder attacked as prescribed by Luftwaffe Intelligence at the time, head-on. This exposed the oncoming fighter to fewer guns and it also kept the firing pass shorter, since the two aircraft were on a converging course. He passed above the B.17 after firing, also the proper tactic according to Luftwaffe training at the time.

The contrast between a German fighter mission and an Allied one at this stage of the war is interesting. German pilots flew short missions after a very long alert period, in several different stages, the last sending them into their cockpits where they again waited, for as long as an hour. Since Allied pilots were on the offensive at this time, the form for them was completely different. They flew long missions, there was little waiting after they got in their aircraft and they enjoyed no effective radar help over the battle area once they were well inland over the continent. Thus the roles of fighters had been completely reversed in the three years since 1940 and the Battle of Britain. German fighters had the benefit of radar and ground direction and control and knew exactly where their foe was when they took off. Allied fighters at this time were staying reasonably close to the bombers (later they began to range outward more freely) and were, relatively, in the dark. Moreover, a badly damaged Allied aircraft had to go down in enemy territory; the pilot (or crew) was captured, if he landed safely, and lost for the war. Partly because of these advantages the Luftwaffe fighters won the air war in 1941 and 1942 and were probably still winning it when this mission took place. It was not to be until December of that year—1943—that P.51s were seen over Germany.

Eder transferred into Me.262s toward the end of the war and was indeed a fighter pilot with at least eighteen lives, having been shot down seventeen times between the day he reported to an airfield near Coquelles, France in 1940, and that day in January 1945, when he was shot down in a jet east of Munich. He was taken to a hospital on the Tegensee after his last crash and there taken prisoner by the Americans when they overran Bavaria in the spring.

28

DECLINE OF THE GERMAN FIGHTER ARM

If there was a single day which represented the high tide of the German fighter defense against the U.S. daylight bombing offensive in the Second World War, it was probably 6 March 1944. On that day German fighters shot down 80 U.S. aircraft, 69 of them heavy bombers—the biggest loss of the war for the Eighth Air Force. On this day the Americans carried out their first really heavy bombing of Berlin. The grim losses, however, didn't stop the assault, as such losses had in the autumn of 1943. Two days later the heavies went to Berlin again; again losses were heavy—54 aircraft.

On the third attack on Berlin a week later, on 15 March, the overall result for U.S. forces was strikingly better. Luftwaffe fighters failed to shoot down a single heavy bomber of the 669 sent out! Flak accounted for a dozen. The reason was that Luftwaffe fighters had suffered very heavily in both the 6 and 8 March raids, particularly from wide-ranging U.S. fighters. And though the raid on the 15th came after a respite in the Berlin offensive the German fighter arm had suffered so heavily it needed a respite to regather its strength with replacement pilots. Interestingly, German fighters never again brought down anywhere near the number of bombers that were lost on 6 March.

Flying on both these missions was the second-highest scoring U.S. fighter pilot in the European theater, Robert S. Johnson. On earler escorts Johnson had realized that U.S. fighters were tied too closely to the bomber stream and had helped bring about a change in escort tactics.

U.S. fighter pilots, then, had learned a valuable lesson

in the year since they had begun escorting the heavies into France and Germany. They had learned that fighters should not stay in a close formation on escort and that individual pilots should be allowed to break when they saw enemy fighters closing. Using these more effective tactics, fighter units now ranged out ahead and to the sides of the bomber stream to find and break up German fighter gaggles before they reached the heavies.

Johnson at this time was a First Lieutenant and had only a limited voice in devising tactics in the famous 56th Group; only after almost having been shot down holding formation, being afraid to break without orders, and only after having been "chewed out" for diving on four enemy fighters one day without orders—and shooting one down—did he finally impress his ideas on tactics on his superiors. The highest-scoring U.S. fighter ace of the European war, Frank Gabreski, was at this time Johnson's squadron commander and he, after questioning Johnson's ideas, accepted them as sound and advised others to follow Johnson's example. The same lesson was being learned in other U.S. fighter Groups at this time, but no other two fighters in the U.S. Army Air Force in Europe learned the lesson as well as Gabreski and Johnson, who between them shot down 59 German aircraft.

On a cold winter day in New York recently I reminisced with Johnson about the tactics he and the Germans used in this decisive Battle of Germany. The first American pilot in Europe to equal Captain Eddie Rickenbacker's First World War victory total, he flew the heavy P.47 and has always been an admirer of this big U.S. radial-engined fighter. He thinks it held its own in encounters with the 190s and 109s and recalls a mission when one of his comrades out-turned two 190s. It was in April 1944 and he cited this incident to show what a good pilot could do in a Thunderbolt, to demonstrate that in a fight much depended on the pilot's performance.

"This day—it was 23 April—we were over Kiel and I was flying with Sam Hamilton, from Mississippi. Any greenhorn or new boy could out-fly Sam over the base or on a training mission. But in combat—that man could fly an airplane! Sam spotted several enemy fighters and chased them to the deck. I was staying high, as I was tied up with some others, when I heard him calling on the radio: 'Hey, Bob! Come down here and get these Krauts off my ass!' I couldn't get away for a time and he continued to call, two or three times; finally I got free and started down.

"Hamilton was in a desperate fight with three F.W.190s and as I dove down he shot one down in a head-on pass and went into a turning duel with the other two. I watched them as I approached and he was out-turning them. I still had my belly tank attached and as I came down the 190 pilots noticed me, with my tank, and maybe they thought I would be easier game. They seemed to relax in their turns and in an instant Sam was behind them. But one of the 190s suddenly pulled up after me and darn near got me. I pulled up with full throttle and we hung noses until he stalled. I saw the 190 falling off to the right and as he went down I winged over and went down after him, and though he started first I caught him.

"When he saw me behind he began to whip back and forth, left and right, as violently as he could. I followed, but it was hard to line him up for a shot. Finally, as we kept whipping back and forth, right and left, I began to shoot before he whipped and he had to fly through my fire. I was only about a plane's length behind him, that close. This finally shook him and he seemed to be ready to land somewhere. He suddenly banked hard and tried to gain time to get out. I managed to stay with him in the turn and hit him, I think, when he was climbing out of the cockpit, about half way out. He baled out anyhow, and his chute opened and he went down but I think he was hit."

Assessing the relative performance of the P.47 and the F.W.190, Johnson had no illusions about the turn radius of the Thunderbolt as compared with German fighters, despite the outstanding flying job done by Hamilton that day near Kiel. "Sam was out-turning them that day and he was right over the water—they were flat turns, there was nowhere to go, down, and he did it. But, generally, we couldn't out-turn them in the P.47. We could out-spiral climb them and outdive them after we got the big paddle prop on the T-Bolt in early 1944.

"We had been told by the British we couldn't turn with the German fighters, couldn't outclimb and couldn't outrun them. But we could outrun them and we could outdive them. I think with the big prop we could climb with them, outclimb them, though the paddle prop took about five miles an hour off our top speed."

Johnson remembered reading a book by Heinz Knoke[1] and wondered if Knoke could have been one of his victims on an early 1944 mission, because the one Knoke described sounded familiar. Knoke's squadron was later so decimated trying to check the daylight bomber offensive that it was largely inoperative from mid-March until late in April. Knoke had flown three times on 8 March trying to check this second bombing attack on Berlin and had been badly shot up on one mission, chased by forty Thunderbolts on another, and had watched Thunderbolts destroy an F.W.190 on the ground that he was about to climb into on a third. In his diary he writes that his Staffel—after interceptions on the 8th—was left with only two pilots. This was the toll being exacted by U.S. fighter escorts roaming deep into Germany. On that day the U.S. Army Air Force sent 801 fighters over Germany, more than the number of fighters the Luftwaffe was able to send up. On the 15th, the third big Berlin raid of the month, Knoke's squadron managed to send up only six fighters.

I asked Johnson to describe his aerial combat tactics, in general, in fighting the 109 and 190.

"Well, they were primarily interested, of course, in going for the bombers. They weren't interested in us. They would almost invariably be high and dive on us and come through, have a shot, and go on for a strike at the bombers. That's where we got a lot of them. They seldom seemed to take advantage of their great speed and come back up—when I was flying. As for my personal tactics

---

[1] Heinz Knoke, *I Flew For The Führer*.

fighting them I didn't often engage in a lot of turning or maneuvering. I used the dive and a zoom back up, utilizing the tremendous speed I had gained in the dive and the tremendous power of the P.47. The key was altitude. Once a pilot had the altitude advantage he could keep it, diving for a firing pass and then using speed and power to pull back up. As I said, the 47 would climb with them or outclimb them."

Asked about the performance edge he considered most important in a fighter in the Second World War Johnson chose "dive velocity and speed," and added: "I don't believe in sitting in a circle. While you're doing that you might be up against some hot pilot who gets inside you. And he might do that without being able to out-turn you, which some people don't realize. I did that sometimes against 109s and 190s, although they had a better rate of turn. I shot some down like this.

"I couldn't out-turn them but I could slip inside them in a turn. I'd kick the aircraft up and slip it inside them. I spent a lot of time thinking about this maneuver at night and I reasoned that the average pilot, flying with his right hand, usually turns left if faced with a sudden break; it's the more natural movement, the average pilot can go into a left turn quicker because of the more quickly available muscle strength in the right arm in that position. Torque also had something to do with it in some of our aircraft. So when I was behind a German fighter and saw that tell-tale puff of smoke, meaning he had cut back the throttle, I pulled the nose up, slipped to the right with the left wing down, and skidded inside him, often got a shot that way. Others could do it also—so I didn't advise sitting in a circle. In fact, we taught our pilots in the 56th to use the dive and zoom back up to altitude to keep their height advantage, to stay out of circles."

Two years after I had heard how Sam Hamilton out-turned the three F.W.190s near Kiel and had discussed Second World War tactics I again questioned Johnson, in Huntington, New York. On this occasion he recalled the first time he had seen the German jet.

"I think I saw the German Me.262 before I came

home, in June 1944, but I didn't know what I had seen. Intelligence had warned us that we might encounter the jet fighter and had even warned us about the Me.163 rocket fighter. We were coming back from an escort mission, and saw an airfield below. We decided to go down and strafe it and as I was flashing over the field I saw, from the corner of my eye, two or three of them between hangars. I didn't recognize it as any type I was familiar with and it wasn't until I saw one at Wright Field in America long afterward that I realized what I had seen. This field wasn't a trap like the one at Calais, on which the Germans staked out dummy aircraft and surrounded them with flak—and shot down a number of Allied aircraft.

"Intelligence had told us, by the way, to keep our speed down if we encountered and were fighting the 262; it had to keep its speed up, the theory went, thus wouldn't be able to turn with us.[1] As for the Me.163 rocket aircraft, we were told to wait for it, that it would zoom up at a terrific speed but that its flying time was very short and that if we waited it would presently come floating down very slowly. Fortunately, I didn't have to test these prescribed tactics in the air.

"We also encountered various souped-up conventional Luftwaffe fighters. I think we called one of them the Me.209.[2] I've forgotten much of it, but they had high performance and, I believe, could be identified by the slightly different shape of the nose. Generally speaking, I'd say the best 109s and the P.51 were very close in per-

---

[1] If the aircraft Johnson saw were Me.262s, they would have been prototypes or pre-production evaluation models, the first thirteen of which were completed in March and April 1944. The Me.262 went into operation first as a bomber during the Allied invasion of France, which began on 6 June 1944. See William Green, *Famous Fighters of the Second World War*, pp. 117–23.

[2] Baumbach, *The Life and Death of the Luftwaffe*, Chapter 26, recounts the effort to modernize the Me.109, and notes that the Me.209 and Me.309 were technical failures, only a few having been produced.

formance; the difference was probably in the pilot in these combats."

Because Johnson worked in the aircraft industry for many years after the war and remains abreast of military aviation development, continues to fly today, and keeps in touch with U.S. pilots who have seen action in Korea and Vietnam, his appreciation of air combat, aircraft and conditions in the seventies is of interest.

"They're still dogfighting today. It's relative. If two pilots are in comparable aircraft the dogfight is still part of the picture. Speed and turn are still deciding factors, and many other things. Of course, fighters fly much faster today and while I think you could say it's a dogfight, it's very different and it's all relative, as I said."

Were the MiG-21s as good as we read they are? "From what I've been told they're very damn good." I asked about the F.4 Phantom, the U.S. fighter which has seen the most action against MiG-17s and 21s (about which we will learn more in a later chapter). "The F.4s are very good but I've been told by our pilots the MiG-21s are even better, in some ways, in air-to-air combat."

29

THE GREATEST ACE

The most successful fighter pilot in the history of air fighting is Erich Hartmann, who shot down 352 Allied aircraft. Hartmann retired from the new Luftwaffe in 1970 and was the subject that year of a book[1] done by two Americans long his admirers. There is no question about his truly remarkable talent as a fighter pilot, even though the overwhelming number of his aerial victories came against Russian pilots in the East. (He shot down seven American fighters—P.51s—when he got a brief opportunity to do so in Rumania.) His record is remarkable in several respects. He flew some 1,400 missions, but was never wounded and never lost a wingman, though he was shot down and crash-landed on many occasions.

Hartmann developed his own style in fighter combat and though led and taught by some of Germany's greatest pilots he realized relatively early that he should develop his own style according to experience, ability and analysis, tactics which he felt offered the best chance of success and survival. The discriminating reader will note in these tactics similarities to those of other aces in recent chapters— aces who flew in the last part of the Second World War. All recognized the unneccessary hazard of the traditional dogfight. Hartmann was, if one analyzes his tactics, similar in his philosophical approach to Manfred von Richthofen. Both were careful in selecting the opponents and conditions under which they engaged. Both were good shots, though one suspects Hartmann was the better (if any fair

---

[1] Toliver and Constable, *The Blond Knight of Germany.*

comparison can be made), both approached foes as closely as possible and both were usually satisfied with a limited number of victims per mission or day. Most important of all similarities, both were very cool in combat situations—Hartmann so much so that once when captured by the Russians he continually faked injuries until his Russian guards became lax, thinking him badly injured. Then he escaped, jumping from a truck, running into the woods and outdistancing his captors. Calmly hiding by day and travelling at night, he returned safely to the German lines.

Hartmann reached the Russian front at the age of twenty late in 1942 and therefore didn't fly during the comparatively easy years in the East, 1941 and 1942. It was not until the summer of 1943 that he began to demonstrate his unique potential as a fighter pilot. His early missions had been inauspicious; he fled from the enemy in some confusion in his first encounter. Luckily for him and for the Luftwaffe in Russia, he had a patient and understanding leader and teacher, Major Walther Krupinski, who didn't humiliate or berate him for first-combat jitters. From that time onward Hartmann steadily improved and, even among the many highscoring German fighter pilots of the Second World War, he emerged far in the lead of all others in aerial victories—by a 51-kill margin.

What is so different about Hartmann? What were the combat tactics he followed in the air? What set him above all the fighter pilots of the Second World War in the victory column? As a one-time fighter pilot I was for years cuious about the answer to this question and when living in Germany began a personal inquiry by paying Hartmann a visit. I had already spent some time looking into his record and discussing it with Luftwaffe fighter historian Hans Ring and with Adolf Galland, General of the Fighter Arm of the Luftwaffe in the war. So in our meeting I was seeking to discern superior talents, a will, or nature, or whatever, in this remarkable pilot. But it is extremely difficult decades after the war, after Hartmann's ten years in Russian prison, after the mood and times have changed so much, to recognize such a fine edge, or the elusive differences in a great pilot's combat flying years ago. The strongest clue and perhaps part of the answer may be Hartmann's quiet, cool nature, which would exclude anything impetuous. He was unquestionably a remarkable shot and enjoyed excellent vision, and these assets, plus exceptional flying ability, are obvious. His most singular talent might have been a unique ability to size up a situation carefully and coolly in all its dimensions before acting, thus avoiding mistakes.

Hartmann's conception of fighter combat stressed four stages. He believes one of the most vital parts of every aerial encounter is to see the enemy first and to decide how to begin the action or whether to avoid combat. Seeing the enemy first requires not only good eyes but concentration, the best position from which to see and a certain amount of knowledge and intelligence in knowing what to expect, from what direction. It is not always possible to see the enemy first but it is an advantage Hartmann always sought and often utilized.

The next step, deciding whether to attack, is one Hartmann viewed somewhat differently than did many aggressive pilots, some of whom attacked under almost any circumstances. Hartmann was very careful to size up his enemy and aerial conditions and to wait for the right moment to attack, which was usually possible on the Eastern Front. This, more than any other tactical principle, perhaps more than his technique in the firing pass itself, is the most overlooked difference between Hartmann and the majority of fighter pilots.

If he decided to engage, Hartmann followed one of the firing pass patterns which he had concluded offered the maximum chance of success and the minimum chance of being hit, and always attempted to surprise his foe. In good weather he preferred a pass from above, usually from behind. The pass could vary, however, because of the defensive armament of the enemy aircraft. After an early tendency to lower speed in the firing pass, he decided to approach at speed, fire quickly and break away more quickly. He often opened fire at less than one hundred yards, and closer than fifty yards on many occasions.

But he was able to make the longer shot also, leading his target with great accuracy. If his foe was not flying the treetops he would break away quickly, usually by a split-S, and dive several thousand feet. This quickly cleared him from the defensive area of fire and made it all but impossible for the enemy to follow. Pulling out of the dive, he would translate his speed back into altitude, climbing at maximum power, and thus regaining a position for another pass if necessary.

In some cases Hartmann rolled over the wing of the very heavily armored Il.II (Shtolmovik) fighter-bomber and dived down on the other side after a firing pass, to avoid return fire.

If his enemy were on the deck, Hartmann would pull back up for another pass, at speed, turning sharply away after firing to avoid defensive fire.

In cloudy skies he dived for speed when possible but in any event approached fast from below. In winter the top of his 109 was painted white and this made his aircraft much more difficult to detect from above. In general, the Germans paid more attention to painting and camouflage than did some of their adversaries. Hartmann notes[1] that even in the last days of the war American fighters, glistening silver in the sun, announced their arrival time and time again at great distances. In summer German fighters were usually painted a brown-green color on the top and a blue underneath. From above they blended with the landscape and seen from below they blended with the sky.

After a firing pass, Hartmann didn't hurry into a second pass automatically. Instead, he again surveyed the situation before deciding to continue the attack, which he usually did, but only when satisfied that conditions were still favorable and he could make the kind of pass he wanted to.

This pause in combat testifies to Hartmann's careful approach to aerial fighting. It reflects a steadiness and concentration which enabled him to execute flying and gunnery

---

[1] Toliver and Constable, *The Blond Knight of Germany*, p. 172.

patterns in the right conditions with consistent effectiveness.

The most successful ace in history avoided traditional turning and dogfighting. His tactics tended to give him the advantage at all times, whereas a dogfight could become something of a test of turning, aircraft performance and luck—because pilots so engaged were unable to check the surrounding skies and could be surprised by other attacking aircraft.

Hartmann used these offensive tactics from the time he developed them until the end of the war and considers them valid today. They have been used successfully in both Korea and Vietnam. Hartmann was not the only pilot in the Second World War to devise this approach, as we have seen, but he was the most successful in the number of aircraft shot down in following it.

On defense, which Hartmann had to concentrate on more than many would imagine, because the Germans were almost invariably outnumbered in the last years of the war, Hartmann's tactics were uncomplicated but effective. He preferred to turn into the firing pass of an opponent closing him from the rear, after allowing him to get almost within firing range. If the enemy pilot was above him, coming down in a firing pass from one side, Hartmann turned as sharply as he could toward the side from which his foe was approaching, climbing at full power as he did so. To disengage, if he was at a very dangerous disadvantage, he used either that famous tactic of so many German pilots which was already a German ace-in-the-hole in the Battle of Britain and before, the split-S, or another tactic he worked out himself. (German pilots employed the split-S initially because their engines had fuel injection and didn't cut out in rollovers or inverted flying.) Hartmann often preferred to use, in an emergency, the negative-gravity diving turn, which enabled him to shake off a pursuer by requiring him to adopt an unnatural and unusual maneuver few pilots were proficient enough to accomplish. The negative-G dive out of a turn meant pushing the stick forward and applying bottom rudder, so that the fighter began what would appear to be the beginning of an outside loop. Gravity forces, which when turning tightly in a circle pushed the pilot harder and harder into the seat, now pulled the pilot off the seat, only the seat belt keeping him from crashing into the glass above his head. This negative-G escape procedure could be begun from a turn or from more level flight. The pursuing pilot was forced to follow with the same maneuver and it was almost impossible to follow it, hanging upward off one's seat belt, vision impaired, turning and diving. This escape tactic was a major reason why Hartmann was never wounded in the more than 800 combats in his more than 1,400 missions.

In discussions about fighter tactics Hartmann stressed the importance of lead (forward allowance) in gunnery. "You must know how far to lead the target. Coming up from below after a dive, very fast, it's important to learn this lead factor.

"In fighter combat the most important thing is to be high, to have altitude. In gunnery the important thing is to be as close as possible and to close fast, if possible taking your opponent by surprise."

Hartmann is among those who never were dissatisfied with the Me.109 (though post-war statements of other German pilots reveal a conclusion, as early as 1942 and 1943, that the 109 was in some ways technically outmoded). In combat Hartmann flew the Me.109 in the G7, G10, G14, G16 and R4 models.

"The P.51 was faster than the 109 only above 15,000 feet. Below that height the 109 was better. I could get 480 m.p.h. indicated at 12,000 feet from the 109 and I have pulled away from P.51s in the 109. Once there were eight Mustangs behind me, only about a thousand yards—this was during the raids on Plosti—and I left them, in a 109."

Hartmann was posted to an Me.262 unit near the end of the war but was unhappy because the unit flew only periodically. He requested to be posted back to his old squadron in the East; after his return he fought there until the end of the war, claiming his last Russian victim on the last day of combat. (He surrendered to the Americans, who naïvely turned him over to the Russians, who in turn imprisoned him for ten and a half years.) Of his combat achievements, one of which he is quite proud is his record with wingmen.

"In all my combat I never lost a wingman under my leading; a few got ground or air hits. Near the end of the war I almost lost a transferred bomber pilot who left my wing during an air battle with four Yaks. When I realized he was no longer on my wing, I looked for him and found him in a turn with a Yak on his tail. I interrupted my attack on one of the enemy planes to help him and got behind the Russian quickly. But before I could get there I saw hits from the Yak striking the 109 and I immediately called to him to bail out, which he did, and I sent the Yak burning to hell. My bomber pilot friend did a nice descent in nylon and is still alive."

Other than that, Hartmann protected every wingman so well that none was ever shot down, a remarkable feat considering how often German pilots were outnumbered in Russia. "I bailed out twice, once in flying school, and crash-landed fourteen times but was never hit by an enemy fighter in combat. I was hit by flak and hit by bombers," he recalls.

Speaking of the more traditional dogfighting tactics, Hartmann said: "There was not too much dogfighting for us. It requires a large area and is absolutely defensive. We had a speed advantage and, as I have said, I liked to have altitude and come in fast for a firing pass, if possible a surprise pass, and I liked the whole front of my windscreen to be full of the enemy aircraft when I fired. Then I broke away quickly, and could make another pass if I wanted to, from good position again."

Probably because Hartmann is still alive, a modest, even quiet individual, the post-war years have not built him into a legend similar to that of Manfred von Richthofen, killed in 1918 in the First World War. Of course, death plays a part in building nostalgia and a romantic legend. And the years to come are certain to romanticize Hartmann because of his unique record. Worldwide interest, however, has already begun to manifest itself, especially in England and America. Recognition came more slowly, understandably, because of the nature of the regime for which Hartmann fought so brilliantly, the Hitler regime. But, of course, he joined the Luftwaffe as a teenager and could scarcely be held accountable for the political or social crimes of state. Nevertheless, and even though West Germany, England and America are now allies in NATO, there are some who have not forgiven the Germans for their Hitler and I was reminded of that in 1967 when my book, *The Fighter Pilots,* was published in England. (The title in the United States was *The Greatest Aces.*) My publisher and I were hosting a London dinner party in honor of the great aces featured in the book and Erich Hartmann accepted my invitation to come as the representative of the German aces. Also attending were famous R.A.F. aces, the legendary Douglas Bader, R.A.F. top scorer Johnnie Johnson and Ginger Lacey, the hero of the Battle of Britain.

I was informed that some people in England still felt intensely enough about the war not to take too kindly to pictures of the kiss-and-make up type. But it was good that we could all sit together and enjoy dinner with Europe at peace, with all agreed that war is futile.

A year later, when *Die Jagdflieger* was published in Germany, at the party in the Rhine Hotel Dressen, in the room in which Chamberlain met Hitler in 1938, was Hartmann; the wartime commanding General of German fighters, Adolf Galland; the Inspector General of the present Luftwaffe, General Johannes Steinhof, and others. Representing the R.A.F. was Wing Commander Stanford Tuck, one of the greatest of the R.A.F. aces.

Frau Hartmann, who had unknowingly played a role in the fighter history of the Second World War by preserving the letters Hartmann wrote to her every day while he was in Russia, added much to the evening.

The kitchen staff surprised everyone in serving dessert.

On top of each pudding were small flags—German, British and American. I like to think this gesture will prove an accurate symbol of the future, that the flags of these democracies will be together in any future crisis.

Part Five

KOREA: FIRST JET WAR

The German Luftwaffe went down to defeat, overwhelmed in the air and overrun on the ground; three months later Japan surrendered, after two atomic bombs had shown that further fighting offered no hope of victory. The Japanese had produced no jet near the end, and were simply crushed by superior quality and quantity. The closing stages of the war had, however, introduced the jet, and it was clear that the next chapter of air fighting would be written by jets. What wasn't known or expected at that time was that the next chapter was only five years distant and destined to involve U.S.F.80 Shooting Stars and F.86 Sabres and Russian-built MiG-15s and MiG-17s.

Galland had been prophetic when he said in a conference in 1942: ". . . Our development of jets may well start something of which we cannot see the end. Under some circumstances the use of these things can anticipate events and lead to our giving away a weapon before we possess it in a really effective quantity. But I believe we need not be afraid of our own courage—assuming that we go all out. But I have the impression that we are not doing so. . . ."

By April 1944 Galland desperately needed a jet fighter:

"The problem with which the Americans have confronted the fighter arm is—I am speaking solely of daytime— quite simply the problem of superiority in the air. . . . As things are now, it is almost the same thing as command of the air. The ratio between the two sides in day fighting is between 1:6 and 1:8. The enemy's proficiency in action is extraordinarily high and the technical accomplishment of his aircraft is so outstanding that all we can say is—something must be done! In the last four months we have lost

well over a thousand men in the daytime. . . . I have gone
so far as to talk of the danger of a collapse.

"What must we do to change this? The first thing is to
alter the ratio. . . . Second, just because we are numerically inferior, and always will be, technical performance
must be raised. . . . I am absolutely convinced that we can
do wonders with a small number of greatly superior aircraft like the Me.262 or the Me.163. For the fight between the fighters—which in the daytime is the preliminary for going for the bombers—is largely a matter of
morale. We must break the enemy's morale. . . . We need
higher performance to give our fighter force the feeling of
superiority, even when we are much inferior in
numbers. . . . I prefer one Me.262 to five Me.109s."[1]

Airmen on the German side were not the only ones to
appreciate the potentialities of the jet. The British were already flying their Meteors, though not in combat, and Major General Fred Anderson, chief of Operations under
U.S. air commander General Carl Spaatz, was quoted as
having told Supreme Commander Dwight Eisenhower in
February 1945 that unless ground forces occupied Germany by June German jet fighters would make it impossible for the daylight bombing offensive to continue.
Though this might have been over-pessimistic, had 262s
been available to the Luftwaffe in numbers in late 1943
or early 1944, the daylight bombing offensive might have
been checked.

In addition to ushering in the jet age, the Second World
War demonstrated the enormous and growing value of air
power over the battlefront—a trend which began toward
the end of the First World War. Luftwaffe co-operation
helped to produce their *Blitzkrieg* in the opening stages of
the war and by the last year of the war Allied tactical air
power was so overwhelming that it ensured success of landings in France and produced conditions on the fighting
front which resulted in the decisive breakout at Saint-Lô
in August. Assessing the result of the U.S. decision to use
its strategic bombers (as well as mediums and fighter

---

[1] Baumbach, *The Life and Death of the Luftwaffe*, pp. 195, 199.

bombers) tactically, to clear a path for U.S. ground forces, Galland writes:

"... The Allied strategic bombers were only sent into action at particularly important times. Thus on 18 July, 1,600 heavy and 350 medium English and American bombers intervened in the particularly bitter fighting at Saint-Lô. Within a few minutes 7,700 tons of bombs came down on the battlefield. So far this was the heaviest bombing of the war of this type. A few days later von Kluge reported to Hitler the result of a conference of commanders. In the face of such complete air supremacy nothing else could be done except to give up territory. The report ended with these words: 'The psychological effect on the fighting troops, especially on the infantry, caused by the cascades of falling bombs, of the elements, is a factor which gives cause for serious consideration.'

"A week later, on 25 July, the attack was repeated on the same target, but in much greater strength: 1,507 heavy bombers, 38 medium and 559 fighter bombers attacked the position. According to a statement from the commander of the Panzer Training Division, 70 per cent of his troops were either 'dead, wounded or had a nervous breakdown,' and von Rundstedt called the bombing 'the most effective use of air force I have ever witnessed.' "[1]

This was, of course, the decisive battle of France and the decisive breakout, and it is significant to note that Germany used its Me.262 jet for the first time in this struggle, though it was available only in small numbers. Allied fighters, however, ruled the skies to such a degree that the heavies went about their bombing almost unmolested. Had German fighters retained their 1941-2 edge in the skies above France, such uninterrupted bombing would have been impossible. Thus Allied fighters, which had won air supremacy over France, in effect opened the door on the ground to the U.S. Third Army's breakout. The tactical co-operation of U.S. and British fighter bombers in this campaign also far surpassed anything seen in the First World War, the British using Typhoons and

---

[1] Galland, *The First and the Last*, p. 288.

other aircraft with rockets very effectively and the U.S. relying on the sturdy P.47 and other types, some of which also carried rockets. When the Germans launched their desperate counter-attack in the vicinity of Mortain, their last chance to close the gap through which General George Patton's army was pouring, fighter bombers decimated German panzers leading it. The German Seventh Army reported: "The attack failed because of unusually lively activities on the part of enemy fighter-bombers."

The air advantage had also often been decisive in the Pacific. Now, five years after the end of the Second World War, it was to save desperate American and South Korean forces grimly clinging to the Pusan perimeter in southeastern Korea.

When North Korean forces invaded South Korea, in June 1950, Yak fighters attempted to clear the way for their ground forces. U.S. F.80 Shooting Stars soon shot them out of the sky. But the ground retreat had been so rapid that U.S. and South Korean forces in the Pusan perimeter were left with no safe airfields and no communications system—a necessary part of tactical air cooperation. For a time two F.80s were kept over the perimeter at all times, flying from bases in Japan, but because of fuel limitations they had little time over the battle area and were not as effective as the situation demanded.

Then the U.S. Air Force worked out a communications system utilizing small, light planes and jeeps with radios as spotters for the F.80s and F.84 Thunderjets, which were now on the scene, and jeeps which radioed targets to the jets above. Johnnie Johnson, at that time in the area and attached to the U.S. Air Force, writes that the U.S. Army commander at Pusan told him that without the fighters and fighter bombers overhead his troops could not have held the perimeter and would have been driven into the sea.[1]

The pattern of tactical air co-operation in Korea was much the same as in the Second World War. Small, light

---

[1] Johnson, *Full Circle*, p. 264.

planes (called Mosquitoes) or ground parties spotted for strafers, which flew in the same finger-four formations as in the 1939–45 war. Smoke bombs were used to mark enemy positions, either fired from guns on the ground or dropped from Mosquitoes, and then the jets took turns in making runs with bombs, napalm fire bombs, rockets or machine-guns. Napalm proved highly effective for, being a liquid, it ran into trenches and spread over the ground for many yards and could destroy the very effective T-34 tank from as far as fifty or sixty feet.

With predominant air power, American and South Korean forces drove northward under the command of General Douglas MacArthur, recaptured all of South Korea and invaded North Korea, which had launched the attack. By November 1950, five months after the opening of the war, practically all of North Korea had been occupied. In this period U.S. forces had introduced a new form of tactical co-operation, night intruder operations against supply lines. The famous British night-fighter ace, Peter Wykeham, came to lend his skill, teaching flying in mountainous territory at night, and soon this most difficult form of air attack was being pursued over much of North Korea. It was a needed technique because United Nations air forces had been so successful that the enemy moved virtually all his supplies at night.

The first air fighting between jets occurred in November when U.S. F.80s chased a formation of MiG-15s out of North Korean skies and into Manchuria (across the Yalu River). The MiGs fled but once inside Manchuria climbed into the sun, recrossed the river at high altitude and bounced the Shooting Stars. The U.S. pilots escaped, but they learned in this action that the MiG-15s were faster than their F.80s and could outclimb them. The MiGs were flown by Russian pilots, who impressed the Americans and other Allied fliers with their ability. Their tactics were excellent and almost identical to those of Luftwaffe formations in the Second World War. For a time they made things difficult for the F.80s, the British Meteor 8s, and the American B.26s and B.29s. Major General O. P.

Weyland, commanding U.S. air forces, realized he would have to have the F.86, and by December they were flying from a base near Seoul, Kimpo. (The Communist Chinese had meanwhile entered the war and driven Allied ground forces southward.) In their first two weeks of operations the F.86s shot down eight MiG-15s at a cost of only one F.86, even though the Russian pilots enjoyed the advantage of flying close to their bases and were able to escape over the Yalu at any time. U.S. ascendancy over the Russian-built and Russian-flown MiGs then continued for the rest of the war—another three years.

With jets, formations reverted to smaller numbers of aircraft and U.S. F.86 pilots usually fought the enemy in fours or twos. It was found that the F.86 was slightly faster than the MiG-15 below 27,000 feet but above that there was no difference in the two fighters. Because they were flying from Seoul, 200 miles to the south, U.S. pilots had only about twenty minutes over the Yalu (about what German fighter pilots had over England in the Battle of Britain) and only released their drop tanks when the enemy was in sight. The F.86 was equipped with gyroscopic sights (which had been introduced in the Second World War) but because of the great speed and control demands involved in turns at such speed an encounter often produced only one good firing burst. At this time the F.86 was armed with six 50-mm. caliber machine-guns, the same armament as that in the P.51 in the Second World War. The F.86E, which soon arrived, was equipped with a radar computing sight, which was an improvement, though it still mounted six machine-guns. Its more powerful engine made it superior in most categories to the MiG-15. But it was not until the Americans fitted automatic rockets under the wings of their F.86Hs, which homed on the enemy aircraft, that superiority over MiG-17s was most vividly established, by Nationalist Chinese pilots, years later, near Formosa. At the end of the Korean War the scorecard showed about 800 enemy jets destroyed to less than 100 U.S. fighters lost, and a North Korean pilot who defected confirmed these heavy losses, reporting that two Russian units had been completely wiped out in the fighting.[1]

Air fighting tactics in Korea remained basically similar to earlier aerial combat in most respects, though the large fighter formations of the two World Wars gave way to smaller formations and firing at a greater distance became possible with missiles, which appeared at the end. The height of dogfights—which combat was still called—increased. In the beginning engagements were taking place at 30,000 and 35,000 feet but then higher performing aircraft began to meet at 40,000 feet and above as the war continued. Older pilots were, too, one of the characteristics of the Korean War. Most of them were Second World War veterans, not a few with gray hair. They were flying more sophisticated aircraft which could go through the sound barrier. But surpassing the speed of sound in the F.86 in the early fifties was not a routine affair; the plane often became unwieldly and difficult to control.

The pattern of radar control from the ground in the Korean War was similar to that in the Second World War, but improved. The U.S. listening system (the Y system) regularly monitored Russian ground controllers across the Yalu with surprising efficiency. American fighter pilots were told when the enemy was rising from his fields, where the various groups of fighters were and when they might be expected to appear. The enemy usually flew in large formations which were easy to detect. One of the advantages of flights of four F.86s, taking off at five-minute intervals from Kimpo, was that these small formations were more difficult for the Russians to locate with radar. Usually, however, Russian pilots were well informed by ground radar on the whereabouts of U.S. fighters. The Russian pilots were much more closely controlled by their ground controllers, who told them when to enter into combat, where to land when hit in combat, and so on. This also remained true when, later in the war, North Korean and Chinese pilots began to take part in the air combat. The Korean air war was thus more closely controlled from the

[1] Johnson, *Full Circle*, p. 272.

ground than any fighter campaign in history; both sides were very well informed. British fighter pilots were closely controlled and guided to interception in the Battle of Britain a decade earlier but German attackers had little in the way of such an advantage over England.

Contrary to the popular belief, U.S. fighter pilots frequently chased enemy pilots over Manchuria, and often shot them down, even though U.S. policy was officially to limit U.S. aircraft to the southern side of the Yalu. On some occasions U.S. fighters in units of four entered Manchuria from offshore (to avoid detection by radar) and thus were on the northern side of the Yalu at great height and undetected—in a perfect position to bounce unsuspecting Russian pilots preparing to fly southward to the Yalu. These forays were exceptions to the rule but they occurred repeatedly and were winked at by the Air Force high command, which was understandably in sympathy with the U.S. pilot who, in a life-or-death engagement with a Russian, finally gained the advantage only to see his foe dash across the river in an attempt to get "home free."

The Russians used the Korean War as a training school for their pilots. For a time U.S. pilots didn't understand why some Russian formations stayed on the northern side of the Yalu, others came down for a look at U.S. fighters but didn't engage, and other formations came down and attacked. The answer seems to have been that formations which stayed north of the river were new squadrons which had just arrived, whose pilots were getting acquainted with the area (whole squadrons were rotated from Russian fields to Manchuria), that those formations which came down and flew close to the Sabres were getting their orientation look and that only after that were they allowed to engage the F.86s.

The encouraging thing about air-to-air combat in Korea was the one-sided ratio of success enjoyed by the Americans. It indicated that Russian pilots at that time at least were no match for U.S. pilots, just as they were not, generally speaking, a match for German pilots in the Second World War. With excellent aircraft and excellent radar control from the ground Russian pilots (and North Koreans and Chinese) were shot down at a ratio of between 10 to 1 and 14 to 1. This is a striking defeat however it is measured, even after allowing for over-optimistic claims (which all sides tend to make in all wars) on the American side.

Tactical air support for ground operations, as we have seen, was once again demonstrated to be decisive in Korea. It should be remembered, of course, in concluding this brief analysis of the air war there, that U.S. strafers and fighter bombers encountered little enemy opposition over the battlefield.

Tactical cooperation in the form of vastly increased troop mobility, through the use of helicopters, was a new dimension added to air power's potential in Korea. This new form of air support was singularly successful largely because U.S. fighters controlled the skies; we should remember that, had not this been true, enemy fighters could have destroyed many helicopters. Fighters, then, were again often the key to success on the ground.

31

DEATH OF A MIG-15

The American fighter pilot who shot down the greatest number of enemy aircraft in Europe in the Second World War was Frank Gabreski, with 31 aerial victories. Gabreski was still in the U.S. Air Force when the Communists attacked in Korea and was not long in appearing on the Korean scene. The pilot who had helped make 56th Fighter Group in Europe famous was to become one of thirty-nine Americans to shoot down five enemy jets in Korea. Gabreski had received confirmation for downing 6½ MiG-15s by the time orders rotated him back to the United States and thus ended his combat career with 37½ aerial victories (he retired from the Air Force in 1970). He had brought down his first jet in July 1951 at the age of thirty-two, once considered elderly for fighter pilots. But Gabreski was younger than many other U.S. veterans taking on the MiGs in Korea. Lieutenant Colonel Vermont Garrison, for instance, who shot down 10, after having shot down 11 enemy aircraft in the Second World War, was thirty-six. The second highest scorer in Korea was, like Gabreski, a Second World War veteran. Captain James Jabara had 15 confirmed victories to add to 3½ in the 1939–45 war. A full third of the aces of the Korean War had, in fact, scored victories in the Second World War. One pilot, Colonel Harrison Thyng, had scored in both the Pacific and Europe in the Second World War. He is the only known American pilot to have brought down German, Japanese and Russian (and perhaps Chinese or Korean) pilots in less than fifteen years. The top-scoring American ace of the war, Captain Joseph McConnel, Jr. with 16 kills, was twenty-eight.

252

Whereas the 1941–5 fighter war in Asia had been fought by both land- and carrier-based pilots, the Korean fighter war was primarily a U.S.A.F. show. Of the thirty-nine pilots with five or more aerial kills, all but one—he was Marine Major John Bolt—were Air Force pilots.

Gabreski, as the highest-ranking living American ace, who had fought in both wars, is obviously uniquely qualified to discuss differences in tactics and strategy between the two wars. "One lesson in Korea was that four-fighter units were large enough. The first element (two aircraft) flew ahead and below, about a thousand feet below, and the wingman, who was two or three hundred feet back and to one side, watched the rear. He seldom fired unless he was told to do so or found himself left alone by some unusual circumstance. The number-two man in the flight (the flight leader's wingman) was generally the least experienced of the four; number three, the element leader, the next most experienced of course. Flying from South Korea northward, our flights spread out at the bomb line (the front) and later went into what we called the fluid-four formation. This was further above and behind than the old finger-four. In turns in jets, we had to make all of them gently, and we had to descend to keep our speed.

"Fuel was always a consideration in Korea—we were often flying 200 miles north to meet the enemy. 'Bingo' was the call sign that meant one was going home at maximum altitude, where fuel consumption is less, and in some cases pilots would climb up and flame-out and restart to save fuel. Sometimes there were two or three in the flame-out pattern.

"I sought great height over the Yalu, where they couldn't catch or surprise me. The MiG-15s at this stage of the war could outclimb us. We could dive away from them but they left us climbing. We had about the same speed straight and level but they could out-turn us, so there wasn't as much of what you'd call the traditional turning as there might have been had we been able to out-turn them. We would stall trying to stay with them in a turn.

"We usually went straight up and down the Yalu,

slightly on the south side, at about 40,000 feet. We were not far from their fighter base at Antung, on the west coast.

"The F.86 was the first fighter in which the pilot had no feel of the aircraft. It was one of the first generation of aircraft in which the stick merely controls a valve, which power-operates the controls. In 1951, when I arrived there, we were flying to learn jet tactics as much as anything else. We were still using six 50-mm. caliber machine-guns, for example, and then they did new gun evaluation tests, with the 60-mm. and 20-mm. caliber and eventually put four 20-calibers in the Sabres.

"We had eight channels on our radios—two were tactical channels, one for the control tower, one for emergency, two GCA channels (ground radar control), one for the initial controller and one for the final controller, others for various situations.

"We flew out of a field at Suwan, two miles outside the ancient, dirty city. It was a former Japanese airdrome with a black asphalt runway. At night 'Moscow Molly' would come over and drop a few bombs to keep us awake. We lived in tents, and about thirty-five to forty miles north of us—pretty country—there was much hard fighting."

Gabreski described what a Korean fighter mission was like, one in which he had engaged the enemy.

"On my fifth mission I got my first MiG. We were on a top-cover assignment for the F.84s, which were to strafe airfields in the area of Pyongyang [the North Korean capital] and any rolling traffic they could find. We were up early that morning, checked the orders at the wing Operations Center, then went to briefing. About thirty-two Sabres were going up. I was leading the first four. The Director of Operations read the order and gave general details of the mission and outlined the route. There was a map on the blackboard and we got the altitudes, course and other details and shortly after that went out to our aircraft.

"We took off on a direct vector, climbing into the north. It was only 140 miles and, before we were half way, our radar network informed us bandits were heading down from the Yalu. We spread out more and kept climbing, and were now over 30,000 feet. It was a perfectly clear day with no clouds but we didn't see the fighter bombers. It was only twenty-five minutes to the target and as we moved into the area my wingman spotted contrails in the sky ahead and called me over the radio. There were seven or eight contrails at eleven o'clock, much higher than we were. I transmitted: 'Eagle Leader here. Bandits eleven o'clock high. Advance throttles. We'll climb to contrail level and level-off just underneath.' The contrails were far away up north. I didn't think these were the aircraft our radar had warned us about, but I warned the others to keep them in sight while we made a 360-degree climbing circle over Pyongyang. We reached 35,000 feet and levelled off and continued to circle.

"At that moment, we saw directly beneath us, at about 10,000 feet, twelve MiGs flying south, in abreast formation. We were flying north. I immediately increased our right bank to come down on them from behind but by the time we completed the turn they were almost out of sight—that's the thing about jets. We were closing, when I spotted them, at about a thousand miles an hour! I told the guys to keep their eyes on the other contrails up north and we flew back and forth over Pyongyang. We did this until it was almost time to go home. Then we saw a lone MiG heading north below us—at 10,000 feet.

"We were flying west and I positioned the flight by a quick ninety-degree turn to come down from behind him. We went after him as fast as we could but by the time we were on his course, coming from behind, he was a good six miles ahead of us. I had the throttle wide open with a maximum Mach of .91. He was probably doing about .85 and we closed in on him slowly. By the time I had dived down almost to his level, behind, he was only two miles ahead, but still out of range. I kept on descending until I was about five hundred feet below—in his blind spot. I wanted to overtake him before arriving at minimum fuel for return but the stern chase seemed like an hour. It was probably only minutes. Finally I was in good position, some 1,000 feet behind.

"He was on a steady course, and his MiG was painted red at the nose and had a red rudder. Otherwise, it was a dirty aluminum gray. I had two Sabres on the left and one on the right and we had closed our formation a bit. It was time to pull up the nose and line him up in my sight from below. When the sight was squarely on his mid-section I fired a short burst of armor-piercing and incendiary from the six fifties. I could see strikes all over the lower section of the fuselage. I kept firing for a couple of seconds and was now directly astern, about 600 feet back. I centered the sight on his tailpipe next and gave him another burst. I saw strikes again, around the engine as well as the wings. Now he went into a slight dive and smoke began to streak back from the tailpipe.

"I passed over him and broke off to the right and he started down and I kept him in view. He was losing altitude but, much to my amazement, was still under control. I decided to make another pass from above right; my three Sabres were now strung out behind me. There was gray smoke from the MiG; he had decelerated. In a matter of seconds I closed for another pass, coming in from astern. I got very close and gave him a good, long burst. This time pieces of his aircraft began to fly off. They might have been turbine blades from the engine, and they passed me on the right. The canopy flew off. Then the pilot ejected. His parachute opened. We turned on course for home.

"I remember one of the guys calling in congratulations but also needling me: 'Good shooting, Colonel, but he was a sitting duck.' I answered: 'I like mine easy.' We set course, about 140 or 150 degrees for home and in twenty to twenty-five minutes were back at the base. I called the tower and got landing instructions and we went in. I touched down at about 130, turned off the runway and taxied up to the revetment and my crew chief saw smoke on the gunports and knew I had fired the guns. He immediately asked, 'Have any luck?' and I was glad to be able to say, 'This was one of my better days. One MiG destroyed.'

"I was surprised to see how hard it was to bring down a jet, how much damage he absorbed before he finally went down. Later, of course, we got the bigger guns in the Sabres ... these were fifty-caliber shells. It took a lot of them to bring one down."

The Gabreski mission illustrates the differences in air combat between jets and piston-engined fighters of the Second World War. The speed of closure had become so rapid that a major opportunity (when twelve MiGs flew under the American fighters) was missed because the two groups happened to be flying opposite directions. Had the F.86s been flying south or even southeast or southwest, they could have bounced the enemy. But while they were making a 180-degree turn, the MiGs had had time to escape!

The considerable amount of firing required to bring down the enemy MiG illustrates the toughness of the jet fighter. Contrary to some early reports from Korea, pilots much preferred jets to propeller aircraft on strafing missions because the jets, having fewer moving parts, were harder to shoot down from the ground. They were also harder to shoot down in the air. The Gabreski mission was flown on 8 July 1951, relatively early in the Korean air war. Cannon, rockets and missiles were soon to replace the fifty-caliber machine-guns he used that day to score his first aerial victory.

This mission also illustrates a strict limitation placed on today's fighters by the enormous fuel consumption of the jet engine. Missions lasted perhaps two hours. At full power all fuel could be consumed in an hour and twenty minutes, or less. Though Pyongyang was only 140 miles from Gabreski's base, he could patrol only a limited time over the target, and when he dived after the MiG heading north, the question in his mind was whether he would have enough fuel to complete the chase and shoot his adversary down.

This jet fuel consideration represents quite a change from that faced by P.51 pilots in the Second World War, who could fly seven or eight hours. And while the flying time of jet fighters and fighter bombers has been somewhat increased, it is still (in Vietnam) a major limiting factor in the operation of fighters, especially in areas where they can't refuel in the air—as we are to see in the next two chapters, which deal with the strange air war over Vietnam.

Part Six

VIETNAM: NEW MISSILES AND METHODS

32

SOPHISTICATED AIR WAR

The most recent sustained air combat by fighters took place in southeast Asia, where the United States mounted a major air assault against North Vietnamese and other forces in several countries for many years. After regular bombing attacks on North Vietnam were halted in 1968, air activity nevertheless continued on a major scale. But clashes between fighters became a thing of the past, generally speaking, for they had occurred over North Vietnam.

The lessons learned in the air in the Vietnamese war have been many, and the cost high. U.S. fighter pilots entered the war with the hope that they might duplicate somewhat the severe defeat inflicted on Russian and other fighter pilots in Korean and Chinese skies in the fifties. But in the Vietnam war they were not destined to achieve such results. In fact, in the air fighting between F.4s and F.105s and MiG-17s and MiG-21s over North Vietnam in the autumn of 1967 and 1968 (up to the bombing halt) they probably lost more planes than they shot down. This is a decided departure from the trend in Korea and the earlier trend in Vietnam and carries with it considerable significance in the developing history of air combat.

To understand the fighter war in Vietnam one must understand what U.S. fighters were asked to do, and the conditions, limitations and obstacles facing them in carrying out that task. It should be understood that in south-east Asia there were two wars—the in-country war and the out-country war. The in-country war involved South Vietnam. There, as in Korea, the Communists maintained the claim that the struggle was purely a revolutionary one among the South Vietnamese; therefore MiG-17s and 21s didn't operate in South Vietnamese skies. The U.S. Air Force, of course, operated in South Vietnam primarily against ground targets and in a support role. Fighter combat seldom occurred.

The out-country war was another matter. The U.S. Air Force mounted a major and sustained offensive campaign against North Vietnam over a period of years, a campaign built primarily around fighters. The F.105 was employed as a fighter bomber in these attacks and was often protected by F.4s higher up, acting as top cover (called MiG Cap in this war). In this campaign the 105s flew from two bases in Thailand, Taklai in the south and Khorat in the north. The F.4s—with their shorter range—flew from two other Thai bases nearer the Laotian border (all had to cross Laos on every strike at North Vietnam), Ubon in the southeast and Udorn in the north. In addition to these four fighter wings the early model F.102 delta-wing fighter was also employed in Thailand, based in Bangkok.

The war these fighters and other aircraft waged against North Vietnam was a bitter struggle that became more and more demanding, and costly, as time went on. The F.105s and F.4s were frequently jumped by MiG-17s and MiG-21s when over North Vietnam and it was not long before U.S. pilots knew that neither American fighter was a match for the MiG-21 in the traditional dogfight. The MiGs, lighter and built as interceptors, could easily outturn the heavier U.S. fighters and were quicker in accelerating—a factor of great importance in combat between jets, which seldom fly at maximum speed because of the enormous amount of fuel consumed. (In tests conducted by Israel, after Israeli forces had captured an Egyptian MiG-21, it was found that the MiG was far more maneuverable and could accelerate faster. The F.4, used in the Israeli Air Force, was thought to have a slight edge in speed, though this is doubted by some pilots.)

U.S. fighters encountered steadily improving ground defenses as the North Vietnam air offensive campaign continued, ground defenses which accounted for many of the planes and pilots lost. In the last year of these operations, when losses to MiGs increased, so too did losses to the ground defenses' 37-mm., and 57-mm., and 85-mm. guns and Sam missiles. The U.S. fighter effort suffered in these months for several reasons: the enemy's air defense capability improved greatly; American fighters employed less aggressive tactics in late 1967 and 1968; the MiG-21 proved superior in dogfighting; and enemy pilots were improving in ability. There were other reasons, but these seem to have constituted the four primary ones. The greatest cause of losses, of course, was the nature of the campaign American pilots had to wage.

Among the handicaps—probably more numerous than those facing any fighter force other than the Luftwaffe in the Second World War in a sustained campaign—were the numerous restrictions limiting their freedom to hit the enemy where it would have been effective. There were hundreds of what were called rules of engagement. For example, targets more than a certain distance off main highways could not be attacked in many areas, some North Vietnamese airfields could not be attacked, ships longer than a certain length could not be attacked, all targets in certain areas could not be attacked, and, of course, enemy fighters escaping into Chinese skies could not be pursued over China. Though rules such as that against entering Chinese air space could be understood, others were harder to accept by pilots risking their lives daily in the campaign. The total effect of the rules was that the enemy could not be incapacitated on the ground to the extent that otherwise would have been possible. He also enjoyed the very important advantage of knowing over a long period where the U.S. strike force was coming from; he could detect the exact position of approaching aircraft very early with his excellent radar monitoring system. Thus the attacking force was regularly assaulting long and carefully prepared gun and missile positions and excellent fighters which had ample warning of their approach. That the attack was constantly sustained in the face of what was almost certainly the most concentrated array of sophisticated defenses in history is a tribute to the U.S. Air Force and the morale and talents of U.S. pilots and airmen. And just as in Korea, U.S. pilots were up against

Russian pilots and Russian-operated ground defenses in the campaign.

The sophisticated nature of the defenses resulted in a partial reversal in the trend—seen in the Korean war—toward smaller and smaller fighter formations. It will be recalled that by the end of that war fighters were taking off from bases near Seoul in fours every five minutes or so, approaching the Yalu in these smaller formations as a means of making radar detection more difficult for the enemy and keeping a patrol over the border area for as long as possible with the number of fighters available. In the Vietnam war radar detection and radar and electronic missile defenses became so effective, that U.S. fighters were forced to employ special jamming and other counter measures, and it was found that larger formations of aircraft, each with a suppression device (called Pod), more effectively countered the enemy's defenses; thus four-aircraft strikes, an accepted technique at the beginning of the war, were replaced by larger formations, some of the aircraft primarily engaged in the task of disrupting the enemy defenses. (The four-aircraft flight had in the opening phases of the war approached targets on the deck, zooming up just before hitting them; this tactic had succeeded. As the enemy's ground defense improved, losses increased until on some occasions three out of the four attacking fighter bombers were shot down.)

The Vietnam war produced such a degree of sophistication in defense that losses, always of course partly the result of chance, sometimes became more a matter of technical luck than previously. The aircraft upon which a Sam missile homed could be any in the formation. While pilots could usually dodge the Sams if they saw them coming and timed evasive tactics just right, those not seen could not be avoided. In this connection, it should be remembered that while North Vietnam is a rather large area, the enemy knew where U.S. aircraft could and could not bomb, and therefore defenses were concentrated in the vulnerable areas; this concentration and limitation of U.S. targets greatly facilitated the creation of an effective defense.

The biggest air-power lesson of the Vietnam war was that the aerial-combat fighter is still a must in a major, sustained campaign. The U.S. Air Force was fortunate that the Navy-developed Phantom (the F.4) was available and proved to be a generally satisfactory air-to-air fighter (though originally conceived as a fighter bomber by the Navy) because the Pentagon had in large part succumbed in the post-Korean War years (until about 1963) to the theory that air-to-air fighters would not again be needed or used in warfare. Although this same malady has infected peacetime planners and theorists ever since 1918, as fighters are written off as obsolete after every war, the Vietnam war proved quickly, yet again, that air-to-air fighters are still the decisive factor in air operations.

The main reason why MiG-17s and 21s were superior in aerial combat was that they had been designed for the traditional role of fighters in air war, as interceptors and air-to-air fighters. The U.S. Air Force entered the Vietnam war without a fighter designed primarily as an air superiority weapon. The Air Force, it should be mentioned, didn't deploy its highly sophisticated F.106s in Vietnam, but the F.111 was given a trial. After three of the very few introduced in the theater had crashed, they were unceremoniously withdrawn from operations. Thus these two jets have not had a full test over any length of time in combat. Neither, of course, is an air-to-air fighter. (There are currently greater hopes for the F.14 and F.15.)

The U.S. Navy used the F.4 and the F.8 and the slower special-purpose A-4 and A-7, and the Marines used the F.4 and the excellent radar-systemed A-6. The U.S. Air Force used the F.104 earlier and still other aircraft in the in-country war, their former mainstay the F.100, the F.4, the F.5, the A-1 and the A-37; the A-37 (a fine close-in support weapon which could carry as much ordinance as the F.100) and the F.5 were largely turned over to the South Vietnam Air Force.

The failure of the F.111, in effect, meant failure in an effort to introduce night fighter-bomber operations which could be sustained without unacceptable losses. The F.105 had been used as a night raider (Ryan's Raiders were

F.105 men)—F.105 models with a second pilot in the rear operating radar and F.4s also did much night bombing early in the war but losses became unacceptable. The F.111, it had been thought, would prove vastly superior in night operations. The first crashed just north of the demilitarized zone on a mission into North Vietnam. The theory is that it flew into the ground. A second is thought to have gone down in the mountains of Thailand but its disappearance is something of a mystery. The third experienced a control problem, and its two occupants ejected and survived—in the F.111 the pilots sit side-by-side. The highly sophisticated systems which their designers confidently expected to enable U.S. pilots to achieve impressive results at night didn't perform up to expectations. The future of fighter bombers equipped with all sorts of special terrain avoidance systems for night operations thus remains a question. (A B.57, of twenty converted into special night-time intruders, was shot down over Laos in December 1970; it is too early to assess this aircraft's performance.)

The F.105 fighter bomber, however, was a marvellously successful aircraft in a role which had been that of bombers in the Second World War, and could also shed that role and become a very fast low-level fighter. (Many of today's fighter bombers are heavier than Second World War heavy bombers.) The F.105, though capable of carrying more than 6,000 pounds of bombs, plus other arms and equipment, also shot down its share of MiG-17s and 21s over North Vietnam, one F.105 pilot (Dave Waldrop) having brought down two in less than a minute. It had the range the F.4 lacked and was faster at low altitudes. But it was not designed as an air-to-air fighter; its wing loading was designed for clean speed at the low level a fighter bomber flies, not for turns or dogfighting. It had excellent acceleration, and when F.105 pilots were jumped by MiGs, and saw them in time, they could clear off external encumbrances and plug in the afterburner and pull away from both the MiG-17 and the MiG-21. Therefore, the reason why U.S. pilots did not have an interceptor or air-combat fighter superior to the MiG-21 in Vietnam was not that all U.S. aircraft were inferior; it was because an air-combat fighter interceptor had not been designed, ordered and built in the years preceding the war.

The fortuitous F.4 flew top cover for the F.105s, keeping their losses down, and enabling them and other aircraft to push attacks home. But it should be remembered that very few MiG-17s and MiG-21s were deployed against the U.S. air offensive. That offensive, moreover, was largely a fighter-bomber offensive, (the B.52s were seldom risked in this area) of low-level bombing, and in such attacks ground fire inflicted most of the loss on the attacking force. Had the U.S. Air Force mounted a heavy high-level bombing attack against northern North Vietnam, and had the enemy countered with massive numbers of MiG-21 fighters, it would only then have become clear whether U.S. escorts could have thwarted enemy interceptors. The answer to this question would have largely determined the fate of the heavy bomber effort.

The course of the fighter war which developed from about September 1967 and continued until the end of air combat over North Vietnam in 1968, indicates that it was wise not to employ the giant B.52s over North Vietnam. The interceptors that the enemy employed developed the tactic which Erich Hartmann, John C. Meyer and many others used so successfully in the Second World War. They sought superior altitude and bounced the F.4s or F.105s at supersonic speed. Since on these missions U.S. fighters were not flying constantly at supersonic speed (fuel was a major consideration and tankers accompanied every strike force), when they were bounced they could seldom accelerate quickly enough to catch their adversary. Usually fighter actions in the air-to-air category consisted of one fast pass (Phantom pilots sought to catch MiGs in the same type of pass). The attacker fired his missile or missiles and got out of the enemy's range quickly, either regaining altitude or diving away with greater speed. The MiGs often made a diving pass on F.4 formations on their way down to the F.105s.

The Sidewinder missile, which had proved so effective for U.S. and Chinese Nationalist F.86 pilots in the mid-fifties, again proved a dependable weapon in the Vietnam war, and there was also the radar-guided Sparrow and two types of Falcon missiles, one radar-guided and one heat-seeking. The F.105 carried the 20-mm. Vulcan cannon in its nose, and the F.4E, which arrived after the bombing halt, added it. Ironically, the MiGs were armed with almost exact copies of the 5-inch rocket-fired Sidewinder, and they were also effective.

Both sides in this war, just as in Korea, had excellent radar detection. U.S. and enemy formation leaders were usually informed of the presence of opposing formations, their approximate strength and the direction and altitude they were flying. In addition to radar there was electronic gear for countering enemy radar-aimed missiles and other electronic devices. The special U.S. Shrike missile homed on radar antennaes. Four-engined aircraft accompanied every strike force from the south—loaded with secret devices to counter the enemy's most sophisticated weapons. In addition, U.S. strike forces carried with them a special flight of flak-suppression fighter bombers and, usually, eight Iron Hand F.105s to suppress the Sam missiles. There were also aircraft to jam the enemy's radar and radio, special rescue aircraft (including helicopters) and a reconnaissance aircraft, and in addition to all this, many of the fighter bombers were equipped with the Pod device to interfere with the enemy's automatic radar aiming. And for each four fighter bombers flying from Thailand there were several huge jet tankers, one or more over Thailand and Laos and another, often, over the Gulf of Tonkin—protected by the U.S. Navy.

Thus, in the fifty-odd years from 1914 to the Vietnam war, air fighting has come a long way from the day of sportsmen pilots passing each other in opposite directions in flimsy machines, unable to take offensive action. Today's fighters and fighter bombers are supersonic aircraft with rocket-fired, automatic-aiming missiles; air-to-air combat is largely one fast pass from above, but this of course was a trend evident as early as 1917 and 1918. Jet fighters have merely confirmed and refined that tactic. Basic principles remain the same and there are still long chases and many in-combat tests of flying and shooting skill, and judgment.

Captain Jacob Shuler of the U.S.A.F. was an outstanding F.105 fighter-bomber pilot in Thailand (the out-country war) flying from Khorat, and his words paint a good picture of what a typical strike on a North Vietnam target toward the end of the air war was like:

"We flew in sixteen-ship squadrons. Each day there were two strikes planned, one in the morning and one in the afternoon. We always had several targets; invariably the primary target was in the Hanoi area. The weather determined where we went. We might break up and hit targets in Laos if the weather—reports came to us from a satellite—wasn't right over North Vietnam. Saigon would call in the mission. We could go over either the water or the land route—refuel over Thailand or from over the Gulf of Tonkin. The tankers went as far north as they could. We had fine radar control over Thailand and Laos; we could rendezvous with them with amazing accuracy. Our C.121 airborne radar also gave us many timely warnings. Over the Gulf of Tonkin the Navy possessed a very good intercept capability and monitored us very accurately when we were over the sea.

"A typical strike force would be made up of sixteen F.105s, four of them for flak suppression each carrying six CBUs [cluster bomb units] and the other twelve carrying either six 750-pound bombs or two 3,000-pound bombs. There would also be eight Iron Hand F.105s, eight F.4s above for the MiG Cap—which went in before the strike force and left after it, one tanker for each four F.105s both going and coming, or eight for each sixteen F.105s, two EB.66s for jamming, two EC.121s for radar surveillance and MiG warnings, one C.135 Sneaky Pete carrying secret electronic equipment, two SAR (Sea–Air Rescue) forces consisting of one C.130, four piston-engine A.1s, two HH.53 helicopters and one reconnaissance RF.4. Some of the F.105s were also carrying Shrikes.

"We generally stayed in formation to blank out enemy radar but some of us staying in formation also got shot down—by MiGs. Staying in formation was protection against Sam missiles but Russians were manning the enemy GCI network and flying the MiGs and they shot down many of us. Our releases didn't always tell how many they shot down.

"I flew some missions before Robin Olds returned to the States. When he left, the quality of the top cover we got deteriorated. He did the job. The pilots who flew with him swore by him and though he was called on the carpet for breaking some of the rules there was no doubt that he gave us good top cover." (General Robin Olds commanded the F.4 wing at Ubon—more will be heard about him in the next chapter.)

"We would make only one pass when we hit a target. The idea was to get in and out as fast as we could. We faced a problem of MiG interception about five to ten minutes before we reached the target. About a minute before there was the danger of Sam missiles. But the Pods and Iron Hand were good at whipping the Sams and so they sometimes fired twenty or thirty at us, with proximity fuses. We jammed their tracking and also the return signal from the Sam in flight.

"We usually approached target at about 15,000 feet and in the last thirty seconds before the roll-in started getting 85-mm. fire. They always had our altitude just right—one could see the flak barrage open and it would be just the right height. We'd cut in afterburners and climb maybe a thousand feet and then the leader would call the roll-in and down we would go for the target and usually we would hit it about eight abreast, going down the chute that way after reversing positions in the roll over. The suppression flight and lead flight would go in first and then the last two flights and by this time the 37s and 57s would be sending up a heavy barrage. We released at about 8,000 or 9,000 feet; we couldn't release above 550 knots indicated. And as soon as we dropped our bombs we cut in the afterburner and jinked and climbed and got out of the area as soon as we could; we spread out for protection against MiG bounces going out. Sometimes we lost four or five on one strike; sometimes no one was lost.

"On one mission to Hanoi I recall we lost six 105s and F.4s to Sams and because defenses were that good we didn't risk the big bombers in this area. SAC (Strategic Air Command) had a different war—the Laotian war. And the B.52s, with their saturation bombing, saved Kaesong—also the fighter strikes. The area around Kaesong where the enemy was trying to encroach on the surrounded base looked like the moon after they pulled back. The C.130s and C.123s also hauled in the supplies to maintain the base and shared in the victory."

Shuler's mention of Kaesong reflects a fighter pilot's appreciation of the tactical potential of strategic bombers. The plastering B.52s gave enemy forces attempting to strangle Kaesong was a Vietnam war example of the application of strategic bomber power in a tactical campaign. The nature of the war offered few opportunities for such applications, but this was one in the tradition of that at Saint-Lô in August 1944.

"Before the fall of 1967," Shuler concluded, "I think we shot down more enemy planes than we lost—most of tem with Sidewinders. They key was aggressive tactics. When the F.4s were aggressive they shot down more than they lost."

Aggressiveness, of course, has always been a fundamental rule in the use of fighters on escort or top-cover duty. The same lesson was learned in the Second World War. One of those who learned it at an early date in that war, and who also fought as a fighter pilot more than twenty years later in Vietnam, is the fighter leader with whom we are concerned in the next chapter.

33

F.105 STRIKE AND F.4S AGAINST MIG-21S

If there was a fighter pilot who emerged from the Vietnam
air war with the leadership image and color of the great
aces of the World Wars, he was Robin Olds. As this book
is written he is General Olds, Commandant of Cadets at
the Air Force Academy. He has co-operated in expressing
for this study his views on fighter tactics and strategy and
their use in air combat in southeast Asia. He is singularly
qualified to discuss the development of aerial combat because he was also a leading ace of the Second World War
and a keen student of tactics, tactics which in 1944 and
1945 led to the destruction of many Luftwaffe fighters,
which he attacked forming up or on the ground, as well as
in combat. He was popular as the 434th Squadron Leader
in the 479th Group in the Second World War, and as well
liked in 1966 and 1967, as commanding officer of the 8th
Wing at Ubon, in Thailand. In Asia he led very much
younger fighter pilots (after he had learned the demands
and conditions of the new war flying in position sixteen,
last in the squadron) and shot down more MiGs than any
of them. Most important of all, he taught them the aggressive spirit that is the soul of high-scoring fighter
squadrons.

In the traditional fighter-pilot image, a good image, he
had his crew chiefs paint red stars on the F.4s which
achieved victories, as was done in two World Wars and in
Korea; encouraged celebrations when a pilot did well; and
took other actions to see to it that his pilots' spirits remained high. He believes such personal leadership and aggressiveness is important in the molding of a spirited, ad-
venturous fighter wing. If there are those who frown on

such *esprit de corps,* the history of air fighting strongly indicates it is a necessary ingredient in inspiring men to fly and fight daily for their lives. Luckily in the Korean and Vietnam wars the United States Air Force still counted among its pilots professionals who appreciated the value of such leadership and spirit. In Korea the young pilots learned this tradition from them. In Vietnam the young learn it from both Korean and Second World War pros.

I asked him to look back for the moment to the Second World War to analyze the role of fighters in that conflict.

"I look back on the P.51 as the greatest airplane of the war, and that includes Spitfires, Tempests, Typhoons, the Me.109 and the F.W.190, because it was a true fighter, which could turn and perform and carried six guns and, of equal importance, it has range, which meant the Eighth Air Force could carry the war into the heart of Germany. When the enemy chose not to engage, we could shoot up transportation, trains, trucks, barges and so on, and here was a case when the enemy had to cope with something new, these fighters ranging all over Germany. The Strategic Bombing Survey shows we bombed the hell out of Germany and yet in February and March of 1945 German industry was producing more aircraft than ever before, though about to run out of oil. But the P.51 had an overwhelming impact on the ability of Germany to continue the war, in the field of transportation, training and other essential areas.

"As for fighter tactics, I speak of air fighting as maneuvering. I think of tactics as the way you use your fighters.[1] For example, in World War Two however many fighters the Germans had, the only thing they could use them for was to attack the heavy bombers. The answer was obviously to catch them before they got to the bombers. The question of our tactics was how to use our fighters, our capability as a force, against the enemy. The main thing was to find the enemy fighters before they hit the bombers. If you do that, you're successful even if you don't shoot any down, because you break them up. I also

---

[1] Sometimes also viewed as strategy.

think of tactics as sizing up the total situation you encounter in the air, and how you defeat the enemy's plan.

"Our idea in World War Two was to protect the bombers. For a long time we had to sit there and watch contrails and wait for the enemy fighters to attack. I proposed to the Group Commander (in those days what are today called Wings were Groups) that one squadron adopt different tactics because ours were ridiculous. Soon one squadron would strictly carry out the orders, one would give support ranging out twenty or thirty miles, trying to interpose themselves between the bombers and enemy fighters, and one was an outlaw squadron roaming all over. Once we knew where the bombers were going, it was relatively simple to determine where the enemy fighters would assemble. This takes time. We knew where their fields were and could pretty well determine from which they would probably take off and where they would try to strike the bombers.

"The outlaw squadron would take off earlier than the others and roam all the way to Berlin and then back to Magdeburg. If we found sixty we attacked them with twenty. We spread out wide and could cover a lot of territory. Once a fight started, it worked down quickly to fours and twos. I don't think it should ever break down below two. When you begin to go around and around, that's maneuvering and relates to individual skills. The key is what you can see, retain, anticipate, estimate in a three-dimensional movement of many aircraft. Can you look at an enemy aircraft and know the odds—to get to him before someone else . . . if he can get behind you first, and so on? It's a three-dimension impression; you must get it in seconds. This is essential in aerial combat. The guy you don't see will kill you. You must act instantly, anticipate the other fellow's motives, know that when you do this, he must do one of several things. If you're good at gunnery you flail away, but you must remember where the others are and if you've goofed up on your estimate the wingman better be there. But whoever is in the best position makes the bounce, and the other covers.

"I always thought to go around in circles, slower and

slower, was a ridiculous thing. Soon you'll be seeing goof balls. It's kinda dumb but it happened a lot. It's not the way to fight. The best tactic is to make a pass, then break off and come back. If you don't do this you'll lose people; one can't be greedy."

Asked to choose the most important performance features of fighters, Olds said:

"The P.47 and P.51 had speed, good acceleration, a good rate of climb, which is important, and maneuverability. Maneuverability and range, I'd say, were most important."

Asked to list the qualifications of an outstanding fighter pilot, Olds answered:

"One thing was to know how to fly the airplane. He has to know it, to love to fly, to be aggressive and to have good eyeballs and to know how to use them. I'd say he has to have an instinctive capability for air fighting. The good ones have an instinctive ability to do the things necessary to cope with the situation that faces them at the moment. They know whether it's worthwhile to go after the aircraft at nine o'clock—it usually isn't—and whether to go for the one at five o'clock low, and so on. I think the American fighter pilot possesses these talents in greater abundance than any other, as an innate capability. But not every pilot has the sense of timing or skill to apply the art at the precise instant. Fighting spirit one must have. Even if a man lacks some of the other qualifications, he can often make up for it in fighting spirit.

"It was about 1963 or 1964 that the Air Force began to prepare for air-to-air combat again, somewhat late. We got our first squadron of F.4s, which, thankfully, the Navy had built. When in 1965 we got heavily involved in Vietnam we had a fighter force building."

Olds described vividly the air war in Vietnam.

"The air war in Vietnam was more demanding, tougher and more dangerous than the war over Germany. The American public doesn't understand this and many don't give a damn. Yet my arrival there, in the fall of 1966, to take command of the 8th Fighter Wing, was a pleasant surprise. The base at Ubon was well built, comfortable.

There was even a swimming-pool. The buildings were of a lovely warm color—the wood a form of teak, with a wonderful smell. Rooms were air conditioned. My first impression was one of delight. The men lived in comfortable hootches, the officers in wonderfully comfortable hootches of their own.

"I soon learned the wing flew twenty-four hours a day, around the clock, on a shift basis. In World War Two we were often grounded by weather, got a break for a day or two. Here the wing flew twenty-four hours a day seven days a week . . . it never stood down while I was there. This posed some interesting problems. The late, late show, for example, began at six a.m., the mess halls served five meals a day. Men were having their evening meal in the morning after a mission. It was a strange environment, men living different twenty-four hour routines and the base had to adjust. Thai women did our laundry.

"We had three squadrons of F.4s, later four. I was a new guy and had to prove myself. I flew as much as I could. Soon one got into the routine and didn't recognize the passage of days. I found myself building up to a keyed-up tension. At first I flew tail-end Charlie (16th position) for two or three weeks. I told my guys to teach me well and stay ahead of me. Then I flew 2, then 3 position. I learned a lot, for one thing how much I had to give. The squadrons had suffered heavy casualties—guys were flying every day. They were almost exhausted. I was damn proud of 'em."

I asked what a typical mission was like.

"Well, let's say it was an early go, and that we carry bombs. We'd get the first order in the afternoon before—there were about two strikes a day up north. We'd make up the squadron assignments and post an unclassified version in the club. The kids would check the board there. When they saw they were on the morning mission they didn't show too much emotion. Maybe they'd have a drink at the bar, then supper, and enjoy our really great salad bar, then disappear from the club about eight o'clock. They would be awakened at two a.m.

"At about two we'd go over to the club for breakfast,

eggs and the best pineapples in the world. It was black outside. We could hear the Night Owl F.4s roaring off and see their glow and the flood lights on the flight line. We'd go down to wing headquarters in a van truck at about 2.45. There we'd get all the intelligence and learn about other forces and tactics and plot our maps and fill out our mission cards; we'd get tanker routes, times, rendezvous points, flak maps, navigation checks, speeds, bomb load, aim point, roll-in, sight picture, mill depression and so on and then the weather officer would give us a guess on the weather, intelligence would guess on the enemy and the communications guy would make his talk. The Mission Head would speak to the group. By then we'd know our pre-station time—fifty minutes prior to take-off. Now we'd have flight briefing and then begin to don gear. We took everything out of our pockets except the Geneva Convention and I.D. cards and sealed them in plastic. We put on G-suits and put a radio in one pocket and a brilliant cloth to wave in the jungle in the other. We stuck a two-pint bottle of water in a knee pocket and a 38-caliber Navy Colt pistol on our right hip. Then we put on the Mae West—two little packages which fit under the arm pits, a survival vest with all kinds of things in it—food, a compass, knives, radio—and over all this a parachute harness. Then with helmet, map and mission kit we got in the trucks and started out to the birds. We had added forty-five pounds to our weight.

"In the truck the guys were pretty tense—they knew it was going to be a hard one. At the aircraft we spoke to the crew chief but we didn't often fly the same plane. There was also the Back Seater, who flew behind me and he was busy setting up the inertial guidance system while I checked the forms. The pre-flight inspection took about twenty minutes; we had to check the ordinance load, fuses, wires, and hundreds of other things. Then I climbed up the ladder. By now we were soaking wet. Sometimes the temperature was over 100 degrees. There was an elaborate strap-in procedure. The F.4 seat alone was more complex than the whole P.51! The F.4 was in a revetment and sometimes the fumes from the ground power starting unit were almost overpowering. Now came the pre-flight cockpit check. We checked everything and it took some time and then there was the elaborate ritual of starting engines. The crew chief is plugged in by telephone and talking to you. He tells you whether the by-pass doors are closed, whether things move in response to your controls, and so on. The crew takes about ten minutes just removing pins. If everything goes right you move out ponderously, maybe carrying as much as 12,000 pounds of ordnance, taxi out with engine screaming; the kid in the back checks radar, missile control, the navigation system. We must take off on the second and rev up engines. We push 'em up to eighty per cent—that's all the brakes can hold—check the hydraulics, pneumatics, temperatures, full flow, r.p.m., generators, ramps, and then slam the throttle forward to full and then out and full forward again. That's the after-burner. She leaps forward and when you pass the 2,000-foot mark you must have a certain speed or abort then. At 175 knots (over 200 m.p.h.) you pull the stick back and she bounces and leaps off at 180 or 190 and then you form up and head for the tankers (KC.135s); after a time we refuel about thirty feet beneath them and drop down again and head north, over beautiful Laos. It's like Montana, a wild savage land, gorges, streams. Now the tension is up.

"Soon we're crossing into Vietnam, the Black River, ahead is the Red River. Now all is business, you're in the Sam ring. We alter course and rendezvous with the 105s. From 480 indicated we increase to 500 and then up to 520, change course twice more, add more power, up to 540. We're heading to a target north of Hanoi. Our gear tells us they have us on radar, so we're constantly on the lookout for Sam sites. The only salvation is to see them coming. They'll kill you within 200 feet, so the key is dodging them. We hurtle on and now here come the Sams! The trick is seeing the launch. You can see the steam. It goes straight up, turns more level, then the booster drops off. If it maintains a relatively stable position, it's coming for you and you're in trouble. You're eager to make a move but can't. If you dodge too fast it will turn and catch you; if you wait too late it will explode near enough to get you. What you do at the right moment is poke your nose down, go down as hard as you can, pull maybe three negative Gs up to 550 knots and once it follows you down, you go up as hard as you can. It can't follow that and goes under. In a two-minute period they once shot thirty-eight Sams at us. Sam sights are occupied one day, unoccupied the next. They're moved around. Going into Route Pack Six (a designated area in North Vietnam) was like going to the Ruhr. They had brought in all their guns. They knew we were coming and where we couldn't go and this kind of defense didn't allow us to stooge around. We got out as quickly as we could; we didn't strafe a truck, for instance, in the Hanoi or Haiphong areas.

"Soon we approach the target and see flak—the 85s. When you've seen the muzzle flashes often enough you can tell whether that battery is aimed at your flight and you move a thousand feet to avoid the bursts. About this time here come the MiGs, from above. We keep our eyes on them and if they come in we break at just the right time and pull right back in and get in the stream. If we're not carrying bombs we go for the MiGs, of course. We have bombs on this mission and roll in together from a good height and dump the whole load as quickly as possible, through the 57 and 37 flak, going as fast as we can. Near Hanoi I've seen skies as black as those over Berlin and Magdeburg in the Second World War.

"We're only over the target for seconds and after pickling our bombs we break and really get out. We know we might be bounced by MiGs again over the Red River and don't really breathe a sigh of relief until over the Black River. When we get back to base there's a maintenance debriefing which takes twenty minutes, an intelligence briefing which takes an hour and about two and a half hours after we land we're free. Then you can gauge the success of a mission by what goes on afterward in the club. Sometimes it's quiet, if there were losses. If it's too quiet, it's not good. They're thinking about it too much. That's what it's like, and it happens twice a day. And there are twos and fours going to Laos and southern Vietnam and other places, and guys flying at night in the mountains, which is really tough."

I asked Olds to describe shooting down a MiG.

"When MiG attacks got too strong, we flew MiG Cap in the F.4s and the 105s did the bombing. When MiGs began to appear in large numbers, we then flew armed only with missiles, to attack them. And when we encountered them we had dogfights; there is no choice—we will always have them. Suppose the Germans had had large numbers of jets in World War Two. We could still have been below them in P.51s. A jet could have made passes—and did—but we could, with the better-turning P.51, have turned out of his path of fire and he couldn't have stayed there and fought with us or we'd have clobbered him. Thus the faster speed of jets doesn't mean the end of dogfights.

"I had an especially interesting air-to-air combat on 20 May 1967; we were hitting marshalling yards, about twenty-eight 105s and F.4s. We went in after refuelling over the Gulf of Tonkin. The target was about thirty to forty miles north-east of Hanoi and heavily defended by flak. The yards were just north of an air base. There were eight of us in F.4s as top cover. About twenty miles out I saw twelve to sixteen MiG-17s. They came on fast from above and soon we were being bounced. There were MiGs everywhere I looked and we couldn't hope to match turns with them. We slashed in at them and fired missiles and then back out again and each time three or four were shooting at me as I took a shot. But I put a missile in one and he went down and two of the others got one.

"Meanwhile, down below the 105s had hit the yards. We started home and just then I noticed a MiG down on the deck doing figure-8s. I couldn't pass that up. I went out fifteen miles, got down on the rice paddies and started back in for him, flying at about fifteen feet, and pretty soon I saw him ahead. He saw me coming and began turning but I got behind him. I think he was heading to his base. I stayed behind him and he knew if he ever pulled up I'd put a missile into him, so he stayed low, only a few feet above ground. He stayed there as long as he could.

But then he had to go up over a ridge. I was only a few feet off the ground and put a missile into him when he shot up over that ridge. But I had a tough time getting back to a tanker. I had gambled on fuel and won in the end but I had only 800 pounds when I found the tanker. I never had a tougher dogfight in the Second World War than the one with those MiGs that day."

Olds spoke about tactics of the future:

"The most important thing is to have a flexible approach. As Johnnie Johnson says, formations from the beginning of air war to Korea came round full circle. In Vietnam we used formations for certain advantages. But we don't know what the future will be, or how air fighting will be. We must keep alive our flexibility. If we fall into a sort of trench-warfare mentality or into a rut in our thinking it would be dangerous. We can't say what the future will be. Look at the Middle East. It might be better for the Israelis to go in on the missiles all at once; certainly they don't want to go after them in pairs. We'll have to see. The future will bring us laser-guided weapons, all kinds of new weapons. The truth is no one knows exactly what air fighting will be like in the future. We can't say anything will stay as it is, but we also can't be certain the future will conform to particular theories, which so often, between the wars, have proved wrong."

34

CONCLUSION

In assessing the views of the outstanding fliers in the years 1914 to 1970, certain patterns in the evolution of fighter strategy and tactics have appeared. These patterns have concurrently developed as the dominant nature and principle of air power have been established, upon which modern military strategy and tactics are properly based. That principle is that competitive fighters, flown by well-trained pilots using sound strategy and tactics, are the basic, essential ingredient of aerial (and often ground and sea) success. Since fighters are recognized as the key to so much military success today, let us trace briefly the patterns of strategy and tactics as we have seen them employed by successful fliers in this book.

We can more briefly review, first, the development of fighter tactics, which we will limit, in a simplified division, to air-to-air combat tactics. A careful reading of the chapters in this book demonstrates that the most successful offensive tactics in fighter-versus-fighter combat include the use of surprise whenever possible, a fast pass from altitude, close-in shooting and two elements of mental judgment: the ability to size up quickly and accurately conditions as they are encountered, and prudence. There are other elements, of course, and they have been discussed in this book, but these seem the basic patterns of the most successful pilots in air combat with other fighters or fighter formations. In air-to-air combat involving bombers and fighters tactics have varied, logically enough, with conditions and the capabilities of the machines; but the fast pass from altitude has been utilized as an almost basic tactic here also, except in night actions. Close-in shooting has also been the successful pattern, although the arrival on the air scene of jets and missiles, in the last two decades, has tended to increase the emphasis on speed and lessen the emphasis on close-in shooting. The newest trend in shooting, which applies to fighters against fighters also, is a fast pass, the quick release of an automatic missile and rapid retirement to a safe distance away from the enemy's automatic-aiming missiles. The principle of greater success depending on close-in shooting, however, still holds good even in jet and missile engagements.

Turning to strategy and the strategic employment of fighters and fighter forces since 1914, we have seen that the German strategy in the First World War was, generally speaking, to hold down losses and fight, when possible, over German lines. It would seem to have been largely successful. Among the Allies, the British adopted an offensive strategy of constantly seeking out the enemy—over his own territory if necessary and even when British machines were inferior in performance. It was at times a very costly policy and probably achieved very little during certain periods. German offensive strategy was to concentrate a larger number of their best pilots and aircraft on a certain sector of the front for a specific purpose, such as a major offensive. The German strategy resulted in far greater Allied air losses.

The British, however, pioneered in development of an adequate fighter defense system at home, spurred on by German heavy bomber attacks in the First World War. By 1918 that defense organization was unique among the air defense systems of the world; Britain also had by that year probably the most powerful air force in the world. How ironic it is that the German heavy bombers of that war—strategic bomber beginnings—stung the British into building an air defense system which would save the nation two decades later. For the 1940 fighter defense system, including its many ground installations, was the outgrowth of this First World War system. Also ironic is the fact that the Germans attempted to defeat Britain, in the Second World War, without a strategic, heavy bombing arm, which they had pioneered in the First World War.

But the British and Americans, remembering the German First World War bombing attacks, had both built large strategic bomber arms, consuming an enormous proportion of the industrial capacity of both countries. (In the final analysis, as we have seen, their ability to wage successful campaigns against the enemy depended upon defending fighters escorting them.)

Compounding the irony of First and Second World War air strategies is the further fact that the British and Americans were, by the closing months of the First World War, employing fighters and other aircraft with ground forces to a highly effective degree. The British also pioneered in the field of tanks. But it was the Germans, at the beginning of the Second World War, who demonstrated this technique, further perfected, with such great success.

Between the World Wars both the Allies and the Germans turned their strategic air emphasis toward bombers—not fighters. (This seems to be a tendency after every war; the wars then prove anew the vital principle: fighters are the key to success in the air and often on the ground and sea.) Hitler and the Luftwaffe concentrated on offense, which meant bombers. That is why the Germans were building so few fighters when the war began in 1939 and even in 1940 during the Battle of Britain, when the British were outbuilding them better than two to one. Although the Germans were building more bombers than fighters, they were not strategic or heavy bombers but medium bombers and fighter bombers, designed to cooperate with the armies. Luftwaffe leaders had chosen, with limited material resources, to build many medium and fighter bombers rapidly rather than attempt, at a painful cost in resources, to build a heavy, strategic bomber force. Hitler, of course, did not intend, prior to the war, to invade England. There is much evidence that he never did have his heart in the project, even after war began. His attitude on the question of war with England is clearly revealed in his failure to build a large submarine force, which quite obviously would be the Germans' major naval weapon in any clash with England.

The British, on the other hand, gradually came to look upon war with Hitler Germany as very likely, though only at the last hour did they come round to a rapid and concentrated effort in the field of fighters. Curiously, though it was Churchill, Eden and others who called for a greater defense effort, especially in the air, in the thirties, it was probably Chamberlain who won the Battle of Britain as much as anyone else, since the Munich Agreement of 1938 delayed the showdown. Had the R.A.F. taken on the Luftwaffe a year earlier than it did, the Luftwaffe's Me.109s would almost certainly have shot down R.A.F. fighters at a fearful rate, since many of them would have been obsolete biplanes. And they would have met no Spitfires.

The Second World War, beginning in 1939, proved, in every phase, that fighters were the key to succesful air operations, and often also to battles on the ground and at sea. The Germans, with the best air force at the outset, won lightning victories. They lost the Battle of Britain, because they attempted a strategic campaign without a strategic air force and with a fighter force only slightly superior to the R.A.F.'s fighter arm, but handicapped by having to fight over England and guard vulnerable bombers. Both the German and British commands made mistakes in this great and decisive victory for British fighters, but the German command probably made the more. Yet, contrary to the popular notion, which is supported by most films and books, the German fighters acquitted themselves well, though the brave performance of the R.A.F. fighter pilots won the battle. And as long as the Luftwaffe enjoyed an edge in fighter performance, roughly up to about 1943, the Allied air offensive against Germany accomplished relatively little. Air support of German ground operations proved effective. From 1943 onwards, the Allies gained fighter ascendancy and both their ground and air operations benefited appreciably. And this edge coming at the same time as overwhelming numbers in the air and on the ground, the Allied air advantage spelled the end for Germany, despite the impressive "victory" weapons produced by Germany in the last years of the war, such as the Me.262 jet fighter and the V-2 rocket.

In the Pacific war, fighters were even more influential on the course of operations. Much of the early Japanese success stemmed from the effective use of superior fighters, often flown from carriers because of the vast Pacific expanses of water. The fighters and accompanying bombers aided ground operations but also sank ships, shot enemy aircraft out of the sky and provided fleet protection. When, however, Allied fighters gained a performance edge, and a numerical advantage as well, the tide turned in most areas. The fatal flaw in Japanese aircraft construction prior to the war was the failure of the Japanese aircraft industry to develop and install self-sealing fuel tanks in Japanese aircraft.

The Korean War began in 1950, only five years after the end of the Second World War; the jet age had arrived in the interval. Though some were already arguing that jet bombers and missiles were the decisive air weapons, Korea once again proved fighters the key to success in the air and often on the ground and at sea. In the desperate days when the Allies were clinging to the Pusan perimeter, U.S. fighters patrolling regularly over the shaky toehold probably enabled the Allies to hold on by shooting up enemy troops, equipment and supplies, protecting Allied ground forces from similar harassment and safeguarding Allied supply routes. From then onward, Allied air superiority and supremacy greatly aided Allied ground forces in pushing back the North Koreans. The air war in Korea also demonstrated the U.S. Air Force edge in pilot training, fighter strategy and fighter tactics over the Russian, for F.86 Sabre jet fighters shot down MiG-15s by something like a ten-to-one margin, or better.

The Communist side managed to redress the fighter balance somewhat in the Vietnam war more than a decade later. Though Communist strategy was, as in Korea, to leave the southern half of the country to the opposing air force, in the air fighting over North Vietnam the MiG-21, and its pilots (who were again mostly Russians), performed better than had Communist aircraft and pilots in

Korea. In spite of this enemy achievement, the key role of fighters was firmly established again in Vietnam. They were needed to protect bombers and fighter bombers attacking North Vietnam. They were used in South Vietnam and in Laos and Cambodia to support ground operations, and they guaranteed control of the air over South Vietnam. Enemy fighters prevented U.S. heavy bombers from undertaking certain operations in distant areas and exacted a significant toll of fighter bombers (F.105s) and other aircraft attacking North Vietnam.

In several ways, however, the enemy's fighter strategy in Korea and Vietnam limited the air war, and the results could be misleading. U.S. fighters were seldom challenged over South Korea or South Vietnam. Air installations were seldom raided from the air. U.S. bombers were free to bomb targets in many areas in both wars with little fear of enemy fighter interception. Thus pro-Government ground operations in both wars benefited greatly from effective tactical air support, massive aerial transportation support and other forms of air support. The air advantage, in fact, was perhaps the most valuable trump possessed by the anti-Communists. But this advantage, it should be remembered, still depended on fighters controlling the air. The fact that U.S. fighters were seldom challenged enabled a relatively small number of them to guarantee control of the air over South Korea and South Vietnam.

Over North Vietnam U.S. air operations had become costly by the time of the bombing halt in 1968 because the enemy was employing a high-performance air-to-air fighter, the MiG-21, and other sophisticated defenses, including Sam missiles. American pilots opposed the MiG-21 with both the F.4 Phantom and the F.105 fighter bomber and other aircraft, but only the F.4, and that providentially, was suited ideally to an air-to-air combat role. The air war over North Vietnam up to 1968 showed quite clearly the paramount need for superior air-to-air fighters, though once again, between Korea and Vietnam, fighter development had been relatively neglected in the United States.

The 1967 Israeli blitz of Arab forces depended, to a

large degree at least, on immediate seizure of air control, by fighters. The Israeli Air Force quickly shot enemy fighters up on the ground and out of the sky, in the German Second World War pattern, and from that point on Israeli ground forces were unstoppable, receiving effective air cooperation while Arab forces were practically without air support. This was a classic example of the decisive nature of air power in a clash between armored forces.

The newest evolutionary development concerning fighters was demonstrated both in the Israeli–Arab war and over North Vietnam. It is the present-day capacity of fighters to carry devastating bomb loads, including small nuclear weapons. Today's fighters can carry greater destructive power than bombers of the Second World War and perhaps enough (if nuclear armed) to accomplish the destruction of any target within a range of many hundreds of miles. Utilizing tanker, in-flight refuelling, they can operate even farther from their bases. Thus a pertinent question today is whether long-range heavy bombers, which require so much more time than missiles to strike a long-distance target, should continue to be emphasized. One should proceed cautiously in reaching conclusions, however, for the past has shown that each time fighters have been written off as obsolete the next war has proved them, once again, the key to successful air operations.

But it is obviously true that today's larger, faster fighters, utilizing the increased destructiveness of modern bombs, have an added capability, in addition to their role as a weapon with which to achieve both aerial superiority or supremacy and cooperation with ground armor; they can now be used to carry out practically all missions previously assigned to bombers, except very long-range missions. This is a striking evolution from the capacity of the small, slow, flimsy scout of the early days of the First World War, which carried no defensive armor and no bombs.

U.S. fighters were so used on bombing strikes in North Vietnam, their speed and maneuverability enabling them to jettison bomb loads and fight enemy fighters if necessary; it should be noted, however, that the low-level use of fighters or any aircraft over missile-armed territory has become a precarious proposition. A current question is how effective automatic-homing missiles on the ground will become in the future, and how high their effectiveness will extend.

A tentative assessment, based primarily on Vietnam, indicates that while automatic-homing missiles will undoubtedly make air operations costly at times, just as with antiaircraft guns in the two World Wars, the manned machine will usually be capable of avoiding the unmanned missile, using the decision-making ability of the human mind at the crucial time, plus counter weapons.

In summary, if this study demonstrates anything, it clearly shows the continuing need for the free world to develop highly capable, manned fighters. In recent years the Russians have been developing as many as a dozen models simultaneously, while for many years the United States, the most powerful of the free-world democracies, allowed development of fighters to all but lapse. Currently, several are under development in the United States, Britain and France. Many people, however, are once more convinced that there will be a very limited role for such aircraft in any future conflict. Should one arise, it will prove, again, that modern fighters, with more military capabilities than ever before, are still the key to successful air operations, and often to ground and sea operations as well.

ACES OF THE WARS AND THEIR VICTORIES

First World War

German

80	Manfred von Richthofen
62	Ernst Udet
53	Erich Loewenhardt
48	Werner Voss
45	Fritz Rumey
44	Rudolph Berthold
43	Paul Bäumer
41	Josef Jacobs
41	Bruno Loerzer
40	Oswald Boelcke
40	Franz Büchner
40	Lothar von Richthofen

British Empire

73	Edward Mannock
72	William Bishop
60	Raymond Collishaw
57	James McCudden
54	A. W. B. Proctor
54	D. R. MacLaren
53	William Barker
47	Robert Little
46	Philip Fullard
46	G. E. H. McElroy
44	Albert Ball
44	J. Gilmore

American

26	Eddie Rickenbacker
21	Frank Luke
17	Raoul Lufbery
13	George Vaughn
12	Field Kindley
12	David Putnam
12	Elliot Springs
10	Reed Landis
10	Jacques Swaab
9	L. A. Hamilton
9	Frank Hunter
9	Chester Wright

Second World War

German

352	Erich Hartmann
301	Gerhard Barkhorn
275	Günther Rall
267	Otto Kittel
258	Walter Nowotny
237	Wilhelm Batz
222	Erich Rudorffer
220	Heinrich Bär
211	Hermann Graf
208	Theodor Weissenberger
206	Hans Philipp
206	Walther Schuck
204	Heinrich Ehrler
204	Anton Hafner
203	Helmut Lipfert
197	Walther Krupinski
190	Anton Hackl
189	Joachim Brendel

British Empire

41	M. T. St. J. Pattle
38	Johnnie Johnson
35	Adolph Malan
32	Brendan Finucane
31	George Beurling
29	John Braham
29	Robert Tuck
29	Neville Duke
29	Clive Caldwell
28	Frank Carey
28	James Lacey
28	Colin Gray
26	Eric Lock
25	Billy Drake
24	William Vale
24	Geoffrey Allard
24	Jacobus Le Roux
23	Douglas Bader

American

40	Richard Bong
38	Thomas McGuire
34	David McCampbell
31	Francis Gabreski
28	Robert Johnson
27	Charles MacDonald
26	George Preddy
26	Joseph Foss
25	Robert Hanson
24	Cecil Harris
24	John Meyer
23	Eugene Valencia
23	Ray Whetmore
23	David Schilling
22	Gerald Johnson
22	Neel Kearby
22	Jay Robbins
22	Gregory Boyington

Korea	Vietnam
American	*American*

Korea	Vietnam
16 Joseph McConnel Jr.	4 Robin Olds
15 James Jabara	3 Robert Titus
15 Manuel Fernandez	3 Milan Zimer
14 George Davis	3 George McKinney Jr.
13 Royal Baker	2 Max Brestel
10 Frederick Blesse	2 Richard Pascoe
10 Harold Fischer	2 Everett Raspberry Jr.
10 James Johnson	2 Darrell Simmonds
10 Vermont Garrison	2 Stephen Wayne
10 Lonnie Moore	2 Norman Wells
10 Ralph Parr	

REFERENCES

BAUMBACH, WERNER. *The Life and Death of the Luftwaffe*. Tr. Frederick Holt. New York: Coward-McCann. As *The Defeat of the Luftwaffe*, London: Robert Hale, 1960.

BEKKER, CAJUS. *Luftwaffe War Diaries*. Tr. Frank Ziegler. London: Macdonald. New York: Doubleday, 1967.

BISHOP, WILLIAM. *Winged Warfare*. London: Hodder & Stoughton and Lythway Press. New York: Doubleday, 1918.

CHURCHILL, WINSTON S. *The World Crisis 1911–1918* (2 vols.). London: Odhams Press. New York: Scribner's Sons, 1939.

CUNEO, JOHN R. *Winged Mars*, vol. ii—*The Air Weapon, 1914–1916*. Harrisburg, Pennsylvania: Military Service Publishing Co., 1942.

FREDETTE, RAYMOND H. *The First Battle of Britain, 1917–1918*. New York: Holt, Rinehart & Winston. London: Cassell, 1966.

FULLER, J. F. C. *The Second World War*. London: Eyre & Spottiswoode, 1948. Des Moines: Meredith, 1963.

GALLAND, ADOLF. *The First and the Last*. Tr. Mervyn Savill. London: Methuen. New York: Holt, Rinehart & Winston, 1955.

GIBBONS, FLOYD P. *The Red Knight of Germany* [Manfred von Richthofen]. New York: Doubleday, 1927. London: Cassell, 1930.

GREEN, WILLIAM. *Famous Fighters of the Second World War* (4 vols.). New York: Doubleday, 1957. London: Macdonald, 1962.

HARRIS, ARTHUR. *Bomber Offensive*. London: Collins. New York: Macmillan, 1947.

JOHNSON, J. E. *Full Circle*. London: Chatto & Windus. New York: Ballantine Books, 1964.

KLEIN, BURTON H. *Germany's Economic Preparations for War*. Cambridge, Mass.: Harvard U. P., 1959.

KNOKE, HEINZ. *I Flew for the Führer*. Tr. John Ewing. London: Evans Brothers. New York: Holt, Rinehart & Winston, 1954.

LEE, ARTHUR GOULD. *No Parachute*. London: Jarrolds. New York: Harper & Row, 1968.

McCUDDEN, JAMES. *Flying Fury*. London: John Hamilton, 1930.

293

MELLENTHIN, F. W. VON. *Panzer Battles.* University of Oklahoma Press, 1956.

MEYER, JOHN C. "The Long Reach". *T.A.C. Attack*, Sept. 1970. Langley Field, Virginia: U.S. Tactical Air Command.

MILNE, DUNCAN GRINNELL-. *Wind in the Wires.* London: Hurst & Blackett. New York: Doubleday, 1933.

MITCHELL, WILLIAM. *Memoirs of World War I.* New York: Random House, 1960.

PLATT, FRANK (Ed.). *Great Battles of World War I: In the Air.* New York: New American Library, 1966.

RAWNSLEY, C. F., and WRIGHT, ROBERT. *Night Fighter.* London: Collins. New York: Henry Holt, 1957.

Rendezvous: Journal of the American Fighter Pilots' Association.

REYNOLDS, QUENTIN. *They Fought for the Sky.* New York: Holt, Rinehart & Winston, 1957. London: Cassell, 1958.

ROBERTSON, BRUCE. *Air Aces of the 1914–1918 War.* Los Angeles: Aero Publishers. Letchworth, Herts: Harleyford Publications, 1959.

SIMS, EDWARD H. *American Aces.* New York: Harper & Row. London: Macdonald, 1958.

SIMS, EDWARD H. *The Greatest Aces.* New York: Harper & Row. As *The Fighter Pilots*, London: Cassell, 1967.

SIMS, EDWARD H. *Greatest Fighter Missions.* New York: Harper & Row, 1962.

SPEER, ALBERT. *Inside the Third Reich.* Tr. R. and C. Winston. London: Weidenfeld & Nicolson. New York: Macmillan, 1970.

TAYLOR, A. J. P. *English History, 1914–1945.* London and New York: Oxford University Press, 1965.

TAYLOR, W. P., and IRVIN, F. L. *History of the 148th Aero Squadron.* Lancaster, South Carolina: Tri-County Publishing Co., 1957.

TOLIVER, RAYMOND F., and CONSTABLE, TREVOR J. *The Blond Knight of Germany* [Erich Hartmann]. New York: Doubleday. London: Arthur Barker, 1970.

ULANOFF, STANLEY M. (Ed.). *Ace of Aces* [René Fonck]. Tr. Martin H. Sabin and Stanley M. Ulanoff. New York: Doubleday, 1966.

VARIOS, JOSE. *Combat over Spain.* London: Neville Spearman, 1968.

WILMOT, CHESTER. *The Struggle for Europe.* New York: Harper & Row. London: Collins, 1952.

INDEX

A-4 aircraft, 265
A-7 aircraft, 265
A-37 aircraft, 265
acceleration, importance of, 24, 188, 275
Ace of Aces (ed. Ulanoff), 9n
Air Aces of the 1914–1918 War (Robertson), 10n
Air Defense Zone West, 140
Air Weapon, The, 1914–1916 (Cuneo), 14n
Alam Halfa (1942), 28
Albatros D-I and D-II, 11, 40-41, 79
Albatros D-III and D-IV, 92
Albatros D-V: top speed of, 60n; Jacobs and, 66-67
Allen, Johnny, 129; and shooting down of first Me.109 (May 1940), 125-26
Anderson, Major General Fred, 244
anti-aircraft guns, 137, 138, 140
Asch, 208
attack, decision to, 78-79, 234

B.17 bombers, 30, 154, 220, 222
B.24 bombers, 30, 154
B.52 bombers, 271
B.57 bombers, 266
B.E.2Cs, Grinnell-Milne and (1915), 39-40, 41, 32-43
Babington, Major Philip, 53
Bader, Group Captain Douglas, 4, 6, 194, 239
Balkan war (1912), 8

Ball, Albert, 23, 52, 94; tactics of flying below adversary, 18; shot down, 23-24, 45
balloons, shooting down of, 64, 71-73
Banifeld, Gottfried, 67
Bär, Heinz, 153n, 198
Bardufoss, 130, 132
barrage balloons, 140
Baumbach, Werner, 133, 230n, 244n
Beamont, Wing Commander Roland, P.: his record, 110-11, 116; with Hurricanes in May 1940, 111-16, 117, 122-23
Beaufighters, as night fighters, 108, 146-52
Bekker, Cajus, 143n, 191
Berlin, bombing of, 187-88, 191, 225, 228
biplanes: at beginning of First World War, 9, 11, 17-20, 99-100; tactics, 17-20; in Second World War, 100, 117-18
Bird-Wilson, Air Vice-Marshal Harold Arthur Cooper: with Hurricanes in May 1940, 118-23; belief in fighters and dogfighting, 117, 121; later record, 121
Bishop, Billy, 23, 52; in 85th (R.F.C.) Squadron, 84, 86; his record, 87, 91; on importance of gunnery, 87-91, 94
Blakeslee, Colonel Don, 182-83, 194